Praise for
I Always Did Like Horses & Women

₽·FOR

A fascinating story...I enjoyed the book and admired the research.
— Lorraine Bonney, historian and co-author of the ten
Bonney guides for Wyoming, Kelly, Wyoming

Cal's story is marvelous...a fascinating look at a man, revealing a complexity of character not appreciated in the legends about him. The author really brings Cal and old-time Jackson to life...Should be on every Western aficionado's bookshelf.
— Jeanne Anderson, owner of Dark Horse Books, editor
of *Spindrift: Stories of Teton Basin*, commissioner of the
Idaho Commission on the Arts, Driggs, Idaho

The author has done an admirable job of fleshing out Cal's story and establishing him in his own right as a truly colorful and historic figure...Cal moves between different cultures with remarkable ease and aplomb, but never loses his authentic Western character...a welcome addition to the histories of the Valley.
— Joe Arnold, artist and mountain climber, grandson of
Felicia Gizycka, great-grandson of Eleanor "Cissy"
Patterson, Laramie, Wyoming

The author has diligently researched Cal Carrington's life... what a great job! Wish I could have met Cal; he was a rare and authentic person...a truly unique character of the Western past.
— Doris Platts, Jackson Hole historian, author of eight
books on Jackson Hole and Western history,
Wilson, Wyoming

New and Expanded Edition Praise

Cal Carrington exemplified the restless spirit of the American West's pioneers. From orphan to homesteader to horse wrangler and more, Carrington's larger-than-life character lives on in the legends of Teton Valley and Jackson Hole. Earle Layser's continued relentless research uncovered significant new material relating to this notable Jackson Hole character, and he has carefully detailed those revelations in his new and updated edition. Rumors and myths about the Carrington's early life are further addressed in this latest cache of photographs, documents, and material supplemented with interviews and family lore from early settlers who were acquainted with Carrington. The author has spun a rousing tale of an enigmatic Western persona who lived during rapidly changing times in American's history.

    – Jim Hardee, editor *Rocky Mountain Fur Trade Journal*
    and author of *Pierre's Hole: The Fur Trade History of*
    Teton Valley, Idaho, Tetonia, Idaho.

In this new edition, the author unfolds more layers of Cal Carrington's story, a man whose life holds endless fascination. This engaging book reveals more of Carrington's mysterious past, his magnetic character, and a long, loving relationship with a glamorous Countess, all set within the beauty of the mountainous West. I fully enjoyed reading it for its great storytelling. And, due to its carefully researched details, I depended on it as a resource for my own writing projects. With this worthy book's new edition the author will be giving readers hours of enjoyment and satisfaction.

    – Tina Welling, novelist and author of *Cowboys Never Cry,*
    Fairy Tale Blues and *Crybaby Ranch*, Jackson, Wyoming.

I Always Did Like Horses & Women

Enoch Cal Carrington's Life Story
A Western Classic

Orphaned Immigrant, Old Time Buckaroo,
Professed Horse Thief,
Teton Valley and Jackson Hole Homesteader,
Forest Ranger and Dude Wrangler,
Hunting Guide and Rancher,
Socialite, Gadabout, Raconteur
and
Jackson Hole Legend

Earle F. Layser

Original Cover and Graphic Design by Karen Russell, Fall Line Design, Driggs, Idaho.

New and Expanded Edition graphic design and layout by Rossetti Designs, Wilson, Wyoming.

Published by Dancing Pine Publishing, Alta, Wyoming.

Printed by Create Space in the United States of America

This book is dedicated to Pattie,
my loving wife, who was an unequaled
companion on life's myriad trails —
together we roamed the West
and shared a grand passion for
the Tetons and Yellowstone.
Tender memories of our life together
are folded into these pages.

The Chapters of
Enoch Cal Carrington's Life Story

A New and Expanded Edition

The original 2008 publication of *Enoch "Cal" Carrington's Life Story* was enthusiastically received. In 2009, it was recognized with the Wyoming State Historical Society's award for biography. It continues to be in demand by readers.

So why a new edition?

It turns out, this kind of work is never finished. After the original book was published, I continued to find and acquire significant unpublished materials, photographic images, and additional insights into Carrington's life. In 2012, I published *The Jackson Hole Settlement Chronicles*. The research for it further expanded my knowledge and perspective on nineteenth-century Jackson Hole. The discoveries of substantial new materials and my additional perceptions compelled me to prepare this updated edition.

Important new material on Cal surfaced when a Jackson Hole Historical Society employee found a one-hundred year old memoir and fifteen vintage photographs by Edith H. Bailey among unaccessioned museum collections. It was material previously not available to the author. Another example, the "lost," some had claimed "stolen," brass plate originally intended for Cal's grave marker was discovered. It had been warehoused in the museum's basement for the last fifty years.

After the original book was published, Berger family members contacted me, providing an unpublished family history of James H. Berger. The account of Jim Berger's and Cal's 1897 trip from Cache Valley, Utah to Teton Valley, Idaho, describes what occupied the two young men upon their arrival in the valley. It further lays to rest the myth that Cal was a horse rustler during his early years in Teton Valley and Jackson Hole. Additionally, since 2008, a procession of other long-time Jackson Hole and Teton Valley residents – today's old timers – have come forward with more stories about Cal.

I visited Syracuse University at Syracuse, New York, where the photographs of Jackie Martin, Eleanor "Cissy" Patterson's staff photographer, are archived. Unpublished photos of Cal and the Flat Creek Ranch were found among the University's Special Collections. Moreover, a new biographical work by Amanda Smith on Eleanor "Cissy" Patterson, Cal's paramour and patron, was published by Alfred A. Knopf in 2011. Amanda Smith had access to Patterson family papers and other biographer's notes and interviews. Notable materials that Amanda discovered pertaining to Cal were kindly passed along to this author.

Besides incorporating new findings and previously unpublished materials, I took this opportunity to include reader's suggestions, and make edits and corrections, too. New chapters have been added, some chapters rewritten, and more than a dozen additional photographs added. In short, not only has significant new content been included, but the entire text has been reworked and supplemented with additional images.

Considering this extensive work over, is the book a new edition or a revision? I have chosen to call it "a new and expanded edition." Title it what you will, it was my ambition to improve the telling of Cal's epic life story, making it as interesting and readable, accurate, and complete as possible. With the addition of the new material and reworking of the original text, I feel that goal is much closer to being achieved.

Earle F. Layser
Alta, Wyoming

Acknowledgments

This biography was prepared over a ten year period. The original 2008 version was four years in the making. Another six years has been involved with discovering and recording new materials and crafting this new edition.

During this passage of time, I became indebted to many for the use of published and unpublished works, shared personal knowledge, freely given insights, helpful criticisms, technical support, patience, encouragement and friendship – to all those who lent a helping hand and encouragement along the way, my sincere thanks.

The discovery of two unpublished transcripts from recorded interviews with Cal Carrington – one conducted in 1957 at the University of Wyoming by the late U.S. Senator and Wyoming Governor Clifford Hansen of Jackson, Wyoming; the second, arranged by attorney Harold Forbush of Rexburg, Idaho, and conducted by Teton County Court Recorder, Dwight Stone, in Driggs, Idaho, in 1958 – contributed greatly to this work. Those individuals deserve credit for their insightfulness in arranging and recording oral interviews nearly sixty years ago in order to preserve Cal's unique history and the times he represented.

A number of Cal's friends, acquaintances, and others, captivated by his colorful character, wrote about parts of his life. These included the Berger family, Struthers Burt, Nathaniel Burt, Harold Forbush, Wendell Gillette, Felicia Gizycka, Eleanor "Cissy"

Patterson, and Cissy's four biographers: Paul Healy, Alice Albright Hoge, Ralph Martin, and Amanda Smith. Those works are a rich source of tales about Carrington and his life, which, if they had not been recorded would have been lost to time.

I gratefully acknowledge the information shared by those I interviewed or spoke with who had personally known or crossed paths with Cal Carrington, or who shared similar related knowledge: Gene Berger, Ron Berger, Bonnie Budge, Farrell Buxton, Rena Croft, Harold Forbush, Kay Fullmer, Oren and Eva Furniss, Bertha Gillette, Gene Gressley, Clifford Hansen, Judy Berger Haven, Dawn Kent, Charlie Petersen, Laren Piquet, Monte Piquet, Johnny Ryan, Russell Stone, Margaret "Muggs" Shultz, Clay Taylor, and Grant Thompson. Many of those folks were getting along in years, but all were eager to talk about Cal. They provided personal insights and previously unrecorded material. The longevity of some of these people was amazing: Oren Furniss could still saddle and sit a horse at age eighty-nine in 2007. No doubt Cliff Hansen and Charlie Petersen could do the same when they were that young, too.

My sincere appreciation and thanks to those who contributed their valuable time to review my various working drafts and offer their comments, criticisms and edits: Flat Creek Ranch operator and Cissy Patterson's great nephew Joe Albright, Dark Horse Books owner Jeanne Anderson, Cissy Patterson's great grandson and artist Joe Arnold, historian and author Lorraine Bonney, *Teton Magazine* publisher and editor Eugene Downer, author and historian Doris Platts, former director of the Jackson Hole Historical Society and Museum Robert Rudd, Fall Line Design owner Karen Russell, biographer Amanda Smith, and three anonymous reviewers of early drafts arranged by Jackson Hole Historical Society and Museum Director Lokey Lytjen. And also, the reviewers of this new edition: author and editor of the *Rocky Mountain Fur Trade Journal*, James Hardee; and Jackson Hole author of *Cowboys Never Cry*, Tina Welling. I am particularly indebted to

Jim Hardee for his detailed editing of this new edition.

Special mention is made of my discussions with Washington, D.C. based biographer Amanda Smith, which proved immensely helpful. She kindly shared her knowledge and selected materials on Cal that were uncovered during her research for Cissy Patterson's biography.

Staff, curators, and historians at numerous museums and historical societies assisted me with archival research and in providing photographs: The American Heritage Center at Laramie, Coffrin's Old West Gallery in Bozeman, Encinitas Historical Society in California, Idaho State Museum at Boise, Jackson Hole Historical Society and Museum, Lemhi Historical Society at Salmon, Teton Valley Museum at Driggs, Yellowstone National Park archives, Sharlot Hall Museum at Prescott, Syracuse University Library, photographer Lucas Novak, Valley of the Tetons Library, *Field and Stream* magazine archives, and the National Archives. I also gratefully acknowledge material and assistance obtained from state and local courthouse records and archivists at Teton County, Idaho and Wyoming; San Diego, California; and Cheyenne, Wyoming.

Rumors of Cal rustling horses play a big part of the Wild West glamour and lore of his early years in Jackson Hole. He had a propensity to refer to himself as an "ol' horse thief," too. I want to make special mention of some of the historians who have specifically researched the topic of early day horse rustling in-and-about the Tetons and on whose research I have relied: Mark Anderson, Robert Betts, Frank Calkins, Orrin and Lorraine Bonney, Benjamin Driggs, Doris Platts, Nollie Mumey and Charles Wilson. Additional research was also done on this subject by the author in preparation of his 2012 book: The *Jackson Hole Settlement Chronicles*. Based on those sources, one must conclude, the facts do not support the rumors and allegations that Carrington was a horse thief.

I owe a great deal of thanks to Karen Russell of Fall Line Design in Driggs, Idaho, for her ideas, patience and work in setting up the original book's layout, design and cover jacket, and for her technical expertise in initially making this publication a reality.

Miga Rossetti of Rossetti Designs in Wilson, Wyoming, skillfully and ably assumed the layout and design work for this 2014 edition. Many thanks for her patience, skills, and professionalism that are reflected throughout this edition.

Last, but far from least, for my loving and gracious wife, Pattie, words are not enough. Pattie also researched and authored stories about the Flat Creek Ranch and Cal and Cissy – "The Flat Creek Ranch: Old West, New West, But Always the Real West," *Wyoming Homes and Living* (2005) and "Tracking the Wilderness Wapiti in 1916," *Bugle* (2009). Pattie's research for the latter article provided materials utilized in Chapter 17. Sharing sources, interpretations, and many entertaining and fun discussions between us, we were a team. I was uncommonly fortunate and grateful to have had Pattie's unfailing support and her insightfulness. Her selfless encouragement and smiling helpfulness greatly assisted me in surmounting the challenges and hurdles that arose while producing this book. She was not only an inspiration for this work, but for life itself.

Finally, this history is based on the interpretations, judgments and research of the author, as well as his attempted artful and selective weaving together of varied source materials. Any resulting omissions, inaccuracies, mistakes or failures in its telling are solely the responsibility of the author.

Preface

The author's first glimpse of the compelling Yellowstone–Teton landscape was as a young boy in 1947, while vacationing with my parents. We were what the locals called "tin-can tourists," camping out of an old panel station wagon in the sagebrush. One morning in Jackson Hole a horseback rider approached, and my father, who had cowboyed in Johnson County, Wyoming, in the early 1900s, apologized profusely for trespassing on what he assumed was ranch property. The rider spat indifferently and said, "Doesn't matter, it all belongs to Rockefeller anyway." To put time in perspective, Cal would have still been around yet and very active in those years.

I didn't return to Jackson Hole again until my career took me there in 1976. Back then, nearly forty years ago, Jackson still seemed authentically Western, peopled with genuine and unpretentious folks – the classless society that characters in this book applaud. Where else would a U.S. Senator walk up to a stranger in the airport and start a conversation as Cliff Hansen once did with me.

The Hole has long since undergone unprecedented change and growth. Like much of the country, portion's have been plowed, grazed, roaded, ditched, fenced, mined, and paved over with modern housing developments. While this history provides a look back at earlier times – people's lives, livelihood, events and society – it also affords perspective on the inevitable "progress" we as a society have known and undergone.

Originally, I intended to only write a short article about Cal Carrington, a legendary early day Jackson Hole figure. Straightaway, I was foiled by outrageous tales, conflicting myths, and whopping information gaps. As the material I uncovered continued to grow, and the more I researched and learned, the more unrealistic the idea became of doing the subject justice in a short story. For instance, previously, gaps in the knowledge of Cal's whereabouts sufficed to substantiate that he was indeed engaged in outlaw activities – if you didn't know his whereabouts, it was assumed he was off stealing horses. Few ever realized or imagined the amazing extent of Cal's activities, social life, and travels. I hesitated to simply repeat old conjecture and handed-down yarns about his being an outlaw without some verification. My research instead led to the contradiction of some locally cherished myths and discovery of new and amazing tales.

The "facts" about Cal invariably existed in multiple variants. An eager editor wanting to show their worth at fact-checking could wallow in the contradictions. Some simple examples: Cal's birthplace had been variously given as England, Norway or Sweden; his real name was reported as unknown, changed at immigration's Port of Entry, changed because he was hiding something or derived from a cowboy he admired; popular hearsay claimed he belonged to a gang of horse thieves, all of whom were captured except for Cal – yet no records of outlaws being captured for the place and time exist?

Many such issues were resolved by my research, but some parts of Enoch Cal Carrington's life will always remain a mystery – lost in the murk of time, confounded by those who realized history could be used to manipulate how the past would be remembered or muddled by canards thrown in just for entertainment.

It's true, too, that if powerhouse Eleanor "Cissy" Patterson had not come into Cal's life, it's unlikely that much, if any, of his history would have ever been recorded. He would have been just another cowpoke passing through. Cal himself admitted to

Earl and Sadie Harris, in Driggs, Idaho, before his passing, that without Cissy and her daughter Felicia, he would have had little. Cissy and Felicia were his family.

Nevertheless, while Jackson Hole fondly celebrates Cal's romance with Cissy to this day, it turns out that she and Felicia were not the only important women in his life. He also carried on long-term relationships with Mary "Mamie" Ake of Mountain Home, Idaho, and Goldie Chisman of San Diego.

Cal's relationship with Mamie remains a puzzle. Was she the young cowboy's sweetheart for whom he had an unrequited romantic notion, or did she in fact bear his child out of wedlock, as some evidence in the Lake Forest Patterson Family Papers may suggest? On his deathbed Cal referred to Mamie as an "old pal," and bequeathed half of his substantial estate to her.

And what about Goldie? He kept in touch with her for over thirty years. And others, too, such as an apparent fling with a Ringling Brothers trapeze artist in Sarasota, Florida? Felicia knew about these women and even details of Cal's relationship with them, yet she was discreetly and purposefully silent, disclosing little or nothing about them in her writings.

I've let Cal tell parts of the story in his own words (and spelling), such as his descriptions of working on open range cattle drives in Chapter 2. I chose to describe the entire ten-year saga of proving-up on his Desert Entry at Bates in Chapter 5, rather than interweaving it throughout the other parts of his life during that same time period. I felt this would more clearly demonstrate what Cal – and others of the time – went through in order to gain title on a Desert Entry. It wasn't "free land." Chapter 11 details what a hunt outfitted and guided by Cal and his camp tenders was like back then.

Some of the likely origins of outlaw tales frequently associated with Cal are revealed and traced in Chapters 6, 7, 9. From what I discovered about Cal's early years homesteading in Bates, Idaho, and his working for the infant Yellowstone National

Park and U.S. Forest Service (see Chapters 5, 8-10), he appears to have lived a much different life than the outlaw tradition and legends previously led one to believe.

Many details of Cal's history still remain open to supposition. For example, when Cal, at age 16, allegedly beat up the Mormon elder and ran away from his Utah foster home, it seems unlikely that he lit out on foot. He had to somehow have acquired a horse to have traveled to the Arizona cow camp. Did he vault bareback onto one of the elder's horses, grab a fist full of mane and gallop off – thereby, also, stealing his first horse? Unfortunately, we only know that somehow he made his way to the cow camp, where, as he later claimed, "he learned to ride." It appears, in fact, this may have been at Twodot Satchells' cow camp, which in later years was photographed and described for posterity by L.A. Huffman in 1907.

Other intriguing parts of Cal's life still remain to be filled in by additional research, a novelist, screenwriter or the reader's own inventions, perhaps. However, Cal's life story need not be embellished to make it fascinating; it's a rousing tale of a life lived to the utmost during rapidly changing times in the American West; and catalyzed, too, by his implausible entry into the opulent life styles, wealth, and mores' of high society.

This is a book for people who love the history of the Old West, the Yellowstone-Teton region, and ramped up early twentieth-century America; and for those also, who will derive inspiration and joy from a true story of a life passionately lived – a spirited tale of an illiterate and orphaned saddle tramp who overcame all odds.

I Always Did Like Horses & Women

Enoch Cal Carrington's Life Story
A Western Classic

Earle F. Layser

Left: Enoch Cal Carrington as a young cowboy, c1908.
Courtesy JHHSM, 1958, 2224.001.

Prologue

*Come gather 'round wranglers
and we'll tell us some lies
of cowboys and horses
and bright starry skies...*[1]

Hidden deep within a steep-walled cirque, Jackson Hole's Flat Creek Guest Ranch lays nestled beside a glittering tarn dominated by Sheep Mountain. Within the rim-rock confinements, eagles soar and shaggy moose loll. It is a breathtaking place, though not really a suitable spot for a farm or ranch, but then its original claimants had no real intention of making it into one. It has always been a secluded mountain hideaway, a place of legend, where nineteenth century outlaws secreted stolen horses.

Access to the ranch has not improved much, if any, from when horses and wagons plied the narrow canyon road. One must buck the last four rocky miles in high-clearance four-wheel drive across National Forest. Fortunately, that is the historically authentic access the ranch's owners and managers have preferred and retained. The most recent in a succession of ranch managers being Joe Albright and Marcia Kunstel. However, once at the ranch, the setting and accommodations are incomparable – original owner Eleanor "Cissy" Patterson called it "the most perfect place."

Present day ranch operators, Joe and Marcia, adopted a dinnertime tradition: they recount the myths and legends surrounding the ranch's origin. As the sun dips below the rim rock, the extraordinary tales unfold and the lodge's historic photographs and artifacts come to life. The star characters captivate the guests: Eleanor "Cissy" Medill Patterson, a red-headed countess, heiress, socialite and publishing powerhouse; and Enoch "Cal" Carrington, an old-time buckaroo and self-professed horse thief.

Biographers have scrambled to chronicle Cissy's incredible life. Granddaughter to abolitionist and mayor of Chicago, Joseph Medill, author of several books, and the publisher and editor of the *Washington Times-Herald*, she was once considered the most powerful (and controversial) woman in the United States. Her biographers have generally treated Cal as a chapter in her flamboyant life. However, Cal's life story – he liked to declare his earliest childhood recollections were as an orphan in an Arizona cow camp – is shrouded by early day Jackson Hole myth, and is itself a compelling saga possessing the grand sweep of a sprawling Western epic.

The American West spawned some fascinating and astonishing tales and Cal's life story ranks among those. When he was a young child his zealous Swedish parents gave him up to serve a religious movement. As an immigrant orphan child in America, he was swept along with the Nation's westward Manifest Destiny. He grew up and lived under rugged frontier conditions among reputed outlaws, but was destined to capture the fancy of a wealthy benefactress, Eleanor "Cissy" Patterson, who introduced him to world travel and aristocratic society.

Cissy Patterson was locally known in Jackson Hole as the "Countess of Flat Creek." Cal's involvement with her is considered one of the most romantic and renowned cowboy-dudine affairs to ever hit Jackson Hole, if not the West. As a result of her influence, Cal spent time in Chicago, New York, Washington D.C., Sarasota, Florida, and the Bahamas among the very wealthy. He also toured Europe, hunted big game in Africa, and acquired southern California beachside property. In his later years, he chose to return to his frontier roots and frugally live what appeared to his neighbors to be a simple rural existence; in reality, he maintained two separate lives.

Cal outlived more than one era. He was a young man at a time when the West was still raw frontier. It was a time of rapid transition and growth – the *Gilded Age* as Mark Twain dubbed it. Cal witnessed incredible changes. His life was one of polar contrasts: he grew up among pioneering Mormons, going from a farm laborer to bronc rider, cattle drover and government horse packer to ranch owner, from homesteader to southern California seaside-property owner, subsistence hunter to big game hunting guide to African safari, from cash poor homesteader to worldly socialite and investor, and from tight-lipped rogue to sociable raconteur. The romance of his story is intertwined with and inseparable from the early day mythos and history of Teton Valley, Idaho, and Jackson Hole, Wyoming. The photographic images within these pages help to illustrate the dramatic breadth and richness of his experiences and the mind-boggling changes occurring over his lifetime.

Some might say his story "jumps around" – back and forth between Jackson Hole and Teton Valley, the Intermountain West and California, across the United States and Europe, even Africa and the Bahamas – but that reflects the nature of Cal's life. The events, dates and places do not always lend themselves to a strict sequential chronicling.

Cal's family possessed no land or wealth and judging from his alleged mistreatment and impoverished childhood, no modern day psychologist would have held out much hope for him. From humble beginnings, however, he proved a man was not bound by what he was born, but that in the egalitarian society of frontier America one could attain whatever he had in himself to be. Cal was an orphaned and illiterate cowboy, a common man, who overcame the odds to realize the American dream of unlimited possibilities. Of course, his meeting a wealthy patron along the way helped considerably, too. And so the extraordinary life story of Enoch Cal Carrington unfolds – a tale that goes beyond imagination.

Medieval Orebro Castle overlooking the city of Orebro, Sweden, where Cal Carrington was born.

1

Orphan Beginnings

Cal Carrington, whose real name was Enoch Kavington Julin, was born to Gustof and Julia Augusta Julin on February 10, 1873, in Orebro, Sweden. He is thought to have been the first of five children born into this shoemaker family.[1]

Located in south-central Sweden on the banks of the Svartre River (the black stream), Orebo, in the nineteenth century, was a medieval village of wooden houses and stone-cobbled streets. Its skyline was dominated by the huge Orebo Castle, which loomed forebodingly over the village. Orebo possesses a cold climate and, because of the northern latitude and oceanic influence, it is frequently overcast with fog and darkness and can be depressingly dreary.

In the ninetieth century, Latter-day Saint missionaries systematically and aggressively recruited "worthy souls" from throughout Eastern Europe to join their American pilgrimage. Many peasants eagerly joined, seeking a new life and escape from repressive poverty and famine. The Elders of Zion especially sought converts with "crucial skills," such as shoemaking.

The missionaries found the Julin's in Orebo to be fervently receptive. But the family was poor and not able to raise the required fare. Instead, in a zealous show of faith, the shoemaker family gave up their first and second born, Enoch, age five or six, and his brother, age two or three, to the Mormon missionaries.[2]

The missionaries were proselytizing under the direction of Albert Carrington, a powerful Church figure – an Apostle of the Council of Twelve, an advisor to Brigham Young, and the presiding authority over European Missions.[3]

Through the Church's immigration program the missionaries offered to pay Enoch's and his brother's travel to the Promised Land, providing care and escort for them. The family was told they would meet up with their children again, when they also traveled to Zion. Located in America's Great Salt Lake Valley within Brigham Young's State of Deseret, it was the gathering place for the Saint's religious movement.

When the time came for Julia to hand her children over to the missionaries, the scene appeared sinister – the menacing castle, a drizzling, fog-shrouded morning, the clopping of the approaching horse drawn carriage on the cobble street, bearded and black-frocked strangers knocking at the Julin's door. But Julia's faith remained strong. There was a brief patronizing exchange of promises, scripture citing, and prayers calling for God's blessing, and a final pronouncement: "God has called them to America. Amen."

Enoch cried and clung to his mother out of fright. Being "quick tempered and torn by her feelings, Julia knocked him down."[4] He and his brother were quickly swept up by the promoters and carried away wailing and weeping into the dreary, fog-shrouded night. According to doctrine, Enoch's soul at that moment entered into and became one with the Saints' religious movement.

From Orebro, the missionaries and their newly recruited believers traveled in crowded stagecoaches on cobble-lined streets and unpaved country roads for forty-two miles to the Copenhagen sea port. There they met up with more emigrants and a trip split into two segments: the first being a North Sea crossing from Copenhagen to Hull on the east coast of England and the second by railway to Liverpool, where a transoceanic steamship awaited its human cargo – hundreds of converts gathered from the

European Mission that were being transported to the New World.

No doubt Enoch and his brother, along with most immigrants, traveled in "steerage" below deck – the cheapest passage possible – in order to minimize expenditure of the Church's immigration fund monies. The newly recruited Saints sang religious hymns and recited scripture to keep up their courage. The women appeared passive, tearful. God was on everyone's lips. They cried out, "Farewell, dear Sweden."

Once underway on the interminable long voyage, the stormy North Atlantic Sea transformed the scene below decks into a terrifying experience. The heaving ship violently tossed people about

Ninetieth century steamship of the type that transported emigrants

in the dark and cramped quarters, strangers crowded together, weeping, moaning, the sick calling out to God; all enveloped in the overwhelming putrid odors of unwashed humanity, fouled and musty bedding, vomit, and excrement. We can only imagine the emotional nightmare for Enoch and his sibling – the trauma of abandonment, alone amid frightening and strange people and surroundings.

Where did the money come from for Enoch's and the other's passage? Undoubtedly, they were sponsored through the Perpetual Emigration Fund Company, supported by the Church's ranching operations on Antelope Island at the Great Salt Lake. The hordes of emigrants recruited by the Church to travel to America eventually made it necessary for transport companies to build more and larger ships.[5]

The Church's Antelope Island Ranch was operated expressly to provide monetary assistance to encourage immigration of converts. Special fund-raising drives were also conducted. The Apostle Albert Carrington presided over the Fund Company. The monies the company expended for an immigrant's ocean voyage and railroad fare, however, were considered loans. Repayment of those loans provided a perpetual source of assistance to others in need. Emigrants were required to sign promissory notes to the Perpetual Emigration Fund Company before embarking. It was a Church investment, yielding more than just monetary returns.[6]

After the Atlantic crossing from Liverpool to either the port of New York or Baltimore by steam vessel, the passengers were checked for diseases before they were allowed to disembark. On the waterfront the bewildered immigrants were met by hawkers and swindlers clustered around the gangway. From there, the immigrating Saints, with young Enoch and his brother in tow, boarded the transcontinental Union Pacific Railway for Utah Territory – Church trains to the Promised Land. The "golden spike" had been driven ten years earlier at Promontory, Utah.

Boarding the train was a euphemism, in actuality the emigrants were herded into railroad cars with straw covering the floor and locked in for the six-day trip west. After investing in an emigrant's fare, the Church wanted assurance that no one could decide on the spur of the moment to drop off somewhere along the way.

A more romantic version might have had Enoch traveling by sailing ship to America. Indeed, in later years, one of Cal's fanciful tales was that he had been taken onto a "sailing ship." The use of covered wagon and carts on the overland trail by emigrant pioneers mostly ended after the transcontinental railroad was completed. The railroad shortened what had been a six-month trip to Deseret to less than six days.

Upon arriving in the Mormon Kingdom at Salt Lake City, the fatigued and disoriented new converts, having had their faith tested by the long and arduous trip, were conducted to the "Emigrant House." From there they might find themselves deployed by Brigham Young's attendants to different and far-flung parts of the Utah Territory.[7] Unquestioningly, they abided by the canon that "when Church officials had spoken, the thinking had been done." God, it was known, worked in no other way.

Enoch's surname name may have gotten recorded as Carrington because he was traveling with the Apostle when they came through the immigration port of entry at New York or Baltimore, but more likely it was a result of a Mormon "sealing practice" referred to as the "Law of Adoption," wherein younger men were called "sons" and took the surname of an older man, generally an elder or Apostle, whom they then called "father." The sons were to give the fathers the benefit of their labor in return for security, counsel and direction. The reason for this practice was that the rapid westward migration of the Saints commonly estranged members from their families. The Church's adoption practice was an attempt at compensation for the sociological upheaval. Mormon Apostles in this time period not uncommonly had thirty or more young men sealed to them. Enoch may well have been sealed to Albert Carrington.[8]

Taking forty years to complete, the Salt Lake Temple was dedicated in 1893. After it was completed, adoptions were ritualistically sealed to foster parents in the temple, which according to Mormon doctrine was the equivalent of an "earthly" or legal adoption. However, this ritual would not have been in practice at the time of Enoch's arrival, the temple had not yet been completed. Instead, it is likely Enoch was simply unceremoniously handed off to foster parents.

Enoch's birth family believed they would follow closely

Latter Day Saint Apostle Albert Carrington.

behind their children when conditions and finances permitted, but once gathered into the Mormon's immigration system, there was, at the time, no way to track their offspring's location. The rest of the family did, in fact, follow to America some short time later, but there were no records on the where about of Enoch and his brother. As it turned out, Enoch's young brother, who had endured the trip with him, died shortly after their arrival in Utah and was buried in the Salt Lake City cemetery. And Enoch would never see his family again, until a sibling, Zeniph J. Julin, finally reconnected with him in the 1950s, nearly seventy-five years later and hundreds of miles from Salt Lake City. By then, Enoch was in his mid-eighties and the parents were long since deceased.[9]

Enoch's father, Gustaf, succumbed to chronic Bright's disease in 1917; his mother, Julia, died in 1919, reportedly of intestinal parasites. Both are buried in the Salt Lake City cemetery.[10] A sister, also named Julia, was listed as an inmate of the Utah State mental institution at Provo in the 1930 census.

Enoch's namesake, Albert Carrington, had a distinguished career with the Church of Jesus Christ of Latter Day Saints. But he was also a polygamist with many wives and a womanizer. His career was destroyed when he caused an embarrassment to the Church. It was proven that he had forced himself on another man's wife. In 1885, he was accused of infidelity and excommunicated for "lascivious conduct and adultery."

The fact Enoch was given up to strangers by his real family in Sweden and then taken on a long and difficult journey to a strange country, where he had little or no understanding of the language, was undoubtedly an extremely frightening and emotionally traumatic experience for him as a child. He harbored an intense life-long bitterness toward his family and the Mormon Church for it. His virulence was reflected in refusal to even proclaim his true country of origin, when, years later, he sought United States citizenship. Instead he renounced fidelity to the King of England.[11]

In any case, Cal would always facetiously maintain he had ended up as an orphaned child in an Arizona cow camp, "where the men would dry their hands on my long curly hair after the evening wash-up."[12] More to fact, after arrival in Utah he was handed over, or you could say "farmed out," to a Utah family at a Mormon outpost north of Logan, a place called Summit, Utah. Later, the name was changed to Smithfield, after the Ward's first bishop, the Elder John Glover Smith. Approximately sixty-three families formed this frontier community around this time period. At that time, all practicing members of the Mormon Church were "fundamentalists" and much of community's schooling would have taken place in private homes.

There may also be some reason to think Enoch's foster family had later been among settlers dispersed by Brigham Young to Mountain Home in the Boise Valley, Idaho, when Enoch was 8-years old.[13] But the latter accounts are uncertain and most likely are a result of Cal's propensity, as we will later see, for purposely confusing his early origins.

In popular psychology's parlance, Enoch had "issues." He was no doubt a stubbornly angry and resentful adolescent. His Mormon foster parents allegedly raised him under harsh impoverished frontier conditions with little or no formal schooling. He resentfully claimed, "My education was on the back door step."[14] Moreover he was subjected to grueling dawn to dusk labor. We may conclude his childhood consisted of the day-to-day drudgery involved in frontier subsistence farming and homesteading, amply salted with religious fervor and righteousness: fetch wood, carry water, milk the cows, feed the livestock, clean the stables, plow, plant and irrigate the fields, put up hay, read scripture, pray, and attend the Ward's gatherings – a Latter-day Saint administrative unit presided over by a Church appointed bishop. Church members were apt to be cautioned: "Be in the world, but not of the world."

In his later years, Cal reminisced: "I rode my first bronc when I was 15." In reality, it was an unglamorous event. A plow horse he was riding to the field began bucking. Enoch clutched and hung onto the flapping harnesses, bull-headedly sticking with the big draft horse until it quit: "But by God I stayed with him," he proudly exclaimed. "I was the tickeledest kid ever!" From that incident, an identity as a horse breaker and bronc rider took seed. [15]

In his own words, he "hated" the stern Mormon elder, who was the head of his foster family and, perhaps, was the Ward's bishop, too. Time passed and Enoch grew to be a stalwart youth, as his physical stature in adulthood later testified. "At age 16," he confided years later, "I beat the hell out of the S.O.B. [elder] and run away." [16]

He never forgave his real family or the Mormon Church; although in his later years, he was generally on good terms with some of his Latter-day Saint neighbors in Teton Valley. However, instead of being diminished by his traumatic and emotionally painful childhood, he developed a strong instinct for survival and a hard-as-nails self-reliance; still others say he had a tamped down anger which sometimes surfaced as a hatred for the human race. [17]

Many years later, late in his life, when asked in an interview where he was born, he retorted: "No. I don't know where I was born. You got something else there? That [subject] is out." [18] In his final days, it became obvious he did know, but he remained reticent on the subject of his childhood all his life. Only near the very end did he disclose the true story, as told here, of his childhood.

Twodot Stachel's open-range cattle drive. L.A. Hoffman photo. Courtesy Coffrins Old West Gallery, Bozeman, Montana.

2

Open Range Cattle Drover

Not much is known about Enoch's immediate history after he broke away from his Utah foster family. As a runaway, he drifted south, an orphan saddle tramp riding grub line. Around 1890, he ended up in Arizona cow camp: "I was down there bumming around when I was a kid, y'see. That's where I started out, learned to ride."[1]

L.A. Hoffman's 1907 *Scribner's* magazine article, "The Last Busting at Bow-Gun," describes firsthand what cow-punchin' and an Arizona cow-camp was like back then. In those days, a hand was expected to ride out his own string of saddle stock wherever or whenever it was given to him. One would certainly have to "learn to ride."

Cowboying was a rough way to make a livelihood; those who did were justifiably proud of their abilities. Some men chose to wear heavy wooly chaps, even in the hottest weather, and large rowel spurs, as badges of their profession.

Characteristic of Carrington, and no doubt reflecting the soured feelings he harbored for his family, at some point he chose his own name, California, after a cowboy he admired. Later he shortened California to Cal, but continued using the surname name Carrington.

He was fond of playing with his name, and even tried the

sobriquet Calvin, perhaps a takeoff on his given middle name, Kavington. It is uncertain why, ironically, he continued with the name of the Mormon Apostle Carrington, who was no relation. As was explained earlier, there was a good chance he received this surname through an early-day Mormon adoption ritual.

He kept Enoch for a first name. In early documents, it is spelled Enock, perhaps initially by the immigration port authority when it was recorded on his entry into the United States. He even tried "Eunuch" at one point, because he said he liked the way it sounded, but a friend carefully called his attention to its meaning.[2]

Generally, he used the name Enoch, rather than Cal, in his early business dealings, or C.E. Carrington and E.C. Carrington, as documents show. But most of all, he became identified as Cal Carrington, or as his friends called him, Cal. For his entire life and beyond, however, confusion has existed over his name.

Beginning around age sixteen, Cal independently and solitarily roamed the western frontier from Old Mexico to Alberta, Canada, working as a cattle drover, herding livestock from the Southwest up into Montana and Canada. He became a top cowhand and bronc rider.[3] Late in his life, when asked about his early day bronc busting, Cal replied, "They was rough treatment, but I had to make my livin' some way."[4]

Montana mining camps had a pent-up demand for beef. On one cattle drive pushing cattle from the Southwest up through Colorado to Helena, Montana, "Slater and Twodot [Satchel]" were said to have been the cattle owners or trail bosses. "The drive took about two years, making less than twelve miles a day."[5]

Generally, herds consisted of several-thousand head of longhorn cattle. Cattle would be strung out in a mile-long drift. "What laggards the first herd left behind, the trail herd picked up," Cal recalled. To keep the cattle moving, the drovers, choking in the heat and dust, would ride behind them whistling and loudly yelling – *Ha-yah*.

Cal claimed, "If there was no noise, the cattle was nervous... jackrabbit or anything and off they'd go. I believe that stock likes music. Oh God, yes, we sung to 'em. After you've been on herd three to four weeks you ain't hoarse [from singing] anymore."

Riding night herd, a cowboy would start up a tune, singing a stanza: "Green grow the lilacs, all sparkling with dew..." The rider on the opposite side of the herd would answer back with the second line: "I'm lonesome, my darling, since parting from you."

It was all before barbwire fencing. "Oh, my God, no," Cal responded to a question on fences, "There were no bob-wahr fences [in those days]. We didn't even have corrals to rope in. It was wide open country with buffalo bones still lying around."

Cal allowed that it was easy to lose cattle on those drives with "three to seven thousand trailing along ... cows and calves drop out ... one man's got a bunch of cows over here and that animal gets in that bunch ... and if the man rides looking for something of his, it's fifty-fifty whether he'll see his own animal." He added, "Course, I didn't know nothin' about rustling cattle at that time [as a kid], but since then I've learned a few things.[6]

"When they got to Helena, they [the cattle owners] had a row among themselves over strays. They said thar was eight-hundred head of strays [missing cattle]," Cal recalled. "Twodot shot Slater and killed him [when he found out]. I didn't see it, but I was thar... a little bit north and west of Helena, on a creek."[7]

"The boys would take a notion to go in to town along the trail once in a while and have a little celebration, sorta 'hurrah the town'," Cal called to mind. "If they destroyed anything or shot a light or two, they always paid for it. The bartenders or saloon managers hardly ever objected." When asked if some of the boys celebrated quite a bit? Cal replied, "Yeah, I've heard tell quite a bit." Characteristically, in his telling, it was always the other guy, not himself.

Asked, "When a cattle drive ended, did the men ride through

the town real fast discharging their guns?" Cal responded defensively, "I was never a desperado."[8]

Along the way, cattle sometimes ended up being driven past and right through homesteads, which irritated the farmers, to say the least. Cal commented, "Well, I never seen a quarrel, but I heard some of them cussin'. About as big a stir as affected me was one day passing along a farmer's place with our cattle, there was some tame green-head ducks.

"The cook says to me, 'Bet you can't hit one of them.'"

"I had an old cap and ball six-shooter loaded with shot. I killed one of them and the farmer came up and about eat me up. So the boys had to take him apart – little stunts like that about happened every day."[9]

Enduring the less romantic side of a cowboy's life was also a part of it: short pay; ten to twelve hours a day in the saddle; a home and kitchen on wheels serving up chuck wagon fare – beef, beans and bread; extreme weather; sagebrush for a bed; tents and drafty cabins for shelter; dangerous and unpredictable horses; saddle sores on both horses and riders; and nothing dirtier and lower than "riding drag." Cal said, "Half the time I just slept out on the ground. If it rained, I'd just let it wash me and the dirty camp bedding out."[10]

Still, Cal became proficient at skills that served him his entire life – riding, horse packing, bustin' broncs, handling livestock, all aspects of ranching, and most of all getting along with some pretty rough characters.

By the late 1800s, the railroads had penetrated inaccessible parts of the West and it became unnecessary to drive cattle long distances to market. Cal had been engaged in open-range cattle drives as that era of the American cowboy was coming to a close. A cowboy's remark in L.A. Huffman's 1907 *Scribner's* magazine story summed it up: "Hain't goin' to be no room on this earth for 'ery real cow-hand a few years more."

Similar to his childhood years, Cal generally did not discuss his early buckaroo and saddle tramp days much, or if he did, he did not get into details – stories he told to Teton Valley children and the University of Wyoming interviewers late in his life are the exceptions. Invariably, this has been misinterpreted that he was hiding something from those years. One thing is certain though, he never frequented or even passed through Jackson Hole in those years as an open-range cowboy.

Taming a bronc. Courtesy American Heritage Center, University of Wyoming, Laramie.

3

A Horseman and Cowboy

Who was this enigmatic man, Cal Carrington? It might be said he lived multiple lives over the course of his lifetime. Perception of him, often contrasting, changes with the places, people and times. No single description is satisfactory, but if a snapshot of his character must be chosen, it might best be taken from his early years as a Western horseman and cowboy. It's an image that most certainly would have pleased Cal, too.

People were inclined to photograph him – vacationing dudes, ranch owners, socialites, friends, and historians all did. There is an uncommon amount of photographic images of him spanning his adult life and chronicling his appearance. Included in this biography are the images of a grinning, mischievous-looking young cowboy; a hunting guide and horseman; and a strapping, handsome man with neckerchief, leather cuffs, and his signature angora chaps. Later, a middle-aged man in a formal suit with silk socks and tea cups, sitting next to a groomed poodle. And, toward the end, a tough-looking, colorful character appearing disheveled, cantankerous and toothless, who hung out in Jackson's Wort Hotel – a crusty old timer who had outlived more than one era.

When Cal first rode into Teton Valley in 1897, he was a young cowboy, yet his demeanor and mannerisms already commanded people's attention and comment. He stood out from the average man both in appearance and competency. But this, along with his

Enoch Cal Carrington with leather cuffs, vest, and neckerchief, c1916.
Courtesy of Joe Arnold and family.

rugged and handsome looks, when combined with a tight-lipped countenance and solitary nature, often inspired and elicited fanciful rumors and small-town gossip about him.

As a grown man, Carrington was over six-feet tall, perhaps 6'2" – 6'3", around two-hundred pounds, with taffy-colored hair, clear blue eyes, a narrow waist, great chest and large hands – a ruggedly handsome and powerful man. Jackson wrangler, Rex Ross, once pointed out that, "While Cal didn't look like a real tough guy, he was, and he was afraid of no one."[1]

In his heyday in Jackson Hole, when he dressed up, he sometimes wore silver-studded leather cuffs and a black and yellow neckerchief tossed airily over one shoulder. Along with a tall cowboy hat, angora chaps, and spurred high-heeled boots, he presented an imposing figure. Later in life, in formal dress attire, he was still a dashing figure summoning respect.

The Burt family, who authored numerous novels in Jackson Hole, patterned their Western characters after him, including Katharine N. Burt's cowboy figures in her book *The Branding Iron*. In Struthers Burt's *Diary of a Dude Wrangler*, his character Nate was based on early impressions of Cal:

> "Nate was from Arizona...he wore big spurs, high-heeled boots covered with fancy stitching, chaps of leather or angora wool, flannel shirt, neck handkerchief and sombrero...[he] had been a cowpuncher all his life and had to the fullest extent that curious baffling pride... [which can make] a man with whom you have camped and slept and talked leave you suddenly without a word of explanation... sharp as moonlight and as cold as a knife."[2]

Cal epitomized the glamorous image of the competent Western horseman. Struther's son, Nathaniel Burt, also a writer, considered Cal to be an archetype:

> "Lank, sardonic, profane and dictatorial, with an aura of glamour and expertise... [he] treated horses with a mixture of affection, callousness, care, amusement, irritation... with

a low steady drone of curses... [and] grave deliberation in all movements derived from dealing with spooky animals; [there was a] quiet quick sureness in each act of horse catching, saddling, mounting–precision, economy, grace, effectiveness."[3]

Struthers Burt penned another narrative further reinforcing the image of Cal's superb horsemanship:

"Riding across the country with Cal at dusk, when he was in a hurry to get back to camp or the ranch was an experience to be remembered. Shale rock, fallen timber, gullies, grass slopes so precipitous that a horse sat down on his tail were nothing to him ... There wasn't a horse he couldn't gentle nor ride...[he was] the prototype of the old time cowboy."[4]

People also read into Cal's taciturn nature a reckless or dangerous side which added to his mystique. Cissy Patterson's initial impression was that he "reminded her of a wolf – lone, savage and quick on his feet." In her 1926 novel, *Glass Houses*, she modeled her aloof and darkly brooding character, Ben, after Carrington. In her story, he jealously and very coolly murdered a long-standing rival, the scarcely disguised Senator William Borah of Idaho. Cissy described the rivalry as "two dogs quarreling over a bone for years;" the object of the jealous rivalry in her story was a woman named Mary, a composite representation of herself.

One sometimes gets the feeling that Cal was a man who would give you his last dime, but the next time he'd break your neck instead, and you'd never know why he had done either one. It was said, "Anyone who wanted to make friends with Cal had to make the initial overture, and then he might, or might not, reciprocate."[5] Clay Taylor, who's family homesteaded at the mouth of Flat Creek Canyon commented, "Cal was a rough guy, he could be intimidating."

On the other hand, perhaps because of being orphaned and without family, evidence points to Cal being loyal and generous

Cal Carrington in Western garb resting on a log while his horse waits nearby c1916.
Courtesy of JHHSM 2004.0102.602.

to those he considered his friends or neighbors. He maintained strong, lifelong friendships with some. For those people, he went the extra mile to do considerate or helpful things.

Cal's words, when he chose, could be "cuttingly laconic or sardonic."[6] Some say he taught himself to read and write.[7] No doubt that is partly the case. However, his friend Felicia Gizycka, Cissy Patterson's daughter, wrote about a person in his life named Mary Frances Ake, a well-educated and much younger woman at Mountain Home, Idaho. Felicia claimed Mary Ake nursed Cal when he had Rocky Mountain spotted fever – the deadliest of all tick-borne illnesses – and taught him some of his reading and writing skills.

Cal's signature on documents is a practiced bold calligraphy, and he readily carried on correspondence in letters –"splashing

Enoch Carrington

some ink," as he referred to it. He also owned and used what he called a "word machine"– a typewriter. Cal's spelling, however, was creative; akin to the phonetic spelling in the original journals of Lewis and Clark. Still, Felicia characterized him as "barely literate."[8]

Carrington was a man of polar contrasts and contradictions. He successfully integrated into high society in midlife, yet at the same time, in Teton Valley, he was considered by some as a "kinda rough guy who'd seen rough times, certainly not a Sunday school boy."[9] Nathanial Burt referred to him as a "wild man," who added spice to Jackson Hole's Bar BC guest ranch setup, especially for the dude girls.[10] Yet, conversely, Jackson Hole homesteader and author, Bertha Gillette described Cal as "jolly... never known to be without a broad smile."[11]

Cal, like many Westerners in those times, was skeptical of government red tape and procedures. He appears to have made a lifelong practice of avoiding and mocking it whenever possible. He did not leave a paper trail, intentionally or otherwise, if he could avoid it. For whatever reasons one wants to imagine, he appeared skittish about drawing attention to his name or doings. It went against his grain.

It is probably no accident that his name doesn't show up in any early census records for either Idaho or Wyoming. But his "it's none of their business" attitude could not avoid paper trails associated with, for example: his Desert Entry claim, Forest Service employment, the World War I draft register, his 1906 National Forest Homestead Act paperwork, water right applications, and real estate transactions. The frequently manipulative manner in which he went about satisfying paper requirements demonstrated a distrust, indifference, or impatient scorn for such things.

Reminiscent of nineteenth-century adventurers, Cal had an incredible wanderlust. Some might say he was always searching. His lifetime of roaming boggles the mind – from Sweden to America; throughout the Intermountain West and Yellowstone; from the West Coast, Southwest, Midwest, and East Coast to the Bahamas, Canada, Europe, Africa, and even the goldfields of Nome, Alaska – all before commercial air flights.

When Carrington first rode into the Teton country, he was a young buckaroo, vigorous and energetic, good at what he did and raring to prove it. That is how he is best remembered: a roguish cowboy and horseman and, some would have you believe, an outlaw, too.

Those who only know about Cal Carrington through the romantic Wild West myths circulated in Jackson Hole find it hard to relate to him having had a more mundane life as a cattle drover, a wrangler and horse packer for the government, a Teton Valley rancher and farmer, or as a gadabout socialite and California snowbird. They don't want to hear about those parts of his life, preferring to remember or think of him only as a reckless outlaw, regardless of whether or not it was true.

Crabtree Hotel proprietors Henry and Rose Crabtree's son, Hank, in an interview with Cissy's biographer Ralph Martin, recalled, "Cal was a big, tall guy, built like Gary Cooper – tall, rangy and slim. He looked the part, wore Western clothes the way they were meant to be worn."

When Cal worked at the Bar BC guest ranch in Jackson Hole, there was a characterization of him by one of Cissy's biographers which pretty much summed it up: "Easterners photographed Cal to prove to their friends back home that the frontier still existed."[12]

Cal never allowed his homesteading and farming activities in Teton Valley to tie him down. Grubbing out a homestead at Bates – in Idaho near Driggs – was only one of his many endeavors, sort of a hole card. He apparently didn't talk about his homesteading at Bates much during his glamour years in Jackson Hole, but it, like his other ventures, ambitions, and skills, seasoned with a measure of good luck, all came together and paid off in spades over his lifetime.

There were four things Cal despised: his family, the Mormon Church, sanctimonious Mormons, and sheep. "I had no use for sheep, wouldn't even wear woolen socks, or such trash as that."[13]

Late in life, Cal did make one indisputable statement about himself, saying: "I always did like horses and women."[14]

The view from Harrup's Hill when first entering Teton Valley, undated.

4

Coming into the Tetons

The Shoshone called the expansive mountain valley on the west side of the Teton Mountains "Broad Valley." The mountain men named it Pierre's Hole. Later, Mormon settlers called it Teton Basin. Today, it is known as Teton Valley.

In a sepia-toned scene out of the past, Cal, and a nineteen-year old traveling companion, James "Jim" H. Berger, first rode into Teton Basin in April 1897 on a rattling, light iron-tired wagon pulled by a team of horses. Two more horses trotted behind them tied to the wagon.[1] The men wore Western work clothing common to the era consisting of overalls, blue denim shirts, boots, tall hats and loose neckerchiefs. Cal was about twenty-four years old at the time.

Three of the four horses belonged to Cal, and as he told it years later, Jim had asked if he could come along with him. Berger, who owned one of the horses, also had twenty-five cents in his pocket. Jim was originally from Milville, near Providence, Utah, in the Cache Valley.[2] His father had been among Salt Lake Valley's earliest Mormon pioneers. Although neither of the two men could have articulated it, both, typical of the era, were restlessly searching for something: new country, adventure, and livelihood, perhaps.

Cal and Jim had followed the old Mormon Trail, a muddy wagon road, from Cache Valley, Utah, where Cal had spent the winter. When asked some sixty years later where he had been before then, he growled defensively, "That's none of your damn business," which only added to the mystique of his early years.[3]

They were forced to hold over near Menan, Idaho, for nearly a month while the winter's accumulation of snow along the route to Teton Basin finally receded enough to get through.[4] Settled in 1879, Menan was the first Mormon community to be established in the Snake River Valley. A ferry had been built there; Cal and Jim undoubtedly used it to get their wagon and horses across the Snake River.

Only nine miles from Menan, Market Lake (later named Roberts, Idaho) consisted of a saloon, post office, store, and livery stable. Serving as a stage stop between Salt Lake City and the gold fields in Virginia City, Montana, Market Lake boasted a railroad terminal by 1879.

The Menan and Market Lake vicinity, like most river bottom and mountain meadow areas, swarmed with clouds of mosquitoes.[5] Bears and wolves were not much worry, more alarming were the fearsome mosquitoes. In desperation, sheep dip – a concoction of carbolic acid, coal tar, and kerosene used to disinfect sheep – might be used as a repellant, if the ingredients were available.

Cal and Jim carried provisions with them. The menu items consisted of a sack of flour for Dutch-oven biscuits, dried apples and peaches, a container of honey and a ham.[6] In addition, they had hauled a plow and a mower belonging to Cal, along with their bedding, in the wagon.[7]

Columbus "Lum" Nickerson, driving a four-horse team with a wagon load of hay, was the first person they encountered when they were approaching Teton Valley.[8] Nickerson was a reformed outlaw, one of valley's toughest characters.

Ten years earlier, Lum, along with two others, Ed Harrington and Jim Robinson, had tried their hand at rustling livestock in Teton Basin. A posse caught up with them; Robinson was shot and

James "Jim" Berger portrait, c1897. Courtesy James Berger family.

died. Harrington and Nickerson were jailed. In a failed jail escape, Harrington was shot in the foot. Both men were recaptured and did some serious jail time.[9]

Of course, Cal and Jim Berger didn't know all that, they were simply pleased to make Lum's acquaintance. Seeing Lum's load of hay impressed them with the valley's potential for farming.

Rumors buzzed ahead of them among Teton Valley's Mormon

settlers: "Look out for those two strangers, they're claim jumpers." Years later, Cal still remonstrated angrily when recalling this malicious gossip.[10]

As early as 1889, Latter-day Saints in Salt Lake City had extolled the natural wonders and resources of Teton Valley in the *Deseret News*, encouraging its settlement.[11] It's reasonable to assume that the two young men seeking to make a start had been influenced by those stories while living among Utah settlers.

Historian Fredrick Jackson Turner declared the American frontier "finally closed" in 1892, five years before Cal's arrival in the Tetons, but conditions in the isolated high mountain valleys arguably didn't agree. Surveyor William Owen described the country surrounding the Tetons that same year as "rugged and wild beyond the power of words to convey."[12]

For the Nation, this was a time of enormous and rapid growth. The first ship carrying gold from the Yukon arrived in Seattle, Washington, that year, while Mark Twain responded to rumors that "the report of his death was an exaggeration"; and, Cheyenne, Wyoming, advertised its first *Frontier Days* celebration. But Cal and Jim knew nothing of outside events, they were exhilarated with the potential of their natural surroundings and having the time of their lives exploring Teton Basin.

Cal and Jim arrived in Teton Valley twenty years after its native inhabitants had been forcefully evicted to the Fort Hall and Wind River Reservations, and only around fourteen years after the valley's first pioneers had settled there. It was the same year in which cattlemen first threatened that they would not permit sheep to cross Teton Pass into Jackson Hole. Mountain man Beaver Dick Leigh who had once noted in his journal, "Teton Basin was the beautifulest sight in the whole world," was still living and guiding hunters at that time.[13]

But the springtime quagmire on frontier Driggs' Main Street was anything but beautiful. It was a thoroughfare for large numbers of cattle, sheep and horses on the way to pasture. Melting snow, mud and manure combined to give it the mucky look of a lazy man's barnyard. It was a springtime mien which characterized downtown Driggs and other frontier towns for decades.[14]

Camped near David Breckenridge's homestead along the Teton River, Cal and Jim spent several days hunting sage grouse and fishing. Breckenridge was a rugged frontiersman, one of the first pioneers to permanently settle in Teton Basin. After a couple years of trapping in Jackson Hole and surviving formidable winters, he had taken up a homestead near present day Tetonia in 1884.

In their exploring the north-end of the valley, Cal and Jim walked to Hank Goes' homestead at the mouth of Packsaddle Creek, where they bought a slab of bacon for fifty-cents. The bacon furnished grease essential for their cooking.[15]

Generally, in the progression of a settlement's development, a store comes first. Located in an old homestead cabin, Don Driggs' mercantile, the "Star Commercial," served that purpose. There Cal purchased additional staples, including a year's supply of blackstrap molasses in a two-and-a-half gallon can for $1.75. In the process, he questioned store owner Driggs about the prospects of homesteading in Teton Basin. A man named J. Moffat, who later served as a witness on Cal's Desert Entry submissions, overheard and advised Cal about unclaimed tracts at a place called Bates – named after Tom Bates, who had first taken up land there near the mouth of Mahogany Creek around 1888.[16]

Cal squatted (took up residence without title, as was the practice) on a near level 160-acre tract near the mouth of Mahogany Creek, and according to Bureau of Land Management General Land Office (GLO) records, Berger settled a mile northwest, on a +159.64 acre parcel. A patent for the latter tract was issued under the Homestead Entry Act to James H. Berger on March 1, 1904.[17] What may not have been evident to Cal at the time was that the Bates area was sparsely settled for a reason – there were

Replica of Don Driggs' store, the Star Commercial. Photo by the author.

few streams and little readily available water. Water rights and availability would be issues that were to plague him in later years.

In fact, Cal first attempted to claim a parcel east of settler John Holland's 320-acre Horseshoe Creek Ranch. In April 1897, he filed a water right for "the surplus water from John Holland's spring."[18] But when it became obvious that was not going to be very workable, he moved over to the mouth of Mahogany Creek location.[19]

John Holland employed Berger at cutting and skidding logs from Twin Creek in the Big Hole Mountains for construction of corrals, barns and buildings on his Horseshoe Creek Ranch. Berger worked dawn-to-dusk six days a week for twenty-dollars a month. Holland offered the fringe benefit that on Sundays Jim was free to use the horse team to skid logs for his own cabin, if he felt like it.[20]

Jim Berger took two days off that summer to ride to St. Anthony and back in order to pay the nineteen-dollar filing fee for his homestead application, leaving him a whole dollar to live on that month. When snow began to drift in the valley, Berger headed back south, over wintering that first year in Utah. Returning the next spring, Jim earned a reputation for being a hard worker – cutting timber, working with stock, and cutting and stacking hay for ranchers as far way as Rexburg for $1.25 a day. Jim soon acquired his own team of horses and half-dozen head of cattle.[21]

Holland's Horseshoe Creek Ranch operation was mostly involved with raising horses. Cal was employed applying his cow-camp riding experience breaking horses for Holland. Working with horses back then meant not only could one ride, but also train, shoe, and provide all manner of needed equine care.

Bronc busting in those days was literally that, breaking a horse to the point of submission. The horse would be fore footed from the string with a no-fuss throw of a catch-rope, known as a hoolihan, wrestled squealing to its knees – called "earring him

Jim Berger's original homestead cabin near Bates, undated. Courtesy of James Berger family.

down"– and a saddle gotten onto it. It would then be Cal's job to ride and buck the horse, spurring it unmercifully with sharp rowels, while the horse plowed up the earth, until it finally either quit or crippled itself. Then it was run around the corral until both it and its rider were exhausted.

Other forceful methods were sometimes employed, too. Unbroken horses were tied to the saddle horn of a strong, dependable horse with a short halter and made to travel along for miles. For hard-headed cayuses, harsher methods might be used, such as "cross-hobbles" or "scotch hobbles"– tying a hind leg up to the horse's brisket, then hitching it to a snubbing post, leaving the horse standing for hours, preferably in the heat of the day. When the horse finally quit struggling, his hind leg was released.

All horse breaking methods essentially consisted of putting pressure on the animal when it resisted, and relaxing it when the horse quit fighting. Generally, it was brutal business, definitely not for the timid. There were no "horse whispers" in those days, only steady streams of threats, yelling, and lots of cussin'. Asked about his bronc busting years later, Cal responded, "I had to make a livin' somehow, that seemed easiest at the time."[22]

Near the end of his life, Cal was asked what he remembered most about coming into Teton Valley for the first time. No doubt the interviewer expected him to wax nostalgically about unsettled prairie or the rugged, snow-covered mountains, but men who engaged in the struggle of frontier existence rarely displayed such sentiment. Instead, Cal's reply echoed the simple pragmatism of the time: "The grass, grass everywhere, it was a damn good place to picket a horse."[23]

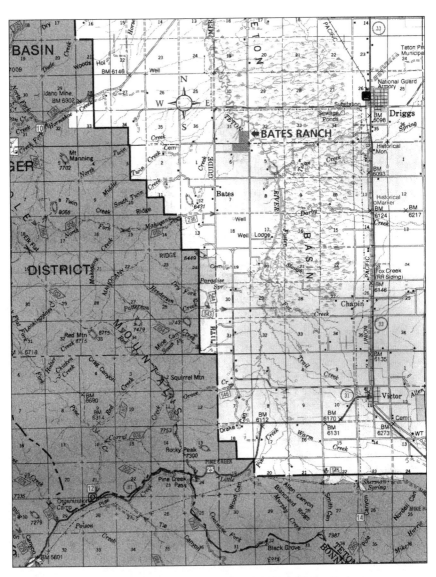

Map of the location of Cal's Bates Ranch in Teton Valley, Idaho.

5
Teton Valley Desert Land Entry

To locate the 160-acre Bates tract southwest of the Driggs settlement, where Moffat directed him, Cal had to first ford the overflowing Teton River. Springtime crossing of the river in those days could be difficult. One historic ford was located south of Bates, near Fox Creek.[1]

The tract Cal located and "squatted on" (took up residence without title) ominously qualified as "desert land," meaning it was incapable of producing an agricultural crop without artificial irrigation. Anyone who wanted to take up the challenge of developing it through irrigation and successfully producing at least 80 acres of crop land within a four-year period could then purchase it from the government for $1.25 per acre under the 1877 Desert Land Act. The process was referred to as a Desert Entry.

A bargain? Perhaps, but in practice it was not free land. Pioneering a farm and proving up required hard work, time, coping with adversity, and a rare item in those days, money.

After staking his squatter's claim on the land, Cal, with the help of neighbors, including probably Jim Berger, set about building himself a stout cabin and stable shelter for his horses. Connecting to his stable he constructed a lodgepole pine rail corral. He also worked at putting up wild hay, cutting a supply of firewood, breaking horses at Holland's ranch, and subsistence hunting. As Cal himself said, "There was plenty of hunting to keep a fellow alive." It was all part of establishing his land claim and

NOTICE OF WATER RIGHT.

STATE OF IDAHO,
County of *Fremont* } ss.

To All Concerned Notice is Hereby Given:

1st. That *George W Allen* and *Enoch Carrington*
of *Bates, Fremont Co, Idaho*

hereby claim the use of the waters of *The South Fork of Mahogany Creek*
in Fremont County, Idaho

to the extent of *Ten* cubic feet per second.

2nd. It is intended to divert said water at or near the point where a copy of this notice is posted, and more definitely described as follows: *on the South Bank of the*
Main Channel of Mahogany Creek, at a point
about 40 rods east of the NW Corner of the SW¼ of
SW¼ Section 6, Tsp 4 N R 45 E, B Meridian as
previously claimed and recorded

(In above description give legal subdivision of land or describe the place with reference to some prominent landmark.)

3rd. The purpose for which said water is intended to be used is
Agricultural and domestic use

The place of intended use is *near Bates, Fremont County, Idaho*

4th. It is intended to divert said water by means of *a reservoir to hold*
all the high water of Said South Mahogany Creek at a
point in the Canyon about 3 miles above the headgate described in
~~this order~~
~~The general course of the proposed canal is~~ *dam*
The length of the proposed ~~canal~~ is *for this reservoir is about 200 ft*

It is intended to use said water for irrigating the following described land: *NW¼ Section*
5, NE¼ Sec 6, Tsp 4 N, W½ SW¼ Section 32, E½ SE¼
Section 31, Tsp 5 N R 45 E.

5th. It is intended to have the works for diversion and use of said water as aforesaid completed within *five* years. (This must in no case exceed five years.)

Witness *our* hands at *Bates Fremont Co*, Idaho, this *29*
day of *October* 1901.

George W Allen
Enoch Carrington
} Claimants

Notice of Water Right filing.

insuring himself the means to survive Teton Valley's brutal winter. Similar to Jim Berger, it didn't leave him much time for anything else that first summer in 1897.

Topographically, Cal's Desert Entry parcel was on a bench west of the Teton River, with the eastern part of the tract being close to the river at what was then the mouth of Mahogany Creek. But he had no way to raise water from the river onto his land. In 1900 and 1901, he filed claims on water from Mahogany Creek. Establishing water rights and developing irrigation for his land was a required step in the Desert Entry process. Cal's water right claims were recorded at Blackfoot, Idaho. Neighbors who recorded water rights from Mahogany Creek around the same time were homesteaders George Allen, B. Dustin, and G. E. Stone.[2] Decades later, the Dustins would challenge Cal's water right share in court.[3]

On June 5, 1901, Cal submitted a Declaration of Applicant at Oasis, a small community located southeast of Tetonia on Packsaddle Creek. Located at the foot of the Big Hole Mountains, it was then part of Fremont County, Idaho. The document was his sworn testimony that the tract qualified as "desert land" and it stated his intention to "reclaim" it. At this point he paid an application fee of fifteen dollars, plus twenty-five cents per acre. His application was identified on Department of Interior, General Land Office (GLO) records as "No. 3116."[4]

He also filed a Declaration of Intention in St. Anthony, Idaho, stating under sworn oath it was his "bona fide intention to become a citizen of the United States, and to renounce forever all allegiance to the King of England of whom he was a subject." A provision of the Desert Land Act required that the applicant be a citizen of the United States or to declare under oath his intention of becoming one.[5]

During the years from 1897 to 1907, Cal doggedly submitted the required witness statements, various sworn proofs, and underwent investigations of his improvements, labors and veracity, in order to prove up and gain title to his Bates tract. National

DECLARATION OF INTENTION.

I, Enoch Carrington, do declare, on oath, that it is bona fide my intention to become a CITIZEN OF THE UNITED STATES OF AMERICA, and to renounce and abjure forever all allegiance and fidelity to all and any foreign Prince, Potentate, State and Sovereignty whatsoever, and particularly to the King of England of whom I was a subject.

Enoch Carrington

Sworn to and subscribed before me, at my office, this 5" day of June A. D. 189- 190 6

A. M. Carter
Clerk of the District Court.

By Rose E. Drew
Deputy Clerk.

Fifth Judicial District Court in and for the State of Idaho.

Sworn 1901 Statement by Enoch Carrington of intention to become a U.S. citizen.

Archive documents record a saga of Cal's persistent labors, trials, and more than his share of bureaucratic tribulations: building a house, stable and corrals, digging two miles of irrigation ditches with his neighbor Ed Seymour, clearing and grubbing fifty acres, building fence, planting twenty acres of timothy and oats, annually cutting wild hay, involvement in water right disputes, and traveling to Oasis, Blackfoot and St. Anthony, Idaho, to submit timely sworn and witnessed statements to the GLO.[6]

The application witnesses signing for Cal in 1901, for example, included neighboring rancher Ed Seymour, rancher Carlos Moon, saloon keeper George Allen, rancher John H. Holland, and others residing at Oasis, Idaho. James Berger was a witness on Cal's improvement affidavits in 1902.[7]

Cal's witness and part-time employer, John Holland, was a well known, but controversial, historical figure in early day Jackson Hole. One of the Hole's original settlers in 1883, it was suspected (but never proven) that he may have lived on both sides of the law in his early years in Jackson Hole.[8]

Holland originally took up a homestead in Jackson Hole on Nowlin Creek, just north of Miller's Butte. He carried mail, served as the Hole's first Justice of the Peace, and also merchandised goods in Teton Valley and Jackson Hole. Don Driggs' store, the "Star Commercial," was initially financed, in part, by Holland.

After he married Maud, Dan "Dad" Carpenter's youngest daughter, sometime around 1894, Holland sold his homestead in Jackson Hole. They moved to Horseshoe Creek in Teton Basin around 1895-96, so they could be near her family. Dad Carpenter was a Civil War veteran living in or near Teton Basin.[9]

Irrigation ditches that serve parts of Jackson Hole's National Elk Refuge today yet are attributed to Holland. They were dug using a fresnos, a scoop pulled by horse teams, and by hand methods, both requiring a lot of hard labor. Cal's relationship with Holland is particularly relevant from the standpoint of horse rustling stories that later circulated and which are addressed in following chapters. Cal boarded with and did ranch work for Holland during his early years in Teton Valley and Jackson Hole; notably, breaking horses at Holland's Horseshoe Creek Ranch.[10]

Cal submitted his final Desert Entry proof December 1904. And in August 1905, a full eight years from when he first saw the property, he made the final purchase payment of $160.29 (a dollar per acre) to the GLO in Blackfoot, Idaho. Some might care to speculate on how a foot-loose cowboy like Cal ever came up with $160.29? Turns out, Cal had somehow also wrangled seasonal employment with the fledgling Forest Service and Yellowstone National Park in those years, jobs which paid in cash money.

Taken at face value, all his labor, improvements, proofs, timely filings, and payments should have served to satisfy the cumbersome bureaucratic proving-up process, but there was a hitch. The Desert Land Act had a notorious history of producing fraudulent claims. According to the Bureau of Land Management, a majority of Desert Entry claims in the western United States were bogus.[11]

Claimants were inclined to fudge. With a wink and nod local witnesses went along with it. They were expected to be "credible," but the unstated code was: "you witness mine, I'll witness yours"– you scratch my back, I'll scratch yours. Together they were united by the land, labor and common destiny. It was a part of the culture, place, and time; the common man against the government. It fit a notion expressed in a popular 1850s song –"Uncle Sam is rich enough to give us all a farm..."

Not surprising then, but contrary to Cal's filed statements, in an August 1905 field inspection of his Bates tract, following his final proof submittal and payment, a government examiner noted: "... [only] twenty acres have been prepared for irrigation, [and only] five acres have actually been irrigated and cultivated, [and further] it is believed the water supply is insufficient." As a consequence, it was recommended Carrington's case be "specially examined" by a GLO agent. It was, after all, understandably difficult to keep as many irons in the fire as Cal had going and

In reply please refer to   FHN   and date of this letter.

SUBJECT: Desert land entry.

Address all communications to
"Director, U. S. Geological Survey,
Washington, D. C."

DEPARTMENT OF THE INTERIOR

GBF

UNITED STATES GEOLOGICAL SURVEY

WASHINGTON, D. C.,   August 19, 1905.

Commissioner of the General Land Office,

Washington, D.C.

Sir:

Referring to your letters of January 19 and May 2, 1905, relative to D.L.E. No.3116, Enoch Carrington, lots 1 and 2, Sec.6, T.4 N., E$\frac{1}{2}$SE$\frac{1}{4}$ Sec.31, T.5 N., R.45 E., Blackfoot, Idaho, land district, I have to state that from a field examination of this tract made July 5, 1905, it appears that while 20 acres have been prepared for irrigation, but about five acres have been actually irrigated and cultivated. It is believed that the water supply is insufficient and therefore recommendation is made that the case be specially examined by a representative of the General Land Office.

Very respectfully,

Acting Director.

Denial of Enoch Carrington's request for his Bates Desert Entry patent in 1905.

Cal Carrington's original 1897 Bates homestead cabin as it appeared in 2004.
Photo by the author.

still make all his necessary improvements. Patent was withheld pending the investigation.[12]

It was July 22, 1907, nearly two years later, before special agent Henry Brighton, from the GLO Field Division at Salt Lake City, traveled the two days, first by rail (the Oregon Short Line had reached Rexburg in 1899 and St. Anthony by 1902), and then by buckboard or saddle horse to Bates in Teton Valley, to carry out his inspection and render a determination.

Inspector Brighton interviewed Teton Valley residents and neighbors J. Gale, J. Moffat, J. Black and B. Homer, all of whom vouched for Cal's veracity. Brighton determined the water rights, improvements, and water being run over broken and previously cultivated land to be sufficient; although, he did remark on the uncertain fact that no crops were presently growing and Cal was nowhere to be found. His neighbors covered for Cal, telling the inspector that he "was off working for the Forest Service." Brighton also noted, "The claim was improved with [a] fair log house and stable."[13]

In his easygoing two-page report Brighton found in favor of Cal, and in October 1907, it was recommended the claim go to patent.[14] One consolation, at least Cal did not have to pay taxes on the property for all the years he was waiting for patent approval. Cal finally received title to the property ten years after he had first taken up squatter's rights. It was granted by President Theodore Roosevelt's authority October 26, 1907.

Still, it was nowhere near a record for time required to gain a Desert Entry title. Early day Jackson Hole settler John Cherry took nineteen years to finally prove up and receive his Desert Land certificate at Willow Flat (today's Hatchet Ranch) near Moran, Wyoming.[15] Willow Flat along the Buffalo Fork of the Snake River has abundant natural water and was a curious Desert Entry. The GLO had challenged Cherry's claim, charging it was "fraudulent." Time and persistence worked for Cherry and he finally prevailed in gaining title.

There's more to Cal's story, however. He had not hung around tilling his land and fretting the outcome during all that time. While he managed to squeak by on the Desert Land Act requirements, work which totally occupied most men, he was simultaneously fully engaged elsewhere after the first year, as will become apparent. There was a reason GLO inspector Brighton couldn't find him on that day: Cal was variously living in Jackson Hole, Yellowstone National Park, and northern California, places he had found employment, during those ten years while proving up on his Desert Entry.

Cal was smart, ambitious and energetic. He had not put all his eggs into the Desert Entry basket, nor did he let any grass grow under his feet during those years. The truth is he actively pursued and successfully developed two separate and distinct lifestyles and personas: a Teton Valley homesteader and farmer, and an adventuresome cowboy and wrangler in frontier Jackson Hole and elsewhere.[16]

No. 46986

THE UNITED STATES OF AMERICA

Desert Lands
Certificate No.   1494

To all to Whom these Presents shall Come——GREETING:

WHEREAS,   Enoch Carrington

has deposited in the General Land Office of the United States a Certificate of the Register of the Land Office at

Blackfoot, Idaho   whereby it appears that full payment has been made

by the said   Enoch Carrington
according to the provisions of the Act of Congress of the 24th of April, 1820, entitled, "An Act making further provisions for the Sale of the Public Lands," and the acts supplemental thereto, for the

Lots one and two of section six in township four north and the east half of the south east quarter of section thirty one in township five north of range forty five east of the Boise Meridian, Idaho, containing one hundred sixty and twenty nine hundredths acres.

according to the Official Plat of the Survey of the said Land, returned to the General Land Office by the Surveyor General, which said Tract has been purchased by the said Enoch Carrington

NOW, KNOW YE, That the United States of America, in consideration of the premises, and in conformity with the several Acts of Congress in such case made and provided, have GIVEN and GRANTED, and by these presents do GIVE and GRANT,

unto the said   Enoch Carrington

and to   his   heirs, the said Tract above described.

TO HAVE AND TO HOLD the same, together with all the rights, privileges, immunities and appurtenances of whatsoever nature thereunto belonging, unto the said   Enoch Carrington

and to   his   heirs
and assigns forever, subject to any vested and accrued water rights for mining, agricultural, manufacturing or other purposes, and rights to ditches and reservoirs used in connection with such water rights, as may be recognized and acknowledged by the local customs, laws and decisions of Courts, and also subject to the right of the proprietor of a vein or lode, to extract and remove his ore therefrom, should the same be found to penetrate or intersect the premises hereby granted, as provided by law, and there is reserved from the lands hereby granted a right of way thereon for ditches or canals constructed by the authority of the United States.

IN TESTIMONY WHEREOF, I,   Theodore Roosevelt   President of the United States of America, have caused these letters to be made Patent, and the Seal of the General Land Office to be hereunto affixed.

Given under my hand, at the City of Washington, the   twenty sixth

day of   October   , in the year of our Lord one thousand nine hundred

and   seven   , and of the Independence of the United States the one

hundred and   thirty second

BY THE PRESIDENT: Theodore Roosevelt

Title for Cal Carrington's Bates property issued by the authority
of President Theodore Roosevelt in 1907.

6
Over the Mountains into
Early Day Jackson Hole

Cal first drifted across Teton Pass into Jackson Hole in 1898, the year after his arrival in Teton Valley and having taken up squatter's rights on the Bates tract.[1] The pull Jackson Hole exerted on Cal was no less than destiny. In later years, he put a colorful spin on it: "When I first rode into Jackson's Hole I didn't have nothin' but a long rope and an old buckskin horse."[2]

Riding his saddle horse and leading a pack mare and extra mount, Cal followed an existing wagon road on the west side of the Teton River along the foot of the Big Hole Mountains. It led toward the tiny Mormon settlement of Victor. The town had been platted in 1895 and named after Teton Valley mail carrier George Victor Sherwood.[3] By traveling along the west side of the river he avoided the springtime problem of fording the Teton River, although the route was still beset with swampy ground and tributary crossings.

Before heading out, Cal had put in a couple months' work on his Bates place that spring – grubbing sagebrush, digging irrigation ditch, improving his buildings and corrals – all a necessary part of proving up and maintaining his Desert Entry claim and squatter's rights. Once that was accomplished though, it wasn't his style to just sit around watching wild hay grow.

Locating a wagon road going south, he proceeded along it from Victor up Trail Creek. It was early summer in the valley, but the rutted mountain road was steeped in mud and runoff, and rivulets flowed down the deep ruts. At higher elevation, he was required to dismount and lead his horses across snow banks. Mormon settlers had improved the wagon track across Teton Pass in 1889 and again in 1893. Although wagon traffic was common by the 1890s, the road was mostly impassable in the early muddy months.[4]

The whisperings Cal had heard about the Hole stoked his imagination; like a magnet, the stories drew him across the pass. At the 8,431-foot-elevation summit it's likely he paused, gripped by views that had left trappers, explorers and early settlers before him agape, and countless others who have since followed.

Before him lay the astounding panoramic sweep of Jackson Hole, bisected by pastel-green cottonwoods and meadows outlining the Snake River, bordered by vast drab green foothill prairies and buttes, behind all of which rose the Gros Ventre Mountains – Jackson Peak, Sleeping Indian, Crystal Mountain – with black-green forest and contrasting snow-capped summits. Breaths of mist magically appeared and disappeared as though the land was alive and breathing – a dramatic scene, which even today, remains among the West's most compelling.

On the Jackson Hole side, the wagon road descended steeply in a series of muddy, snow-filled, tight switchbacks to the base of the pass where Elijah Nick Wilson and other Mormon settlers had raised a scattering of log cabins ten years earlier. When Cal returned along the same route at the end of summer, he would discover a newly built hotel, store and saloon at the eastern foot of the pass.[5]

Wyoming had been granted statehood eight years earlier in 1890, but there was no town of Jackson yet. It didn't exist. The valley's post office, consisting of nothing more than a canvas-covered wagon box, had recently been moved from its Marysvale location to the Simpson homestead on Cache Creek. Post-mistress, Maggie Simpson, named the new location Jackson.

The "Clubhouse" had been built in 1897, which served as a center for Jackson Hole's community activities – dance hall, courtroom, and commercial building. The next year Charles "Pap" Deloney would open his general store – featuring a barn full of building materials – around which a collection of buildings would begin to gather a few years later. It was a pivotal time in Jackson Hole's history; settlement was beginning to gather momentum throughout the valley.[6]

At best it was an arduous, dawn-to-dusk horseback trip from Cal's Bates ranch to Wilson's west bank of the Snake River in those days. For wagons or buckboards, the Pass could be a two-day trip or more. Roadhouses would be constructed along the route in years to come. Undoubtedly, Cal discovered a roiling Snake River, swollen with snowmelt and running too fast to ford or risk swimming his horse across. He probably camped on the riverbank, waiting for morning to cross by a crude ferry or rowboat. The Wilson-Jackson ferryboat operated by local residents and Menor's Ferry, twelve miles upriver as the raven flies, were at that time, the two high-water crossings for the river.

In those days, the river was a major obstacle, effectively dividing the valley. The first settlers seasonally forded the braided channels southeast of Teton Pass, like the mountain men had done. But this was only readily possible during certain months of the year. Drowning was not an uncommon occurrence while attempting river crossings.

One dicey method used to get horses across the river in high water was to tie each horse to another's tail, then with a long lead rope, while riding the lead horse, swim them across. Another way was for a man to ride in the rear seat of a rowboat holding a long lead rope, while an oarsman paddled across. Either way, it was risky business. The strong currents and having to dodge driftwood made it even more hazardous.[7]

The first bridge at the Wilson crossing would not be constructed for another thirteen years, in 1911. In 1915 it washed

Cal Carrington unloading pack horses at Jackson Hole's Menor's Ferry, 1916. Courtesy JHHSM 2008.0018.005.

out and a steel truss bridge was built. This bridge also washed out a few years later, and after it was rebuilt, the Kelly Flood of 1927 took it out. The Wilson crossing continued to present problems for travelers and settlers until after the late 1920s. Menor's Ferry remained the only consistently reliable option for high-water crossings.[8]

Over the years, going back and forth from his Teton Valley property to Jackson, Cal became intimately familiar with the uncertain nature of both the Snake River and Teton Pass crossings. In an interview Cal said, "Never worried about the river, it had [braided smaller] channels. When we got to it, we crossed it."[9] Maybe, but Cal was wisely apt to use Menor's Ferry whenever possible.

In those early years in Jackson Hole, Cal boarded with Dick Turpin and John Holland. He also probably did ranch work for them. In his words, "I was around Bob Miller some, too."[10] These were some of Jackson Hole's original settlers, men with dubious reputations, who were tougher than rawhide and who had only recently morphed into "respectability." Cal knew and referred to them as the Hole's "old timers."[11]

Dick Turpin (aka William A. Swalley), a fiery, bushy-bearded frontiersman, after moving to the Hole around 1887 or earlier, first lived out along the Gros Ventre River. It was rumored he was running from his past, that he had killed a man in a knife fight. Turpin Meadow and Turpin Creek, where he had trapper cabins were named after him, but his final homestead was located immediately north of today's town of Jackson on Flat Creek. Turpin also had a felonious assault charge brought against him in Jackson, which was dismissed by John Holland, the Hole's Justice of the Peace at the time.[12]

After Pap Deloney opened his general store in 1899, Cal apparently boarded with him a time or two, also: "Living with Pap at that time the way I did, I lived as good as the rest of them. It cost me about ten dollars a month for groceries, a little pig meat,

Jackson Hole early settlers Dick Turpin (left) and Frank Petersen, c1905.
Courtesy of JHHSM 1958.0340.001p.

n' lard, flour n' syrup – goes a long ways, ya' know. Potatoes, canned goods – couldn't keep them from freezing."[13]

While it was never proven, settlers John "Johnny" Carnes, John Holland and Robert "Bob" Miller were suspected of providing outlaws with supplies during their earliest years in Jackson Hole.[14] Holland was the posse leader at Jackson Hole's infamous 1892 Cunningham Ranch shootout, where two alleged horse thieves were gunned down. Still, despite his rough reputation, Holland was the first bachelor settler ever to plant a garden in Jackson Hole. And he also carried mail across Teton Pass in winter.[15]

Traveling on snow across the mountains was called "snowshoeing," but in fact, it was not done with snowshoes. Instead, ten-foot-long, home-made skis were used. Strips of elk hide with the hair on them were tacked to the bottom (referred to as "skins"), allowing the heavy ski to glide forward, but to not slide back when going uphill.

Jackson Hole had earned a reputation as a hideout for horse thieves and outlaws in the 1880s and early 1890s. In 1876, Lt. Gustavus Doane, on his epic winter trek through Jackson Hole, had reported, "It was a favorite rendezvous for desperadoes and thieves." Jackson Hole's 1890s residents were characterized by frontiersman Thomas E. Crawford (aka the "Texas Kid"), as: "homeless, reckless, straight-shooting and hard drinking." Crawford was also one of the citizen posse members at the 1892 Cunningham Ranch shootout and Jackson Hole's Indian War of 1895.[16]

Historian Robert Betts points out that Western communities frequently prided themselves on their bad men, "a form of inverted civic pride."[17] Certainly, nowhere else was a reputation for badness more unequivocally celebrated than in early day Jackson Hole. But for whatever reason in a 1957 interview, Cal was ambiguous on the subject: "I [didn't] know any real bad men. [But] I guess some weren't too nice in a way."[18]

Stories about Cal's early years in Jackson Hole are colored by local lore and myths from that era. To put these in perspective,

Cal had a life-long habit of being close-mouthed about some things, but conversely, he excelled at spinning yarns, a common practice of the times, essentially creating his own history. For those who badly want to believe the outlaw tales about him, this may be a disappointing revelation. Nonetheless, it may be heartening to learn that more factual accounts still contain a strong measure of Wild West melodrama.

Cal's reluctance to openly discuss his early years – which is particularly evident when historians interviewing him late in his life were told: "None of your damn business," or "Let's not talk about that"– was a survival habit learned from living in uncertain times and among men of questionable repute.[19] The unspoken code to avoid altercations or trouble on the frontier was to say little and mind your own business.

Some have maintained, based on his taciturn behavior, name changes, and his propensity for spinning yarns, that Cal was hiding something; notably, involvement in organized livestock rustling. No doubt the intentional protection and boosting of Jackson Hole's Wild West image and myths for posterity entered into it in later years, too – an unstated but commonly understood pact among the Hole's old timers and residents. They were the original "spin-doctors."

The previously incomplete story of Cal's early life in Jackson Hole and before he came into the Tetons only served to bolster his mystique and stature in some circles. In his final years, Cal did loosen up somewhat, revealing parts of his life to friends, Teton Valley neighbors, and by giving two recorded interviews. Still, his early history was fragmentary, frequently based on hearsay, often contradictory, and blurred by time. It's been further confounded by Cal's own tales, and Cissy Patterson's and Felicia's subsequent writings, which, while adding currency to his reputation, were sometimes contrived.

In the Western tradition for "stringing greeners," Cal, like many in that era, had a swaggering fondness for devilment;

fabricating fanciful tales and embellishing stories for the benefit of those he considered greenhorns, pilgrims, tenderfeet, or dudes; and also, especially for the ladies. Another euphemism for the practice was "stuffin' dudes."[20]

Cal's stories appear to have drawn upon and incorporated local historical events, tales, and scandals, as well as his own imagination and life experiences. To merely have secondhand knowledge of an event was enough to claim a personal association or involvement. Typically, he and others gave dudes what they wanted to hear, glamorous tales of lawless roguery and romance in which Cal generally enjoyed putting himself in a starring role. He played to his audience.

Sometimes his tales were purposefully laced with subtle barbs, or were designed in an allegorical fashion, to vindicate or justify himself. This was generally the case, for example, when he made any references to his family. Author Nathaniel Burt characterized him as using few words, but those could be disdainfully mocking when he chose.[21] Jackson Hole old timer Charlie Petersen, Sr., amusedly recalled, "Cal was always trying to make a joke out of everything."[22]

Nevertheless, both true and cooked-up events have been equally passed along by journalists and in local folklore or otherwise handed down as fact, making it difficult to distinguish between real happenings and contrived ones. For example, Cal apparently told Jackson hotel proprietress and member of the first ever all-women Town Council, Rose Crabtree, "His mother was a cook in a lumber camp and had run off with some man and left him." Similarly, he confided to Cissy Patterson, "His mother had sold him to the captain of a ship sailing from England."[23] And in *Glass Houses*, Cissy wrote, "His mother had deserted him, left him to wake up one morning crying alone in an upstairs room of a mining camp dance hall."

Two of Cissy's biographers recorded: "Cal had apprenticed to cattle rustlers and lived with Indian tribes ... was in San Francisco during the 1906 earthquake ... had seen the inside of a jail ... and had escaped a posse by plunging his horse into the ice-swollen Snake River as he clung to the horse's tail." And, another time, "a California sheriff started to close in on him for rustling."[24] It all makes Hollywood seem tame!

Had Cal ever "seen the inside of a jail"? Yes, no doubt he may have looked inside one. But there is no evidence he ever did any jail time; nor did he live with Indians. In fact, in a recorded interview when asked about Indians, Cal responded, "No, we had no Indians."[25] After the Indian War of 1895, Native Americans were shut out of Jackson Hole.

Was Cal really in San Francisco on April 18, 1906? He claimed he was, but there is no certain way to know. Possibly he was roughly 170-miles northeast of there working on the Plumas National Forest at Quincy.[26]

The 1906 earthquake was felt from southern Oregon to south of Los Angeles. One of the worst urban disasters in American history, the 7.8 magnitude epicenter was located at the city of San Francisco. Fires started and raged out of control destroying 30,000 homes and buildings. The mayor issued a shoot to kill order to stop the looting. The Forest Service was likely called on to assist in disaster relief. Maintaining that he had been personally associated with the scene of this disaster adds more glamour to Cal's image.

Did he really apprentice to cattle rustlers and escape a posse by holding on to his swimming horse's tail in an ice-swollen river? That Cal worked for or was "apprenticed to" men who may have been reformed outlaws is probably true, but his work for them appears to have been wrangling or ranching, not rustling. Swimming an ice-swollen river with a posse in pursuit is a tall tale, amusing for its outrageousness.

The origin of the escape by swimming the river tale can be found in Cal's 1957 interview, wherein he tells how a citizen's court in Jackson recessed while trying a game poacher. They all went to the saloon. After a few drinks, the defendant, Ed Hunter, slipped out the back, got on a horse and managed to get across the river, leaving his pursuers behind him on the far river bank – "he walked out the back door, swum the river, and away he went." As the tale came to be retold and embellished, Cal became the escapee, the river dramatically swollen, and even more inventive, flowing with ice.

Less dramatic, but more to the facts regarding river crossings, author Struthers Burt wrote: "There wasn't a river Cal wouldn't swim on a horse, although he never learned to swim himself."[27] However, you can be certain Cal had better sense than to try to swim the ice-swollen Snake River on horseback or otherwise.

Did he really ever have a posse pursue him for rustling? Anytime a posse was assembled in the Old West, it generally made headlines in local newspapers; and, for that matter, so did the capture of any outlaws. Regarding the often repeated story that "all the outlaws in his gang were captured except Cal," no Jackson Hole posse is known to have been assembled fitting the time period, nor were any outlaw captures ever recorded.

The most persistent, but unsubstantiated, rumor circulated about Cal, is that when he first came into Jackson Hole he was an outlaw, a horse thief. Author and rancher Struthers Burt wrote, when he first met Cal, "He had a reputation for badness." Burt was warned: "He'd steal the rope off my saddle – while I was looking, too."[28] However, we now pretty much know, from descriptions in Jim Berger's family history and Cal's interviews, how he actually did spend his time. The rustling stories that came along later appear to have evolved from malicious hearsay or in jest.

Long-time Jackson Hole resident, Clay Taylor, recalls his step-father, Joe Madden, greeting Cal by saying: "I trailed them stolen horses you wuz drivin' all the way from Cheyenne;" to which Cal replied, "Lost me comin' into Jackson, eh?"[29] Cal and others entertained themselves by perpetuating the horse thief rumors and playing up the outlaw reputation. Jackson buzz to this day still has it that Cal and his gang hid stolen horses in Flat Creek Canyon, where, with a running iron, they would change the brands.[30]

And this type of tittle-tattle and intrigue still continues to still be passed along. As recent as 2003, award-winning author Jack Huyler claimed, "[Cal] was hiding from his past, that's why he changed his name."[31] Yet Cal's playing with his name, as was shown earlier, had nothing to do with hiding from an outlaw past. It was directed at his birth family.

Flat Creek Ranch owner Cissy Patterson amused herself by creating and contributing to the outrageous Wild West tales, explaining: "Flat Creek Canyon was ideal for hiding his stolen horses." And Cal, playing along, is frequently quoted as having replied: "In Flat Creek Canyon, I can spot the sheriff a-comin' or a-goin'."[32]

Local historian W. Gillette passed the outlaw tales along, too, writing: "A horse thieving ring was established among Cal and five other men." Two of the men Gillette identified in the gang were proven horse thieves: Ed Harrington (aka Ed Trafton, the Yellowstone National Park "gentleman bandit") and Teton Valley's Lum Nickerson. According to Gillette, Carrington and the other men, would drive the stolen horses across Owen Wister's "horse thief trail," and then use Cal's Flat Creek Ranch in Jackson Hole to change the brands. Afterward, they would take the stolen horses over the Continental Divide to sell to unsuspecting buyers.[33] Jackson's hotel proprietress, Rose Crabtree, who was said to be as "sharp as a whip," handed down the yarn, too, saying: "Cal belonged to a gang of six rustlers, all the men were caught except Cal."[34]

However, those stories simply don't add up chronologically. For example, Cal didn't have or own the Flat Creek Ranch yet in those years – it didn't exist – and Harrington and Nickerson had been busted for stealing horses long before, in 1887.

Nor does it add up geographically. Horses driven across the "horse thief trail," the real name of which was the Conant Trail, would have ended up in northern Jackson Hole. From there, it would have been an inconveniently long way to take the stolen horses through the entire length of Jackson Hole to reach Flat Creek Canyon.

In truth, Cal didn't arrive in the Tetons until after those reckless times, years after the last hoorah for organized horse thievery, when Jackson Hole had earned its outlaw reputation. Ruthless efforts in the early 1890s by Montana stock growers and their paid regulators had dealt out harsh discouragement and abruptly brought an end to any organized rustling in and about the area.[35]

Cal's arrival in the Hole, however, was close on the heels of the outlaw era, and some suspected and known rustlers who had not been sent to the great roundup in the sky were unquestionably still around. Wisely, they were no longer engaged in the pre-owned horse business. But the outlaw times and events were still fresh in the memory and lives of Jackson Hole's settlers.

Regardless, outlaw tales and back-fence lore continue to circulate about Cal today. To further address and lay to rest the recurrent rumors of Cal's connections with organized horse rustling requires some additional examination. For example, what really was Cal's supposed involvement with a purported outlaw "gang of six," the "red bandana gang," and the "Jackson Hole brotherhood?"[36] What were those alliances and, if they really ever did exist, what were their purposes?

Ed Harrington (aka Edwin B. Trafton) incarcerated at the Idaho Penitentiary for rustling livestock, c1901. Courtesy Idaho State Historical Society.

7

Wild West Tales

In describing the afore mentioned organization's purposes and associated tales, other examples demonstrating how bogus stories were concocted and passed along similarly stand out. One was the outlaw Ed Harrington's fondness for telling all those who cared to listen that author Owen Wister patterned his heroic character, the Virginian, after him. Instead, most are inclined to believe Harrington was Wister's villain, Trampas.[1]

After a lifetime as a desperado and thief, trying to emulate his hero Jesse James, Harrington ironically died of natural causes in a Los Angeles ice cream parlor in 1922. He had gone to California with a fabricated story in his pocket to sell to the Hollywood movie industry. The *Los Angeles Times* obtained the manuscript, and taking it for the truth, ran the headlines: "The Virginian' Dies Suddenly–Owen Wister Novel Hero Was Real Pioneer–Blazed First Trails Into Jackson Hole Country."[2]

Harrington wasn't alone among the Virginian wannabes in Jackson Hole. Thomas Crawford, the "Texas Kid," also claimed "he could name the boy who was the Virginian," but he never did divulge just who he thought it might be.[3]

Playing with the truth was not limited to a nefarious few back then. A 1914 investigator, E.N. Moody, assigned to look into questionable Jackson events related to game poaching and illegal squatters on the National Forest, became thoroughly frustrated by the wild stories he was told. Moody complained, "all the townspeople had a compulsion to outdo a character named John Cherry, who excelled in telling tall tales."[4]

John Cherry came into the Hole in 1887. He had a homestead at Warm Springs north of West Gros Ventre Butte, and a Desert Entry tract near Moran that later became known as the Hatchet Ranch. Cherry, who also became a hunting guide and Bar BC dude wrangler, was notoriously careless with the truth, earning a deserved reputation for telling exaggerated tales and falsehoods. He claimed Doc Middleton, the infamous Nebraska horse thief, was his brother.[5]

Retelling and reinventing versions of early-day episodes, and the impromptu substitution of main characters, kept the glamour of the Wild West glowing. It also helped to perpetuate Jackson's reputation as a rowdy place populated with bad men and outlaws – a tough, fearless, and heroic image Jackson Holers liked to identify with and took serious pride in maintaining. After all, "stuffin' dudes" was great entertainment.

Besides, already at the turn of the twentieth century, the glamour of a Wild West reputation helped spur the tourist economy. By the late 1890s, Jackson Hole was known as a mountain resort and was serving sportsmen and tourists alike.[6] Outrageous Wild West tales served another purpose, too, that of distracting attention from those who may have actually had a disreputable past to hide. It made it difficult to tell just who the outlaws really were or had ever been.

There should not be any doubt that Cal would have been acquainted with Ed Harrington and his ilk, the Cunningham Ranch incident, Jackson Hole's Indian War of 1895, elk tusking, and other outlaw lore, especially after living and working among the Hole's old timers. Everyone in Teton Valley and Jackson Hole would have been familiar with the traditional outlaw wisdom in those days. Still, when he was asked in an interview about Jackson Hole's most infamous outlaw, Teton Jackson, Cal gave a curious reply: "I don't believe he was much of anything. I don't believe much in things like that." Asked if he had known him, Cal replied: "The old Teton Jackson I never saw. He was there before I was."[7]

Regardless, Cissy Patterson's biographers and others, to this day continue to perpetuate the myth: "Cal belonged to a 'gang of six' rustlers, identified by the red bandanas they wore... only Cal was never caught."[8] However, Cal could not have been part of the so called gang of six, as will become evident, and a red bandana wasn't an identification for organized rustlers, it was the badge of the "Jackson Hole brotherhood."[9]

The Gang of Six

Back when winter closed off the mountain passes into the Hole, it was a place that afforded a snowbound hideaway for scoundrels wanting to evade the law. In winter, and during spring during runoff, in those days, no one could get in or out of the valley.

In 1885, only seven men allegedly wintered inside the Hole.[10] They were a scruffy bunch, unshaven and rank, overalls torn and patched, denim shirts ragged, neckerchiefs filthy, mackinaws blackened from campfire smoke, soot and dirt, and their boots near plumb worn out. None of them had any cash money, and legitimate prospects to rectify that situation were slim to none.

There were plenty of reasons to be suspicious of these men. Earlier that autumn, a posse led by an old Indian fighter, Pap Conant, had searched the Hole. Whisperings had it that a herd of steers which had mysteriously vanished from the Wind River country was hidden there. Pap and his riders found "a great many horse sign," including two bands of ponies of unknown ownership, one grazing on Flat Creek Meadows and another corralled in Leek's Draw.[11] The posse took no action, but federal marshals were interested to learn what they had found.

When spring brought the seven to the surface, federal marshals somehow corralled one of them, Bill Arnn, and took him in for an official chat at Malad, Idaho. (This is not the same Arnn who rode with Butch Cassidy's gang.)

The origin of a rumored "gang of six" likely arises from a sworn statement given by William Arnn, wherein he testified to federal marshals – who were investigating a report that rustlers were using Jackson Hole for a winter hideout – that "just six men, besides himself, had spent the winter in the Hole." They were John Holland, Bob Miller, Bill Thompson and his partner Hilderbrand, Lock Bye, and Ed Harrington.[12]

Harrington (aka Ed Trafton) was a renowned thief who had already done time for rustling. Thompson and his partner, Hilderbrand, were compadres of the notorious outlaw Teton Jackson (two aliases: William Bradford and Harvey Gleason). John Holland and Bob Miller were suspect by association. There's also some evidence Holland and Miller may have been providing supplies for the outlaws.[13] Teton Jackson himself was, at the time, cooling off in the Boise Penitentiary for grand larceny, a fancy way of saying horse stealing.

Presumably, Arnn's testimony regarding the presence of six miscreants who over wintered in the Hole constitutes the origin for back fence references to a shadowy "gang of six" in the years afterward.[14] The gang of six incident took place thirteen years before Cal first arrived in Jackson Hole.

Red Bandana Gang and the Brotherhood

A few years later, in 1887, Teton Valley ranchers had gotten fed up with having their livestock disappear. Hiram Lapham, credited as being one of the first settlers in Teton Valley, led a posse that caught up with Ed Harrington, Lum Nickerson, and Jim Robertson in eastern Idaho, while they were engaged in rounding up ponies that didn't belong to them. Rumor was they were taking the stolen horses across the Tetons, by way of Conant Pass into Jackson Hole, or driving them south into Utah, where they would alter the brands and then sell the stock to unsuspecting buyers. Settlers would buy them as long as they got a bill of sale to show they didn't do the stealing. In the donnybrook that followed, Jim was shot and died, and Lum and Ed were sent to the local slammer. As stated previously, in a failed escape attempt by the outlaws, Ed was shot in the foot and graduated to four years at Leavenworth.[15]

Owen Wister's material for *The Virginian*, published in 1902, is believed to have been based, in large part, on those outlaw happenings. The old Indian trail across the Tetons at Conant Pass (shown today on maps as Jackass Pass) was Wister's "horse thief trail." Wister captured imaginations everywhere by penning: "Somewhere at the eastern base of the Tetons did those hoof prints disappear into a mountain sanctuary where many crooked paths have led."[16]

However, again, those outlaw events took place long before Carrington arrived in Teton Valley or Jackson Hole. Likewise, the 1892 Jackson Hole Cunningham Ranch shootout with alleged horse thieves was before Cal's time, as was the capture of Butch Cassidy in Star Valley earlier that same year, and the capture of Sylvester Summers at Wolverine, Idaho, and also Jack Bliss and Kid Collier elsewhere in Uinta County, Wyoming. All apprehended by range detectives and Montana stockmen's paid regulators, who were determined, once and for all, to rid the range of rustling.[17]

The notorious outlaw activities of Teton Jackson (aka Harvey Gleason, William Bradford) and his first lieutenant Bill "Red" Thompson were even before those events. Teton Jackson went to jail sometime around or before 1884 for horse rustling, then escaped and returned briefly to Jackson Hole. He was recaptured and jailed again and eventually moved on to Lander after allegedly selling his Jackson Hole "fortress" (log buildings and squatter's claim located south of Miller's Butte) to Robert Miller sometime around or after 1885.[18]

Ironically, some of the Jackson Hole posse members involved in the murky Cunningham Ranch incident mentioned above were themselves rumored to have been involved with or associated with livestock rustlers at times. And the federal marshals who enlisted the Jackson posse members were later believed to have been imposters – hired Montana stockmen regulators. Jackson's John Holland had been appointed, without proper authority, to lead the posse of local citizenry whose family names today are respected as among the Jackson Hole's earliest pioneers.[19]

It is essential to understanding Jackson Hole's early history, and the many contradictory tales surrounding events, to know that the Cunningham Ranch episode resulted in purposeful muddling of the facts by participants and Jackson's citizenry right up until recent times.

After the shootout at the sod-roofed Cunningham Ranch cabin, when Jackson Hole posse members had time to reconsider their headlong involvement and the killing of two alleged outlaws, they feared possible retribution from both the law and outlaws. The participants then became understandably closemouthed about the whole incident. In self-interest, they cloaked the happening in a brotherhood of silence, purposely obfuscating the whole affair with wild and conflicting tales. Settler and posse member, Mose Giltner, pretty much summed up the feelings for all of them afterward, saying: "He was a damn fool to have ever gotten involved."[20]

Meanwhile, the *Cheyenne Tribune* lauded Holland as "the embodiment of law and order," adding, "The impression that Jackson's Hole is peopled by rustlers and thieves is erroneous, their good names should not be sullied by classing them with thieves, rustlers and regulators."[21] A commentary that no doubt made Jackson Hole residents shuffle nervously and self-consciously glance sideways to see the reaction of the men beside them.

The two alleged horse thieves were hastily buried in a lonesome shallow grave in frozen ground east of the Cunningham

Ranch. According to local lore, the graves kept washing open for years afterward, exposing the haunting remains.

The Jackson Hole brotherhood proved successful in covering up and keeping a lid on things. Everyone, it seemed, embellished a different version of the Cunningham Ranch incident. The event's history is comprised of conflicting and inconsistent stories. Early day incidents and events up to 1892 had justifiably given Jackson Hole a reputation for being an outlaw hideout. After that, history was purposefully confounded by a cautious and worried citizenry's cover-up, distortions, and imaginative retellings designed to protect themselves and to string greeners. Behind it all was the pact of the so-called brotherhood that self-servingly protected the early settlers who had participated in the Cunningham Ranch affair.

Because of the historical vagueness and mystery surrounding the brotherhood, it has sometimes been mistakenly assumed to have been involved in organized rustling. This was not the case. The brotherhood was comprised of the Hole's original settlers, some of whom Cal later hung around or found employment with, and it was a notable presence when he first rode into the Hole.

In 1957, in an unusual lapse of guardedness, Cal disclosed the key for this early day Jackson Hole enigma, stating: "The red bandana gang was a brotherhood of old timers, who banded together to do what they wanted to do... they all went together. They all had a red-squaw bandana for a badge. If you saw a man in the country riding around without a red bandana, you knew he was a stranger." Significantly, he then added, "They quit wearing them the year after I hit Jackson [in 1899]."[22]

The brotherhood and red-bandana gang were one and the same. Their origin is presumably attributed to the Cunningham Ranch incident cover-up, not rustling. The loose alliance originated in the self-serving interest of protecting the Cunningham Ranch shootout participants, and evolved to include cover up for any Mountain Law (vigilance committee) activities, shady doings, and the dubious reputations of some of Jackson Hole's earliest settlers in general, during its existence.

In an interview, Cal played down Jackson Hole's lawless reputation saying, "Well, I heard more stories [about outlaws] outside Jackson than I did in. When I got to Jackson, they all said the ones told me them stories was damn liars. Then they told me what [really] happened."[23] Unfortunately, there it was dropped. He was not asked to explain what he believed really did happen, nor did Cal volunteer this knowledge.

All this is not to say that Jackson Hole was not a rowdy, uproarious place back then – it was. Plenty of dubious activities were still taking place: gambling, moonshining, illegal squatting on the Forest Reserve, game poaching in Yellowstone, and some serious elk tusking (illegally killing elk for their eye-teeth or tusks, which could fetch twenty-dollars a pair).

Similarly, in Teton Valley, occasional neighbor's beef were being rustled and passed off or marketed as elk meat, while market hunters hauled game meat by the wagon load to nearby railheads and shipped it as freight to hotels and restaurants in Salt Lake City.[24] In the Old West, poaching and market hunting, although illegal, were not consider as serious an offense as rustling. But market hunting was never a major problem in Jackson Hole because of the distance to a railhead.

If a tourist had asked an old timer where all the outlaws went, he may have gotten a knowing wink with the wry reply: "We're all still here, partner." However, one must conclude the days of organized horse rustling in and about Jackson Hole and Teton Valley took place before Carrington's arrival.

Montana stock growers had ruthlessly put an abrupt end to rustling shenanigans in the early 1890s, swearing to rid the range of the rustling scourge once and for all. They effectively made the penalty for stealing livestock so severe that the pre-owned horse business lost any attraction. Any noteworthy outlaw episodes in

Jackson Hole after the early 1890s would certainly have been documented by legal transcripts, newspaper journalists, and historians, but none were.[25]

Jackson Hole was part of Uinta County in those years. In 1895, Uinta County Sheriff, John Ward, declared: "There has not been a report to this office of any horse stealing or of any other unlawful act [in Jackson Hole] since 1892, [when] two noted desperadoes were arrested [gunned down] for horse stealing. There is no better class of citizens in any place in the state than those who have made their homes in the beautiful region known as Jackson's Hole."[26] Course, gotta keep in mind, too, Ward was hoping to be reelected for another term as sheriff.

Forest Service pack string at Hawk's Rest Patrol Cabin in the Teton Wilderness. Courtesy USDA Forest Service.

8

Government Horse Packer
and Forest Ranger

If Cal wasn't stealing livestock or riding with outlaws in those early years in Jackson Hole, as unsubstantiated rumor has popularized, just what was he doing, besides bronc busting, doing ranch work for settlers in the Hole and Teton Basin, and grubbing out a homestead at Bates?

As it turns out, for the period after he first came into the Tetons – from around 1898-1908 – Cal also worked seasonally as a wrangler and horse packer for Yellowstone National Park and the Yellowstone Forest Reserve, and as a forest ranger for the Teton Forest Reserve. When he was gone from the area from 1906-1908, he was employed with the Forest Service in northern California.[1] In 1906, Carrington's Teton Valley neighbors had correctly informed the GLO Desert Land Entry Inspector, Henry Brighton, Cal "was off working for the Forest Service."[2]

How can we be certain of all this? After all, it conflicts with popular lore that Cal was involved in horse rustling during that time. In 1957, Jackson Hole rancher Cliff Hansen, who was a member of the University Of Wyoming Board Of Trustees at the time, drove Cal over to the History Department at Laramie for a recorded interview.

Somehow Cliff overcame Cal's usual reticence; perhaps, Cliff knew the right questions to ask and maybe he brought along a bottle of encouragement, too. In any case, Cal, at age eighty-four, waxed loquaciously and entertainingly – albeit disjointedly – on subjects he had never spilled the beans on before. Conversely, a year later he dodged similar questions with another interviewer in Teton Valley.[3]

"In 1898-1899, somewhere along there," Cal recalled, "I packed the surveyors on the Lamar River out to Yancy's old stage station [near Tower Falls] and then over to the Canyon Hotel."[4] This may have been Arnold Hague's U.S. Geological Survey party, or perhaps one of Hiram Chittenden's survey crews. Most likely, since it was in the Lamar Valley, it was the former.

The 2.1-million-acre Yellowstone National Park had been established in 1872 under President Ulysses S. Grant's authority. The National Park Service did not come into being until 1916; before then, the park was administered under the command of the U.S. Army. Cal worked for the infant Yellowstone National Park while it was being managed by the Army.

Cal stated the job in the Lamar Valley was his first time in Yellowstone National Park. Where he got the horses to do the packing and how he got the job he didn't say. Generally, horse packers in those days were expected to provide their own gear and pack animals, but it's possible he may also have had use of government stock. Cal recalled, "Once at Norris, sleeping in a soldier's camp on a moonlight night, [I] woke up. A bear was standing at the foot of the bed. Scared us both. [But] he went away."[5]

Cal remembered, "Coming down out of the Park with my pack outfit I overtook "Beaver Tooth" (Charles "Beaver Tooth" Neal) – first time I met him. He was a different character." Neal was renowned in the Jackson Hole area for his game poaching and as a scheming shady character. His escapes from game wardens are legend and provided entertainment for the local citizenry. Somehow he always managed to stay one-step ahead of the authorities. Beaver Tooth operated a store and lodge at the location of today's Heart Six Guest Ranch along the Buffalo Fork of the Snake River near Moran, Wyoming, but his forte' was trapping beaver, illegally.

" 'Lo, have a drink,' Beaver Tooth said.

" 'Yeah', and I took a drink.

" 'Got me another bottle here.'

" 'How much you want for it?'

" 'Dollar.' "

Cal said, "I gave him a dollar. And that night I thought I'd take a drink before I ate. It was nothing but tea – a bottle of trickum. That was my introduction to old Beaver Tooth."[6]

The next summer, by chance, Cal met Colonel A.A. Anderson, Superintendent of Forest Reserves (not to be confused with George S. Anderson, Military Superintendent of Yellowstone, who saved Yellowstone Park's bison from poachers), who was camped at the old Yellowstone Station, today's South Entrance.[7]

"He [Anderson] wanted me. But I told him I was going to work [up in the Park] for Chittenden."[8]

Hiram Chittenden is credited with having designed the road system in Yellowstone, and having engineered other enduring structures, such as the Gardiner entrance gate, around this same time period. He also launched a career as a historian by writing the first history of Yellowstone Park in 1895.

"Anderson said, 'I'll fix it up.' And off he went."

Much to Cal's astonishment, "Sure enough, next morning I was transferred [from the Park Service] into the Forest Service."

Cal presumably was recruited as a wrangler and packer for Colonel Anderson's monumental survey of the boundary of the Yellowstone Forest Reserve – a vast tract of forest and mountainous land encompassing 8,829,000 acres surrounding Yellowstone National Park. It took a party of ten men with thirty-five saddle and pack horses over three months, moving camp almost everyday, to accomplish the job. It was a feat that is unimaginable today.[9]

Cal Carrington on horseback leading a string of horses, c1916.
Courtesy JHHSM 2008.0018.017.

Cal went back and forth between wrangling and horse packing for the Park and Forest Service and working on his homestead in Bates in those years. The trip across Teton Pass was, at best, an all day endurance affair back then. Jackson Hole residents referred to the trip to Victor as "going outside." However, in traveling back to Teton Valley from Yellowstone Park, Cal would not necessarily have followed the old Indian trail along the east side of Jackson Lake into Jackson Hole, and then the length of the valley to Teton Pass; rather, at the north end of the lake, he could cross over the meadows to Berry Creek and then pick up the Conant Trail going across the northern end of the Teton Range. From the divide he could follow the trail down Conant or Bitch Creek into Teton Valley, thus saving a day or more travel.

On September 18-19, 1900, Theodore Roosevelt stopped off in Rexburg on his campaign for vice president. "At that time," Cal says, "John Holland, the old timer from Jackson, was living in the [Teton] Basin and I was breaking broncs for him.[10] Holland

and I rode down to Rexburg – that's thirty-five miles. I was going to ride a bronc [for Roosevelt]... when I got down there the bronc wouldn't switch its tail. The crowd was so thick the horse was scared to death. So I got out of a big chore."[11] As an afterthought, Cal added, "He [Roosevelt] was a nice ol' fella. I liked him. Teddy done more for our whole Western country than any president ever done."[12]

A.A. Anderson divided the vast Yellowstone Forest Reserve into four divisions. It included most of the mountains and forests surrounding Jackson Hole. Charles "Pap" Deloney held the first forest supervisor post until 1902, when he resigned. Deloney hired the first fire suppression crews to work in Jackson Hole at the Forty-Mile Fire in the Hoback in 1900.[13] After Deloney quit, Robert Miller was appointed supervisor of the Teton Division from 1902 to 1908. Local communities generally supported the mission of the Forest Service in those early years.

Cal recalled, "I come down from the [Yellowstone] Park after the surveying was done and Bob Miller put me down on Porcupine [Creek, south of Jackson,] to fight forest fire."[14] "Next," Cal said, "Miller sent me down to Star Valley when they made that drive, the Wind River Rangers and them from Pinedale [Bridger Division.] In fact, there was twenty-two of us in camp on Cottonwood [Creek]... and the sheep was on Piney [Creek]. Covey [the sheep herder] put his sheep right through, didn't pay any attention to the ranger. So we goes up there [with Anderson and his men] and drives the sheep off the Reserve."[15]

In those years, it was the practice of sheepmen to torch the forest to create more area for sheep grazing. Large numbers of sheep were being brought in by owners from Utah and consuming the forage local farmers' livestock might otherwise utilize. They were none too fondly called "transient sheep." Jackson Hole hunting outfitters also feared elk ranges would be destroyed from sheep over grazing. Sometime around 1905, some sixty-thousand transient sheep with forty armed herders were brought onto the

Forest Reserve by four large owners out of Utah.[16]

Anderson gathered all his rangers, about sixty-five men in full regalia, armed and mounted. He told them, "I propose to remove the herders and their flocks from the Reserve using whatever force necessary. Every man who is willing to do this take one step forward." Every man stepped forward and Anderson was told, "Superintendent, there isn't a man here who wouldn't follow you plumb to hell."[17] Cal was undoubtedly among those men.

The rangers confronted the sheepmen, and then forming a line of horsemen behind the sheep, they drove them to the eastern boundary of the Forest Reserve. Meanwhile, an injunction was obtained restraining them from reentering the Reserve. The sheep were caught between the Forest Reserve and irate Green River cattlemen.

"A couple days later," Cal said, "an accident happened to the sheep." The cattlemen killed eight-hundred sheep and burned the herders' outfits. "Covey [one of the sheepmen] cried like a kid. I was in camp. I seen that," Cal recalled. "They [Anderson and his rangers] let him take the sheep back over the Forest Reserve, so he would have some left."[18]

The wild and, literally, woolly incident Cal describes was historically significant for the management of National Forest ranges. By the time it was finished the authority for the Forest Service to regulate livestock operators and require grazing permits was firmly established by the courts.

While all that had been going on, both Cal's Desert Entry application and his Forest Service employment required that he become, or officially swear his intention to become, a United States citizen. In June 1901, he had filed a Declaration of Intention to become a citizen of the United States at the Fifth Judicial District, Fremont County, Idaho. In June 1905, because of the lapsed time, he submitted another similar sworn statement declaring his intention to become a citizen. Finally, later in 1905, he returned to the Fifth District Court and became a naturalized citizen, swearing before a court clerk that he had "behaved as a man of good moral character since emigrating from England."[19]

Following his naturalization, and continuing his National Park and Forest Service jobs, Cal was appointed as an Assistant Forest Ranger on July 1, 1905, for the Teton Division of the Yellowstone Forest Reserve at sixty dollars a month, a seasonal job back then.[20] In any case, it was certainly easier and steadier work than seasonal ranch labor. Most important, it paid a good salary. In those years, there was not much currency in circulation and cash was in short supply.

It was generally the practice for the Forest Service to find the most respected, toughest, no-nonsense person in the local community to appoint as ranger or forest supervisor. In those days, the fledgling Forest Service was an agency with a clear mission. One ranger expressed it this way: "It was a wonderful thing to have a government bureau with nothing but young men in it. There was no sign of inertia or red-tape inhibitions."

In 1905, Chief of the Forest Service, Gifford Pinchot, issued *The Use Book.* A pocket-sized142-page handbook, it contained all the instructions forest rangers, like Cal, needed to know to conduct their duties – it was the ranger's bible. Compare that to the *Forest Service Manual* today, which consists of dozens of large volumes, supplemented by handbooks and guides, in order to incorporate all the regulations and instructions for administering the National Forests. The non-electronic version takes up an entire wall in a ranger's office just to shelve it.

The first rangers were hired for their skills as wranglers and packers, rather than their professional forestry or range management knowledge. One of the requirements a prospective ranger had to fulfill before he got the job was a practical examination which included packing a horse. A candidate ranger would mount his saddle horse and leading the horse he had been required to pack, lope out and back for a mile or so. If the pack stayed on, he passed the exam.

Cal Carrington's USDA Forest Service 1905 Certificate of Appointment to Assistant Forest Ranger. Courtesy JHHSM.

The small log cabin where Robert Miller conducted his Forest Service administrative duties is still standing today at the Miller Ranch historical site on the National Elk Refuge. The ranger examination was held behind the Miller barn located adjacent to the supervisor's cabin. In Cal's case, where Miller was personally acquainted with his riding and packing capabilities, the formality of any exam may have been waived or, at most, conducted in half-serious fun.

Cal and others had a precedence to follow. It was set by Roland W. Brown, the first forest ranger assigned to the Teton-Yellowstone Forest Reserve. Brown held the job from 1898-1910. It covered a vast area, both Jackson Hole and Teton Valley.[21] Carrington claimed "Brown was fired," but in reality he was reassigned to Teton Basin when the Reserve was reorganized.

Rudolph "Rosie" Rosencrans was another well-known, early-day ranger, who worked in the Teton Division beginning in 1904. "Rosie's Ridge," north of Blackrock Creek along Wyoming State Highway 26/287, is named after him. After a long career, Rosie retired due to failing eyesight. He declined corrective surgery, saying, "I have seen enough beauty for a lifetime."[22]

In those days, rangers were solitary, side-armed horsemen whose job entailed regulation of grazing and timber cutting on the Forest Reserves. They were also expected to enforce the game laws where they existed. Cal, however, like most living in the frontier conditions of the time, did not hunt by the calendar. Jackson Hole settlers subsisted on game meat year round.

Cal has been quoted as saying: "The government had no business telling a man what to do in his own mountains."[23] That would appear to be an attitude in conflict with his ranger duties. But on the other hand, Cal's mindset would not have applied universally. This was the era of the elk tuskers and Cal, like other rangers and wardens at the time, had strong support from the local populace to control that activity.

The tuskers killed elk only for their eye teeth or "ivories," which sold for five to twenty dollars a pair, leaving the rest of the animal to rot. Considering wages were generally only thirty-dollars a month, if one could find a job, it was plenty of monetary temptation to become engaged in elk poaching.

Jackson Hole residents were rightfully angry about the wanton slaughtering of elk, which they relied on for subsistence and for the business of outfitting and guiding sport hunters. They finally formed a vigilance committee in 1906, issuing the tuskers a Mountain Law ultimatum: "Clear out or be shot."[24]

Forest Reserve Superintendent A.A. Anderson learned of the difficulty of enforcing the game laws firsthand. He met a young man on the trail who had an out-of-season deer tied on his pack horse and arrested him. At the trial a six-man jury deliberated briefly and returned their verdict: "He did it, but we won't find him guilty this time."[25]

In 1905, Cal was undoubtedly discouraged and angry about the GLO examiner's failure to approve his Desert Entry's final submittal, preventing it from going to patent. A year passed and it still hung fire, awaiting the government's investigation. Cal wouldn't actually learn of its approval until the autumn of 1907.[26] In the meanwhile, he found employment with the Forest Service in northern California.

Two of Cissy's biographers put Cal in San Francisco on April 18, 1906, during the great earthquake. It is believed he was working nearby on the Plumas National Forest.[27] Cal's extended absence from Teton Valley around this time period is substantiated by GLO Inspector Brighton's July 22, 1907 report: "I did not see the claimant. He is said to be in the U.S. Forestry Service and has been for a year or more so employed."[28]

"I couldn't work under Miller," Cal said in his 1957 interview, "I didn't like him. He wanted me to work with his cows and I didn't want cows no more. I got outta that ... I got transferred thru Pinchot [Chief of the Forest Service] to California. I was down there [in California] for two seasons and then I came home and went guiding [dudes and hunters.]"[29]

Further illustrating how hearsay – from remarks no doubt originally made in jest – followed Cal around, in 1979 Cissy Patterson's biographer Ralph Martin described the circumstances under which Cal left California in this manner: "Rustling horses had become his business until a California sheriff started to close in on him. Cal then took a packhorse named Quincy and made the long trek across the West to Jackson."[30]

Cal could have made the long horseback ride from California back to Jackson leading his packhorse, Quincy. It's a romantic image. But on the other hand, he more likely and sensibly made use of the railroad to get himself and his horses home. And it is very unlikely a sheriff was "closing in on him" for rustling while he was working for the U.S. Forest Service. No doubt he named his packhorse Quincy after the town where he was stationed with the Forest Service.

Located in the Sierra Nevada, the Plumas National Forest is headquartered at the town of Quincy. The Plumas National Forest is known as a rugged and scenic area with extensive old-growth forest and abundant streams and lakes. The Plumas' closest large urban center is San Francisco, where the regional office for all of California's national forests is located. Forest Service employees would have undoubtedly been called to assist in disaster relief in the aftermath of the earthquake.

Cal left his Forest Service job in California and returned to Teton Valley when he received word that he had finally been granted title to his Bates ranch. In his 1957 interview, he stated he "returned home to guide dudes and hunters" with John Holland. [31]

The town of Jackson, Wyoming in 1907. Courtesy JHHSM 1958.0225.001p.

9

Rustling Up a Living
in Early Day Jackson Hole

Jackson Hole had undergone radical transformation by the twentieth century. Homesteaders, town-builders, sport hunters, tourists, and frontier riff-raff had poured in. In 1890, when Wyoming Territory became a state, sixty-four people were reported to be living in Jackson Hole. But ten years later, by the 1900 census, the valley had undergone cinch-busting growth from a sparsely settled frontier outpost to having one hundred forty-five farms and mountain ranches along with five post offices.[1] Cal had arrived in Jackson Hole just as this rapid change was taking place. It was the end of one era, and the beginning of a new one.

Beaver Dick Leigh, the mountain man who had guided the Hayden Survey, died in 1899, and was buried on a bluff near Rexburg, Idaho. From his burial site, the Teton Range – about which he had made his home and life – was viewable in the distance. His death at the turn of the century also marked the end of the earlier era. [2]

At the beginning of the twentieth century, sixty-five homesteads had been taken up just within the area that is now the southern end of the National Elk Refuge. The naturally occurring marshes and springs there – referred to as "the swamp" or "morass," the place where not long before Teton Jackson and his outlaw gang had stood off lawmen – provided settlers with plenty of "slough-grass" hay for their livestock. The landmark prominence, originally called Carnes' Butte, became known instead as Miller's Butte to newcomers.

Although it was suspected twenty years earlier that Jackson Hole's preeminent settlers John Carnes, John Holland, and Bob Miller had been accomplices in pre-owned horse dealings, and were in those earlier times providing supplies for outlaws, it was never proven. Maybe they had just been neighborly, since their original homesteads were located next or near to Teton Jackson gang's fortress in "the morass."

As times changed, those men sought to divert attention away from any questionable involvement or shady dealings, metamorphosing into Jackson Hole's most reputable, prosperous and entitled citizenry – the Hole's first settlers, ranchers, hunting guides, a banker, mail carrier, constable, justice of the peace, U.S. commissioner and even a National Forest supervisor.

On the other hand, some early residents failed to graduate from the outlaw line of work. Ed Harrington ended up in and out of jail, as did Teton Jackson, before both eventually became "respectable." Red Thompson meanwhile just faded from the scene.

Some insight into the shenanigans involved in the startup of early day ranches was provided by Pap Conant and his posse's 1885 foray into the Hole. Searching for stolen cattle, they came upon steers at the head of Spread Creek and horses hidden in other locations.[3] Cal also revealed years later how certain enterprising hooligans got their ranching start in Jackson Hole: "They picked up cattle off the Green River trail [and] drove them back up here. Course they'd be some horses and whenever they got a stray, they pushed him in here [too]."[4]

But, again, all this was before Cal's time. John Holland and John Carnes obviously knew the Bacon Creek Divide-Gros Ventre Trail from the Green River into Jackson Hole. They are credited with being the first to bring a wagon and some crude farm equipment into the Hole using that route. There are reasons to believe start-up livestock were brought into the Hole using that route, too.[5]

Most agree, however, cattle rustling never amounted to much in Jackson Hole, because cows were generally too slow moving to be brought in and out of the rugged country. But that was not true for horses. Historian Nolie Mumey pretty much summed it up: "It was difficult to know who was in league with outlaws, for many times men who appeared to be honest and trustworthy, were actually [or had been at one time] associated with the thieves."[6]

Expanding settlement, the telegraph and telephone, fences, and improved transportation, put the outlaws of old decisively out of business. Around this time, Jackson's newspaper even took umbrage with the Hole's outlaw reputation, proclaiming: "Those who had settled there since the first homesteads in 1884 were solid citizens of the first order."[7]

Not all were inclined to embrace the advancement of settlement. Bill Hubbard in Teton Valley complained, "This country is getting to damn thick with Mormons." Another, Old Man Atherton, moved out of Jackson Hole and up the Gros Ventre River in the 1890s because, as he claimed, "people were getting to darn plentiful." Original settler Thomas E. Crawford, also disgusted with the changes remarked in his *Recollections*: "I made my last trip into Jackson Hole during 1900, [it] was filled up with pilgrims and it didn't look good to me anymore." The country surrounding the Tetons had become too civilized for all but rumored or retired horse thieves. Scoundrels of another ilk – game poachers and illegal squatters – replaced the storied desperadoes of old.

Holland and Carnes had applied for territorial water rights already in 1883 and Miller from Cache Creek in 1884. They were the first to do so in Jackson Hole, indicating they had something more permanent in mind than being outlaws.[8] Regardless of the questionable beginnings of ranching in the Hole, by the start of the twentieth century it was pretty much fully legitimate. Not many years afterward, Miller was running one of the largest herds of livestock in Jackson Hole.[9]

Miller married Grace Green in 1893 and they built the large log house (some call it Jackson's first trophy home) on what is today the National Elk Refuge. The Miller's log home is still standing and is listed on the National Register of Historic Places. Many settlers found wives in the sparsely settled country – Holland married Maud Carpenter on the Fourth of July in 1894; John Carnes's common law wife, Millie Sorelle, was part Native American; and Frank Petersen married Rena Peterson, who was from Teton Valley.[10]

In those years, Holland was regularly making snowshoe and horseback trips across Teton Pass to Teton Valley – not to conduct outlaw activities, but for the benign purpose of delivering mail and to check on his property and investments in Teton Basin.

Authors Bonney and Bonney refer to Cal as a "crony" of John Holland's, and an inductee into the brotherhood. But that does not implicate Carrington in rustling. Cal's whereabouts and activities after his arrival in Teton Valley in 1897, and Jackson Hole the following years, have been pretty much accounted for, laying to rest the back fence gossip that he was running with a gang of outlaws in those early years.

Jackson Hole's first settlers, John Holland and John Carnes sold their Nowlin Creek homesteads to David and Ben Goe around 1900, and skedaddled from the Hole. Carnes moved on to Fort Hall, Idaho. John Holland drifted across the pass to homestead and build his Teton Basin Horseshoe Creek Ranch, in order to be closer to where his wife's family was residing at the time.[11]

In 1901, at age forty-six, Holland served as a witness for Cal's Desert Entry application, listing his place of residence as Fremont County, Idaho, and occupation as rancher.[12] He and Cal had become friends and neighbors and stayed in touch. In 1902,

Holland sold his Horseshoe Creek property for the enormous sum of $8000 and moved to Socio, near Salem, Oregon, where he again took up a homestead and created a ranch.[13] He and Maud also purchased and operated the Socio Hotel there. Cal said, "[I] took down a [railroad] carload of horses and cattle for him."[14]

Holland died tragically at age fifty-one from a tetanus infection resulting from an accidental glass cut while fighting a fire at his hotel, but not before suffering two different amputations on the gangrenous leg.[15]

John "Johnny" Carnes, a twice wounded Civil War veteran and Indian fighter died in 1931 at age ninety-two on the Hutchison Ranch at Fort Hall, Idaho. His obituary states, "At one time he was deputy sheriff and was sent to disperse a band of horse and cattle thieves that infested the [Jackson Hole] region." This is undoubtedly reference to his involvement in the Cunningham Ranch incident. Carnes was quoted as frequently remarking: "We were sent in there after them and they are there yet."[16]

Virtually all settlers in Jackson Hole around or before the early 1900s started cattle ranches. While the ranches were generally small, cumulatively they amounted to a large number of cattle and horses. When asked in later years if there were any cattle in the Hole when he arrived there, Cal replied: "No great amount." But then he went on to recall the settlers who ran cattle: "Cunningham, Giltner, Leek, Redman, Miller..."[17] He could have named virtually every settler in Jackson Hole, they all had at least some cattle.

By 1906, 4,072 cattle and horses were being permitted on the adjacent Forest Reserve alone.[18] Jackson Hole's farms and ranches offered work for a skilled bronc buster, cowboy and horsemen like Cal. He likely did ranch work and odd jobs for Holland, Miller, and other settlers at times, in addition to working for the National Park and Forest Service.

Besides running livestock, many settlers also engaged in guiding sport hunters. Guiding and outfitting sport hunters and

Charlie Petersen at the trapper's cabin located near the mouth of Flat Creek canyon, c1927.
Courtesy JHHSM 1993.4807.015 and Rena Croft.

trapping were settlers' primary sources of cash money in those years, more so than ranching.[19]

There has been considerable myth and mystique associated with Flat Creek Canyon and a cabin that once existed there. It figures large in stories about Cal's supposed rustling activities. In Cal's own words about his early years in Jackson: "I sometimes lived [in the cabin] up in the [Flat Creek] canyon where the horse thieves took the horses." In later years, he would embellish it: "All I had to do was to put up two pair of boards and that shut the whole canyon off... from there I could see the sheriff a comin' and a gonin'."

However, his first statement implies the horse thieves were using the canyon before he lived there. A footnote by historians Bonney and Bonney states: "Cal told Charlie Petersen it was Holland who originally built the canyon corrals." Who originally built the cabin up in Flat Creek Canyon is not certain, but one thing for sure, it was not Cal. And he certainly did not live there in winter in those years. The crudely constructed dirt-roof, dirt-floor cabin – a pack-rat manor – would have only been used seasonally. To access it in winter would have required expert snowshoeing (skiing) and winter survival skills, not horsemanship.

Charlie Petersen called a log structure that existed near the mouth of the canyon "the old trapper's cabin."[20] According to a 1972 interview, and subsequent 1998 field trip he led to the moldering structure, trappers Billy Bierer (also spelled Bier) and Albert Nelson built the cabin in the autumn of 1894. Bierer was considered to be Jackson Hole's last mountain man. Others, such as turn of the century sheriff and game warden, Josiah "Si" Ferrin, as well as rancher and hunting guide Frank Petersen, may have also used this cabin at times. This cabin, however, located near the canyon mouth, was not the structure occurring up in the canyon which Cal utilized.

Eastern journalists bought into Cal's and Cissy Paterson's embellished tales about his use of the cabin and canyon for outlaw activities. For example, Cal blandly explained, "he merely helped himself to horses [and] Flat Creek Canyon was ideal for hiding his stolen horses." Cal's alleged use of Flat Creek Canyon for hiding stolen horses simply doesn't match the evidence, but it is consistent with his propensity for spinning yarns and amusing himself by "stuffing" Eastern journalists and dudes with Wild West stories.[21]

Perhaps closer to the truth concerning Cal's rustling activities, Felicia Gizycka remembered Cal earnestly telling her: "He [had] wintered along the southern route, camping in the desert, and Quincy, one of Cal's pack mares, had come along at the end of a rope one dark night in Quincy, California." This if it were actually true, may have been stealing. It was not an uncommon open range practice when traveling through an area to gather up unattended stock along the way, euphemistically called "picking up extras." While it tended to irritate the livestock's rightful owners, it was not on the same level as organized rustling. Felicia later published an assumption that "Quincy was the last horse he ever stole."[22] That date, if it was when he left California, would have been 1908.

But the statement "Quincy had come along at the end of a rope one dark night," once again, has clever double meaning, letting the listener imagine intrigue. It may simply have meant, as was stated, he left California in the evening leading his horse, Quincy. It is similar to the earlier statement "He had seen the inside of a jail"– a double entendre'.

In his later years, Cal was asked, "What breed of horse was your favorite?" He replied, "Kentucky-Morgan." Then he went on to explain the parentage of a local line of horses that came from five thoroughbreds – four two-year old fillies and one valuable stud – Ed Harrington had allegedly stolen while working at the Denver racetrack stables (not rustled from open range on the prairies) and eventually brought into Jackson Hole, after first hiding them over winter on the Fort Hall Indian Reservation, supposedly with

John Carnes' assistance. The exact year is unknown but it would have been the early 1900s.

Once in Jackson Hole, the fillies were bred with the stallion. Then they shot the stud and raised the colts. "They couldn't keep him, y' know. Someone would come along and notice him right away," Cal said. He claimed no part in stealing the horses, but according to his statements he acquired their offspring for breeding purposes, as no doubt did other individuals in Jackson Hole.[23]

Cal's Teton Valley neighbors didn't believe his self-professed horse-thief stories. Lifelong Teton Valley resident Grant Thompson, whose father was born in 1919 in Cal's cabin at Bates, which their family had leased, scoffed at the idea, saying: "Cal wasn't a horse thief."[24] Teton Valley rancher Oren Furniss, whose family's homestead adjoined Cal's, after a thoughtful pause simply allowed, "It was hard to make a living in those days," implying people sometimes turned their heads away from what may have been done out of frontier necessity.[25]

During the time period he was supposedly stealing horses, Cal was juggling the work demanded by his Desert Entry homestead at Bates, simultaneously doing seasonal ranch work for others, and was employed by the Park and Forest Service, too. He was rustling up a living, so to speak, as best he could. Since winter pretty much closed off the way in and out of Jackson Hole in those days, realistically, it wouldn't have left him much time for organized horse rustling.

In addition, the telephone had made its debut in the Hole in 1905. The Forest Service greatly expanded telephone lines in 1907. The influx of honest citizenry into Teton Valley and Jackson Hole, the expansion of settlement, farms and fences, and improved communications through the telegraph and telephone, simply were not conducive to the outlaw activities of old.[26] No longer, for example, was it necessary to ride 250-miles in order to contact the county sheriff in Evanston. And by the first decade of the twentieth century, ranchers and townspeople simply wouldn't have put up with their livestock going missing or having outlaws operating right under their noses, even though many enjoyed perpetuating the outlaw myths.

In summary, it may be true that Flat Creek Canyon was used at some time or another in the 1880s and early 1890s to hide horses whose true ownership was questionable – as possibly were meadows along lower Flat Creek, Leek's Canyon, and the top of Miller's Butte in Jackson Hole. But that Cal himself was actually involved in horse rustling and using Flat Creek Canyon for hiding stolen horses appears very doubtful. More likely, he was joshing folks with stories he had picked up from old timers about events that had actually taken place years before his arrival in Jackson Hole. However, Cal's Wild West tales were, as previously pointed out, eagerly seized upon and passed along in the valley's folklore by local residents and historians, in Cissy Patterson's and her daughter Felicia's writings, and by Cissy's biographers.

It is easy to guess how rumors started and circulated back then. Imagine two old timers sitting around jawing when a scruffy cowpoke rides past them. One of the old men nudges the other and jokingly whispers, "Hey, there goes one of the gang of six." Later, they recognize the same rider again and one of them guffs, "That there's the gang of six horse thief again." The cowboy overhears the horseplay and says, "Yup, they was all caught, 'cept me." Much to their common delight, they've invented an entertaining joke. It gets passed around, the rumor repeatedly replayed and improved upon. After all, what other entertainment was there? Should a wide-eyed dude or journalist take them seriously, hey, all the more fun. And jokes at other people's expense only got funnier with the retelling.

Cal undeniably lived a rugged and demanding life during his early years in Jackson Hole and Teton Valley. A live-and-let-live philosophy and being in with the brotherhood and tight-lipped helped assure one's survival, especially when the only law was

Mountain Law.[27] But the fact remains, around the turn of the twentieth century most Jackson Holers had stopped sleeping with their horses to protect them from rustlers. Historian Doris Platts' summation in *John Cherry: His Lies, Life and Legend*, applies to much of the Hole's early citizenry and history of that era, and especially to the likes of Cal –"We chuckle at how he has succeeded in playing with the truth and in confounding us."[28]

John Holland leading a pack horse with a grizzly bear hide, c1900.
Courtesy JHHSM 1958.2814.001.

10

Outfitting and Guiding

After returning from the Forest Service in California in 1908, Cal became involved with outfitting and guiding hunters. Cal said, "Holland had some big hunters... Boston shoe man, Count de Turin from Italy, Lord Morton, Governor of India."[1] Likely, Carrington got into guiding sport hunters by first wrangling for Holland and his clients.

Some of the first dudes Cal guided after quitting the Forest Service were Struthers Burt and his party around 1908-09. The group included Burt, his wife and sister, Louis Joy and his wife, and Doc Kyle and his wife and niece. "That was Burt's first trip... I bought his first horse."[2] There's a photograph that may have been taken on this trip showing Carrington and Holland with three others. The five men had been hunting antelope.

When Cal had been associated with anybody or anything he would invariably put himself in a proprietary position in his telling about it. His perspective on that first meeting with Struthers Burt was: "That was Burt's first trip, and that fall he wanted me to buy some horses [for] the next year. He wanted to take my [Bates] ranch and go in with me and I wouldn't do it. I dunno how we'd come out, he's ejicated and I ain't. I'm afraid he'd pencil me out. But we was later together [at the Bar BC], I think, nine seasons."[3]

Cal claimed to have had other exclusive clients, too. There was a rich Englishman named John: "We were out six weeks...

got over in Hoback Basin. They brought very little drink. They'd take coffee or tea. Cook would make cake and they'd sit there for hours, chattering and drinking tea."[4]

John, the Englishman, said to Cal, "Better catch a cow and have some fresh milk."

"So I roped one and squeezed out what I could and that impressed him. He wanted to take me to India with him."

In those years, Jackson Hole's elk were being forced off their traditional winter ranges by the continual expansion of settlement and many were dying. Cal recalled, "I didn't see any [elk calves] for three years. All the yearlings died. They was piled [dead] in Flat Creek Canyon. I lived up in the canyon then where the horse thieves took the horses, I seen little elks piled up there three-four high."[5]

Cal apparently spent enough time traveling across Teton Pass from Teton Valley to Jackson and back that the wagon freighters knew him. There was one particular awful stretch of wagon road located on the top of the pass called the "red mud hole." It was so bad that a freighter claimed one day he saw a hat floating in the mud hole. Lifting it up, he found Cal Carrington underneath.

"Gol' durn, Cal, you sure have got into it," the freighter exclaimed, "I'll go down to Victor and get you some help."

"Never mind," Cal replied, "I'm a'horse back, an I'll make it okay."[6]

In traveling back and forth from Jackson Hole, Cal would stop over with his old friend, Jim Berger. Jim sold his original homestead near Bates and moved his family to Victor. They lived on the west side at the main turn in the road at the south end of Teton Valley, where the road led north to Driggs. Cal no doubt looked forward to those visits, since he was probably tired of cooking his own elk meat. On one occasion, Cal gave Jim a 10-guage Damascus double-barrel shotgun as a gift.[7] Jim's life took a different turn than Cal's when he married Odessa "Dessa" Parsons and settled down to ranching.

Dessa was said to be a beautiful dark-haired woman with blue eyes whom everybody loved. Jim and Dessa had five children, the oldest, a son, was born in 1907. Jim had established a reputation as a "colorful pioneer," becoming a well-know community leader, president of the cattlemen association, and even a brand inspector. Berger died in 1963 and is buried in the Victor cemetery. Today, the Spring Creek Resort encompasses what was once Berger's farm. One of the resort's streets is named Berger Road.[8]

Sometime around 1910, Cal and his neighbors had a disagreement with a herder who was grazing sheep in the Twin Creek watershed. "On Twin Creek they was bedding their sheep right alongside the creek, families below was using the water. Allen, Berger, and Briggs come down to the cabin and got me. We went out there and asked if he'd take his sheep off the creek. Well, the young fellow, he claimed he'd as much right there as anybody, and he talked back. I hadn't said anything. Finally, I told him, 'We didn't come up here to discuss laws or anything else. We asked you to move the sheep off the creek and bed 'em back further.' An instead of answering me, he turned up his nose at me. And I smacked him one right now. Wal, he moved the sheep and there was no more trouble there."[9]

Teton Valley, although settled predominately by Latter-day Saints, was not without its rowdy side: "Thar were some good times at Victor," Cal recalled, relishing the memory, "dances at the Old Shanty. I'd go there a'horseback from the ranch at Bates, then we'd go to John's Still to get a bottle. I wouldn't get back to the ranch 'til sun up."[10]

Cal and his cohorts were engaging in the traditional frontier pastime of hell raising. As Maggie McBride noted in her journal, when one of her party's wagons broke down near Driggs on the Fourth of July, 1897, on the way to Jackson Hole. She wrote, "they were invited to a dance, but declined because most of them [the men inviting them] were drunk."[11] Social past times had not changed much in the interval.

Cal recollected that in Jackson Hole, "There was all kinds of parties, generally around Christmas and Fourth of July, never went home 'till the sun come out. Dance, tell yarns. At the time I hit Jackson there was Cora Nelson and two of the Davis girls wasn't married. Then the school mums comes in. We [the bachelors] had a hell'va time pushing one another out of the way. They [the school marms] made up a song"–

> *Jackson Hole, good ol' Jackson Hole;*
> *Nobody's in a hurry;*
> *It's a sin to worry …*

Cora Nelson, who Cal mentioned, was the first Euro-American child to reside in Jackson Hole. Cora was four years old in 1888, when she first entered the Hole. She rode clinging to her mother behind the saddle, while crossing Teton Pass. Her father, "Slough-grass" Nelson, followed behind with a packstring carrying all their possessions.[12]

"Pretty near all the old timers had some kind of music box, accordion, mouth organ, banjo or fiddle – made lots of noise," Cal recalled.[13] By the early 1900s, Teton Valley sported a number of dance halls – at Badger (Felt), Victor, Driggs, and elsewhere in the valley. It was said, "Victor's Log Cabin Inn served whiskey to anyone old enough to push a quarter over the bar." Beesley's Dance Hall in Driggs hosted gifted local musicians, particularly fiddlers. Teton Valley's settlement was not all monotony and work without play, people showed up at those places and events in number by horseback, horse and sleigh, horse and buggy, and in later years, rag-top, wooden-spoke wheeled cars.[14]

In Jackson, dances were commonly held in the Clubhouse,

Locals gathered for a card game in Victor, Idaho, c1915. Lum Nickerson is seated second from right. Courtesy Library of the Tetons.

over Van Vleck's Mercantile Store, or above the drug store. Most dances followed traditional Western frontier custom. Women lined up on one side of the room and the men on the other. An announcer called out the dance and the music started up – a piano and fiddle playing mostly cowboy waltzes. An outsider might have called the instrument a violin, but fiddle was the accepted folk term in those days. The difference between a violin and a fiddle, it was said, was that a violin did not get beer spilled on it.

When the music began the men would ease forward across

the room and gallantly select a partner. Couples promenaded and whirled around the room, generally in a flat-footed glide, because that was mostly all rough floors and hob-nailed work shoes or high-heeled cowboy boots allowed. Style and smoothness were emphasized, no hip-movement and no exhibitionism.

The minute the music stopped, the men took their partners by the arm and escorted them back to their place on the other side of the room. Returning to their side, the men would then discreetly eye the line up across the floor for another dance partner. Contrary to Hollywood, no one cut in, got romantic on the dance floor, or rarely even publicly flirted – it would have been bad manners and led to trouble. A cowboy might buy his girl a soda, however.[15]

Asked if anyone ever got rough at the dances, Cal responded: "Always waited 'till the dance was over. Had a sociable time. Women folks wrapped kids in blankets and danced all night."[16]

Another amusement around that time was "prize fighting" or boxing. In his 1957 interview, Cal remembered "Bed Parker and Lum Nickerson was Teton Basin's prize fighters. They bet horses; didn't have no money. They went over to Jackson, an' Jake Jackson was the fighter there. Wal, it didn't last long, just a spat or two. They lost some horses. Jake was our champeen. They wasn't satisfied with that, so they got a fellow from Butte [Montana] to come down and he was training in the Basin. He was boxing everybody to get in shape. I had the gloves on with him; couldn't hold a hand to him. He'd tap me on the snoot any time he wanted to."

When winter set in, Cal sometimes rode south out of the mountains into warmer climes to, as he expressed it, "winter along the southern route." After 1899, he could leave his horses at a livery stable or with neighbors and take the train from Rexburg or St. Anthony south to Ogden and Salt Lake City and from there the transcontinental Union Pacific to wherever he chose.

Folks back then had an enthusiastic outlook on the railroad's contribution to the settlement of the Western frontier: "The railroads have done more to change a gloomy, uncivilized, sagebrush waste, inhabited only by hostile Indians and a few trapper-like ranchers, into a community of high civilization."[17]

In 1912 the Oregon Short-Line Railroad, a subsidiary of the Union Pacific, was completed into Driggs. The "high civilization" it brought with it was extended to Victor the next year. Victor became the end of the line.

The railroad linked Teton Valley to the outside world, which locals colloquially called "out below." Importantly, the railroad provided a means for ranchers and farmers in the high mountain valleys surrounding the Tetons to get their livestock and produce to market, and also for the clients of dude ranches and hunting guides to travel to Jackson Hole and the surrounding area.

The ranchers and farmers in Jackson Hole had to seasonally drive their livestock and haul produce by horse-drawn wagons across the demanding and hazardous 8,431-foot Teton Pass in order to reach the railhead. To help accommodate commerce, the Forest Service began grading the pass road in 1912.

It was the practice of early-day Jackson Hole ranchers to work together in the annual market roundup. Jackson Hole rancher, Clifford Hansen, recalled that in autumn neighbors would all drive their steers into holding corrals located above Wilson, where they would overnight. The next morning, beginning at dawn, they would bunch the cattle up into one large herd, sometimes 300-400 head. Then they would drive them across Teton Pass in one long day to the stockyards at the Victor railhead.[18] Driving cattle across the mountain pass to market thinned a bit of meat off them, but it couldn't be helped.

Mostly, the cattle drive met little other traffic while trailing across the pass. The drive was probably anticipated, so locals avoided traveling across the pass on that day, if they could.

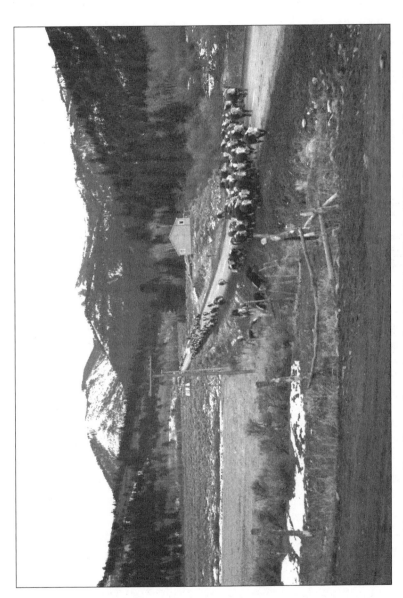

Cattle driven across Teton Pass on the way to market at the Victor railhead, c1940s. Courtesy Snake River Ranch. Collection JHHSM 2003.0131.006

Anyone trying to cross the pass that got caught up in the dusty maelstrom of bawling bovine and irked riders swore to never let it happen again.

The cattle were held in the Victor stockyards or pens provided by the railroad and fed a little hay and water until they could be loaded by chutes into railroad cars. In Victor, the stockyards were intentionally located northwest of the depot to keep the rarified odors downwind. Generally, the cattle were shipped to Omaha, Nebraska.

By the 1950s, Omaha's livestock market had become the largest in the world. Buyers and sellers at Omaha surveyed the herds from elevated walkways constructed above the pens, avoiding the manure, but not the smell.

After the roundup and drive, the cowboys and ranchers were inclined to let off a little steam, spending a rowdy night at the Victor's Killpack Hotel. Sometimes sleeping it off outside on the ground wrapped in their ponchos. It was sort of an annual celebration before heading back home over the pass. Ninety-year old Verl Bagley, who was born and raised in Teton Valley, recalled, "Victor was one of the largest cattle shipping points in the state of Idaho."

But Cal was not just any saddle-warped cowboy. It speaks loudly of his skills that he was hired as the foreman for the newly established Bar BC ranch in Jackson Hole. The Bar BC was homesteaded by Struthers Burt and Horace Carncross. Burt was a Princeton University graduate and a writer; Carncross had been a student of Dr. Sigmund Freud. Burt and Horace were impressed with Cal, as Burt would later attest: "He was a top cowhand. You didn't ask him to do ordinary chores around a ranch, such as fencing, ditching or haying. Those tasks were for a lower order of men known as ranch hands."[19]

Burt credited Cal for instructing him in "the ways of ranching, livestock and the hills." It was a considerable compliment because

Struthers Burt portrait. Courtesty JHHSM 199.0054.001

Burt was no tenderfoot himself. Although local gossips had warned him about Cal's bad character, Burt reported: "I have never known in all my life a more honest man, or one more sensitive to obligation; he refuses to be under obligation to any one, and he is not happy until he has paid a favor back."[20]

Bar BC guest ranch. Courtesy of JHHSM 2004.0004.006

11

Dude Wrangling

The Short Line Railroad into Victor opened the door for a mini-boom in tourism. Struthers Burt and his partner, Horace Carncross, turned their Bar BC cattle enterprise into a guest ranch. It was the second dude ranch to be established in Jackson Hole, and it became the most renowned.

In 1912, Burt and Horace struggled to complete cabins and a main lodge in time for their first guests. Local contractor, Charlie Fox, and his crew were "hired to do some buildin'."[1] Cal recalled, "Burt had a lot of problems before him. The building of that layout, and the carpenters, and a lot of those people under him ... a lot of disagreeable things come up. The boys what he got was none too good, I told him that."[2] The guest ranch was further expanded in 1917.

In spite of Cal's assessment, Charlie Fox, a German immigrant, went on to develop a lumber business in Jackson and was successful as a builder. Some of his structures are much admired in Jackson Hole yet today – the lodge at the AMK Ranch, the Chapel of Transfiguration, and the Flat Creek Ranch buildings, for example. While most are moldering into the ground, some of the old Bar BC cabins and buildings are still standing. The old Bar BC ranch site exists along the river near Cottonwood Creek within what is now Grand Teton National Park.

Burt made Cal "head guide in charge of pack outfits,"

BarBC dude wranglers were a colorful lot. Courtesy JHHSM 2003.0117.098.

declaring, "there wasn't a horse Cal couldn't gentle, and not a wild animal he couldn't outwit."[3] Cal supposed, "It was time for him to get respectable and go into dudin'."[4] He said, "Burt brought out a lot of dudes from the East ... good ones. Most of them was millionaires – Porter, Hemingway, Beau Reece – Reece was Mrs. Ryerson's brother, he got drowned on the Titanic – several artists [and] Princeton students."[5]

John Cherry worked at the Bar BC in the beginning, too, as did many other early day Jackson figures. It was one of the few job opportunities that paid in hard currency. There's no doubt Cherry, a master storyteller, set the bar competitively high for the ranch's wranglers in spinning Wild West tales for the dudes.

Whereas work clothes for Cal before this may have consisted of overalls, a blue denim shirt, neckerchief, and boots, the rambunctious employees of the Bar BC guest ranch were a more colorful lot. The employees went from being gaunt, homely, hungry, and rawboned cowboys to bright, bold, adventurous, and fearless – at least to the dudes.

The Bar BC workers' rigmarole included corked mustaches, fancy boots decorated with steer-head stitching, big spurs, chaps of leather or angora, great gold and silver belt buckles, tight custom-made riders, colorfully designed shirts, loose gay-neckerchiefs, and always a big hat. Struther's son, Nathaniel Burt, summed it up: "They possessed an aura of glamour associated with wranglers, guides, ropers, and horse breakers."[6]

One thing certain to make Cal lose his composure, though, was if one of the dudes, when they headed out with a pack string, asked, "Where are we going to spend the night?" Cal would pretend not to hear. If the dude persisted, Cal would raise both fists to heaven in silent supplication, and then turning on the unfortunate questioner he'd thunder: "Look at them thar hills! How do I know where we're a-goin to camp? I ain't been there for a year. Maybe there's no grass left. Maybe it ain't there no more. How do I know?"[7]

Cal Carrington in angora chaps with horse, c1915. From *Jackson Hole Journal* by N. Burt. Courtesy University of Oklahoma

The ranch's guests would sometimes be taken into Jackson to attend the rodeo. Carrington and other Bar BC cowboys undoubtedly participated in the rodeo events. It was a good chance to show off for the dudes. Nathaniel thought Cal was a "wild man," but conceded "he added spice to the Bar BC setup, especially for the dude girls."[8]

Cal generally stayed at the Crabtree Hotel while in town attending rodeos. Nathaniel Burt, did not hold Cal in as high esteem as did his father, Struthers. On one occasion, Nathaniel was not particularly pleased because he and Cal ended up sharing a room (and bed?) together, "Number 8." Inside the hotel rooms they and the other guests could plainly hear scuffing and

The remains of the original 1912 Bar BC guest lodge building in
Grand Teton National Park, 2004. Photo by the author.

booted footfalls, voices, rowdy laughter in the hallways, as well as
snoring, through the flimsy partitions.

Hank Crabtree said his mother's boarding rates were nine
dollars a week, which included three meals a day –"three of
the biggest darn meals you ever saw." Cal developed the habit,
which he continued over the years, of loitering around in the
hotel kitchen, having coffee and "sittin' and chewin' the fat" with
everyone, according to Hank.[9]

After a season of wrangling dudes at the Bar BC would end,
Cal would ride back across the pass to his Bates ranch. Along
the way he would stop off at his old friend's, Jim Berger's, place
in Victor. Cal liked to tell Jim stories about his experiences dude
wrangling and guiding. Jim would respond disbelievingly, shaking
his head and remarking incredulously, "Them dudes sure was
foolish folks."

Terrain at the head of Granite Creek in the Gros Ventre Mountains where Cal Carrington guided hunting clients. From *The Dairy of a Dudine*. Courtesy of JHHSM 2008.0018.010

12

An Elk Hunt Guided and Outfitted by Cal

In early autumn 1916, Cal got the chore of outfitting and guiding a twenty-two year old dudine on a ten-day elk and bighorn sheep hunt.1 The huntress was from Ardmore, a suburb of Philadelphia, Pennsylvania, where her wealthy family was engaged in the textile business. She was accompanied by a young male friend, who appeared smooth and soft when contrasted to rugged Westerners.

The clients arrived by rail at Victor, Idaho, where they were gathered up and transported to the Bar BC "by stage coach," according to the dudine. What preserved this duo's trip for posterity was that the dudine brought along a camera and kept a diary. She recorded her experiences, which, in her words, were: "a carefree, unconventional, girlhood life in the hills."[1]

Unconventional, yes; but hardly carefree. The "hills" were the rugged high-elevation Gros Ventre Mountains at the head of Granite Creek and the West Fork of Crystal Creek, near 11,107-foot-elevation Pyramid Peak, within what today is the Gros Ventre Wilderness.

The outfit Cal cobbled together for this hunting trip included himself as head guide, and George Ross as a second guide. In addition, there was a wrangler and a cook, along with sixteen head of horses – a "luxury hunt" for its day. Compared to today's standards, though, it was roughing it – low slung two-person canvas tents, blanket bedrolls, manties or pack covers and saddle pads that smelled of horse sweat for ground cloths, cooking over an open fire, and sitting on the ground to eat or relax. The seldom washed pots and pans were blackened and beat up from use. Grub consisted of canned corn, beans, camp meat, and cowboy coffee served at all hours and cooked to a cinder. And for the horses – oats, hobbles, sawbuck pack saddles, extra horseshoes and manila ropes. There were no large cook tents, portable showers, foldable tables and chairs, mattresses, goose-down sleeping bags, propane stoves and gas lanterns, cooler-preserved fresh foods, and 4x4 vehicles, like today.

The hunting and horseback riding involved – as Cal's trips invariably did – hair-raising, precipitous terrain and long hours in the saddle. It was a test of mettle for any dude or dudine. Clients were recklessly put into risky situations – practices that simply wouldn't be allowed today for liability and safety reasons alone – but back then, it was routinely accepted as outdoor adventure. Safe to say, clients never forgot those adventures for the rest of their lives.

Riding at the head of the pack string on a mare named Maggie, with her leggy colt cavorting along beside her, Cal appeared a long, lanky figure in yellowing-wooly chaps, a leather vest, and a felt hat. He was continually urging his tall mare onward, maintaining a fast, ground-covering walk. The pack horses, with their balanced, diamond hitched, 160-180 pound loads, followed along, lined-out single file, alternating between occasional trotting and fast-paced walking to keep up. There wasn't a single dragger, sway-back or barrel-shaped critter among them; nothing rattled or clanked in their packs. Cal's favorite mare, Quincy, was among the pack horses.

Navigating the sagebrush terraces and flats below the Bar BC, they arrived at and crossed the Snake River on Menor's Ferry. From there, they followed east and south around the base of Black

Tail Butte. Passing by homesteads en route, they traveled to the frontier town of Kelly, where they stopped at the Riverside Hotel for lunch.

A thriving hamlet at the time, Kelly was named after Bill Kelly, a local sawmill owner. The settlement consisted of a cluster of rough-built buildings and cabins, including the hotel, a post office, a store called the Grovont Mercantile, a blacksmith shop, livery stable, church, and school.

The community was surrounded by a growing number of outlying homesteads. The town's importance centered on a bridge built across the Gros Ventre River at that location. At the time, Kelly was a serious rival to Jackson for designation as the Teton County seat. But, eleven years later, in 1927, a flood wiped out the town. The Kelly flood was the most serious natural disaster Jackson Hole has ever experienced.[2]

After lunch at the hotel they mounted up, continuing south through Long Hollow to Flat Creek, and then began winding their way up Flat Creek Canyon. Here the dudine's first calamity occurred. Jay-jay, the horse she was riding, stumbled and fell heavily to the side, pinning the client's leg against a boulder. Only the chaps she was wearing and some luck saved her from serious injury.

Shaken, but continuing on over the rough terrain, she complained her shinbone "pained horribly." "At times," she confided, "the world turned black." But Cal was relentless; he had a destination in mind. She stayed in the saddle, Cal pushed onward. After a nine-hour day, with the clients dead-tired and exhausted, they arrived in the upper reaches of Flat Creek Canyon.

They camped at the foot of Sheep Mountain next to a streamside meadow; a beautiful, secluded spot where an old log cabin stood. It was a place, where, in the past, when Cal had first come into Jackson Hole, he had sometimes stayed. Cal was in the fond habit of spoofing his clients into thinking that this spot and cabin was his ranch: "I homesteaded this here place when I was a growin' up, but got so lonely up here all alone, couldn't stay, had to leave it," he told the dudine.

It amused him that dudes actually believed the yarn. No one but experienced trappers on snowshoes would dare try surviving up there in winter belly-deep in snow, and ranching or farming were out of the question. Cal knew it was the spot outlaws of old allegedly used for summer holding pasture for their rustled stock.

Next day, after a leisurely morning and breakfast, the wranglers finished packing up the outfit by ten-thirty. Not long after that they encountered, in the words of the dudine, "a very steep, narrow trail, which ran across an almost perpendicular forested hillside." Clutching onto her horse's neck and mane, shouting "giddy up horse, giddy up," she had almost reached "less terrifying ground," when the tailed-together pack horses, cat-footing along with their dead weight, stumbled off the narrow trail behind her. It came close to being a horse packer's worst nightmare – rolling the pack string. Horrified at the thrashing and crashing, when she was able to look back, the dudine was relieved to see four of the horses clambering back up onto the trail, saved only by the lead rope somehow having snarled around a sapling.[3]

However, it got worse. Soon there was no trail at all, only steeper ground with interlaced fallen timber. The men got out in front, chopping and sawing a pathway, while the wrangler took a dally around his horn and led the struggling, dry-farting pack string through.

Finally, the dudine decided enough was enough. Making the mistake of stopping, she tearfully cried out that "it was foolhardy to continue." When she stopped, it forced the entire pack string to stop, perched precariously and nervously on the precipitous terrain – fidgeting, eyes rolling, nostrils working, sweating, snorting and blowing.

Cal lost his already frayed temper. Riled, he began shouting and cussing, riding recklessly – his horse at one point with its legs locked sliding on its butt down the hill. But he managed to get the pack stock moving again. The awed dudine marveled, "In the grand intensity of his fury, I saw another side to this remarkable man." In her words, "no longer in her mind was he just a chivalrous lady killer."

In the afternoon, they crossed the divide and descended into Granite Creek Canyon; a fortress of remote rocky canyons and few other hunters. It appears to have been country unbelievably rich in elk in those days. They began seeing elk almost at once. George called Cal's attention to a herd with a large bull about 250-yards away on the mountainside. Then began what would be a disturbing part of the hunt to most sportsmen nowadays – shooting and wounding elk, and not recovering the crippled animals. Seemingly, the retrieval of the wounded animals did not overly concern them, there were plenty of elk.

The young dude fired two shots with his .25 -06 caliber rifle at the massive bull. Wounded, the elk ran off into the timber. Cal and the client looked for the crippled animal, but did not find it. The .25-06, also called the .25 Hi Power, was a necked down .30-06 Springfield cartridge with a maximum bullet weight of 120-grains. It is a high-velocity, flat-shooting, accurate rifle, with low recoil, but generally best used for hunting medium-sized game, not elk.

Guided by Cal, the dude got another chance that evening and managed to kill a five-point bull elk, shooting it twice at short-range. Skinned and butchered where it fell, it provided them with camp meat.

The next morning, George Ross and the dudine set out on horses, riding across places she described as "so perpendicular," that while clutching the neck and mane of Cal's mare, Quincy, she "kept her eyes closed and whispered prayers."

Meanwhile, Cal and the other client began hunting for bighorn sheep. But with no success, they started back to camp late that afternoon. On the way, they were surprised to discover a dead six-point elk lying right smack in the middle of the trail. It was the elk the dude had wounded the day before. There was celebration in camp that night – the dude client had bagged the two elk which his non-resident license entitled him.

The next morning Cal and his dude retrieved the trophy heads, teeth (ivories), and feet (dew claws) from the carcasses and then spent the remainder of the day around camp, while George and the dudine set out on horseback again, going down the main canyon. They saw no elk, only a coyote, which the dudine shot at and reportedly wounded, but they could not find it. She noted in her diary: "I had [finally] shot at something, however, and felt much better."

The dudine did not own a gun, but was provided George's .30-30 saddle gun to use. No doubt it was the West's legendary Winchester lever-action Model 94. Although available in bullet weights of 150 and 170 grains, the .30-30's low-velocity cartridge had an effective range of less than 200-yards. Normally, it is not considered a powerful enough rifle to use for elk. However, Cal and his guides made do with what was available.

George and the dudine found a ridge overlooking a secluded canyon and waited until evening hoping to hear the tell-tale bugling of a bull elk. The mountain ridges stretched away forever before them. "My heavens," she said to George, "I wish I could have some little girl, who has never seen anything, on this summit with us for a half second!" "Well," drawled George, "I bet she would not beat me if I was ever to see all them grand buildin's of your'n back East." Afterward, she journaled: "I was perfectly exhausted from climbing and riding, excitement and continued disappointment, and soon fell asleep. We heard or saw nothing, and rode back to camp discouraged."

They all started out together the next morning. Cal promised he was going to take them to "a particularly good spot he usually reserved just for himself." On the way down Granite Creek, a coyote was sighted and the dude killed it with the .25 rifle at what they estimated was "300-yards."

At a selected place in the canyon, they picketed the horses and split up, the dudine going on foot with Cal, and the other client with George. The dudine gushed: "I trotted along behind Cal, excited and almost dead for breath, for he hunted with an air which indicated fatality for whatever species of life lingered just beyond."

After "a long climb," the dudine said, "Cal signaled me from an overlooking ledge." Peering over it, she could see several elk below. "I declare my heart stood still," she wrote. They waited and soon a bull elk began bugling, squealing and grunting. "It sounded to me like a squeaky elevator and I clutched Cal," she wrote. "He swore my eyes bulged out. We crawled to the edge and there was a beautiful bull. I was almost hysterical in the intensity of the moment."

Taking aim, she fired. The herd was startled but didn't run. She shot again, with no effect. "What's the matter with this gun," she exclaimed frantically. Grabbing Cal's .30-30 from him, she fired several more times with it. The bull trotted off. Cal told her she had hit it. He had seen hair fly and the animal hunch up.

"Cal was provoked that I had shot too soon ... he said the elk were in bad light for a shot," she recorded afterward. "But my heavens! What dudine mortal could have waited longer after days of searching? But now we had to go back to the horses to get out of the canyon before dark. We would return to look for him the next day. Then the humor of the situation and consciousness of how excited we had both been struck, and we roared together with laughter and arm in arm hastened back like two rollicking kids... [it was] the sport of a lifetime," she wrote in her memoir.

They arrived back in camp to find George and the dude client "very much wrought up." A bull elk with a "huge spread" had come down a ridge next to camp in full view and was bugling nearby. Taking the .25-06 rifle, Cal and the dudine mounted the horses and tried to head the animal off. Dusk was coming on. Leaving the horses, she declared, "I really did not think I could go another step on foot, but somehow excitement and hope got me to the ridge top.

Through the trees Cal saw part of a head. I could not see it, but he told me to shoot at a certain white spot. As I was about to shoot the bull moved off, [and then I realized] I had not chosen the right spot anyhow."

Although invented in 1906, flashlights were not commonly available until after 1922. In the cold and without any light, they felt their way back to the horses. Where they tried to go down in the dark it was so steep they were required to dismount and "skid and slide" down the slope. At the bottom was a stream and in the pitch black Cal lost his footing. He "landed kerplunk" on his back in the water.

"It certainly was funny, we enjoyed a good laugh. We rode up the main canyon in darkness, keeping hands and arms extended to ward off branches, at one place an unseen tree limb swept Cal from his horse. We reached camp sometime after nine," she wrote.

On the seventh day, Cal decided to try to find the bull the dudine had wounded earlier. Cal and she searched the area to no avail. While leading the horses on a steep descent, Cal suddenly pulled back from the edge: "Another bull elk was below us and another thrilling moment ensued... I was calmer, probably because I was exhausted, and this time waited until Cal told me to shoot, then shot one cartridge as the bull started to move off. I thought I hit him? I was horribly discouraged about my shooting, here I was popping away at elk and they did not fall."

Next, while riding across a rock slide, they lost the trail and wandered around trying to find it. The dudine developed altitude sickness and became dizzy and nauseated. A missed elk, losing the trail, a sick dudine, Cal was frustrated, his temper was on slow burn.

When they found their way back to the main canyon again, they heard an elk bugling, but could not locate the animal. Finally, in the failing light of dusk, Cal spotted two bull elk moving down a ridge toward them. He decided to try to head them off. The dudine confessed, "I can not say I was happy at the prospect. I honestly did not think I could scramble up another mountainside."

The quarry did not show up where Cal planned to intersect them. Instead, darkness came and the two bull elk vanished into the gloom. By the time they returned to their horses it was too dark to even see the ground. It was unusual for Cal not to depend on his horse find the way, but the dudine claimed, he got off and went groping along on foot. The dudine stayed on her horse, Jay-jay, letting him pick his way through the blackness.

All around them, on both sides of the canyon elk began to whistle. One of the bulls began closely following them, "coaxing and whining at the horses with the most appealing grunts. Not until he was almost on us did Cal draw his gun from the scabbard and wait behind a jack pine to ambush him." The elk realizing something was awry went crashing off through the timber.

"It got so dark, I couldn't see my horse's ears," exclaimed the dudine, "I grasped the saddle horn and prayed, while growing numb with cold." They rode through tangles of downed logs and brush, across rushing streams, through boulder fields, and up and down steep embankments in total blackness. Hearing Cal's horse crashing ahead, Jay-jay would jump whatever impediment appeared in the way. "Cold, cold, cold, black, black, black," she recited.

Distraught and exhausted, the dudine called-out into the darkness proposing "they should stop, spend the night out, wait for daylight." From somewhere out ahead in the blackness, Cal came back with: "Wouldn't look nice for me to have you out

Guided hunting party in the head of Granite Creek, 1916 (l-r): Jimmy Manges, wrangler and camp cook; George Ross, guide with .30-30 carbine; a hunting client; Cal Carrington, guide; and Bill Sensenbach, camptender. Courtesy JHHSM 2008.0018.014.

overnight. Besides, I always get my dudes in at night, I've have had men in as bad fixes pretty near this."

They finally arrived in camp some time after ten o'clock. Rather than being met with concerned or worried faces, the men merely allowed "it had been a hard day for a soft dudine."

The next morning the exhausted dudine slept until ten. Not having had a bath for over a week, she made "a firm resolution, she was going to wash that morning." She asked one of the men to bring a basin and some warm water to her tent. George arrived with a tin can that had contained corn, it was filled with greasy warm water. When she asked for more water, the camp tender "howled with indignation," insisting, "there's nothing to heat it in".

Putting on a wrap, she went to the fireside where the men were sitting and picked up a canvas bucket of cold water and took it back to her tent.

Slack jawed, the astonished cook bawled, "Hey, you can't take no bath in my drinkin' bucket."

"I only want the water. Don't you ever take a bath yourselves?"

With this the cook got up and poked at the fire, finally allowing how he "took a bath once or twice a year, whether he needed it or not." The camp tender agreed, nodding his head.

Then the dudine asked, "Is there a towel?"

"Okey-doe-ke," responded the cook, and went and got her a dusty gunny sack.

After lunch, Cal and the woman client headed out on foot with the .25-06 rifle. At the lake where the youth had shot his elk on the first day, they heard an elk grunting and squealing. Sneaking through the timber, they glimpsed a small band of cow elk and "a large bull with a splendid spread."

"I took careful aim," she wrote, "but just as before, [when the rifle cracked] the elk did not drop. I fired a second shot, which went wild. Then in my excitement the gun jammed or I emptied it. I grabbed Cal's .30-30 and again hit the elk, which then disappeared over a knoll. I was so disgusted with myself," she confessed.

She had just described a classic case of "buck fever"– the intense nervous excitement experienced by novice hunters which can result in inaccurate shooting, jamming the gun mechanism, or even ejecting every shell without actually firing any of them. Cal declared, the elk had been "vitally wounded." He said they would return in the morning and assured her they would find it.

Once again, it was getting dark and they were a long way from camp. They repeated the harrowing experience of making their way back to camp in total darkness – slipping, falling, tripping over down trees and rocks, stumbling, and literally feeling their way down the mountain and back to camp. The dudine, gimped-up from all the strenuous riding and hiking, wrote in her diary: "The strain of two nights of this in succession was terrible. It took almost all the joy of the previous hunting away."

The next morning, all the men turned out to look for the crippled elk. Wandering through timbered areas, across hillsides, up and down ravines, scouting along ridges, poking into hidden recesses, they thoroughly combed the area. All to no avail, all they found were two spots of blood. The dudine's prize had escaped again. "How I craved that trophy of what I knew was the greatest experience I had ever had," she wrote.

At the campfire that evening, the huntress rose and melodramatically "vowed to give any man who could get me a shot on the morrow [her last day and chance] twenty-five dollars." That was nearly a week's wages in those days. Since it had already been decided the dude was going with Cal for bighorn sheep, it left it to George to take up the dudine's challenge. She claimed not to have even unlaced her boots to sleep that night, "rolling into her blankets early, ready to spring up and be off within minutes of being awakened."

By eight o'clock in the morning, she and George topped out

of the canyon; by eleven o'clock, they settled into a spot where they intended to wait until sundown, listening and watching for wapiti. Interestingly, Cal and his guides in those days apparently did not try to bugle or whistle the elk in; instead, they waited for the elk to announce or disclose their presence and then attempted to stalk them.

They talked, she asked George about his beliefs. He told her he only needed what was "Western religion – a full stomach, warm beddin', and a bottle of whiskey." He said, "he let his kids go to Sunday school because he guessed it did 'em no harm and they learned 'em to recite and speak nice." Like nearly every aspiring Jackson Hole hunting guide, he had read or heard about Teddy Roosevelt's 1893 book, *The Wilderness Hunter*, and proceeded to tell about it. George impressed her as "one of the most picturesque characters she had ever met."

It was past five o'clock when an elk bugled on the mountainside above them. George guided her on a hard, steep scramble toward the sound. Soon they saw some cows and calves. Then a majestic six-point bull came into view. From behind a rock, the dudine, once again, took aim using Cal's .30-30. This time, the wounded elk was "barely able to move across the hillside." She fired twice more, missing. George directed her to adjust the peep sight and she excitedly shot again. The elk collapsed and rolled end-over-end down the steep hillside. "I was conscious of having sobbed while I shot, but now I was wild with joy," she wrote. "My God," George said, "you are no gladder than I. Think how the fellers would have guyed me if I hadn't even gotten me dude a shot." George field dressed the elk. When they finally stumbled into camp in the dark, they had been out for sixteen hours.

Meanwhile, Cal and his dude, while searching for bighorn sheep, came across "the biggest seven-point bull elk," Cal exclaimed, "that he had ever seen!" The client eagerly agreed to "shooting it on Cal's license." Seven shots were fired at it with the .25-06, before the huge bull finally collapsed. When they approached the downed animal, they were astonished to have it jump up and run off. They tracked it for six hours following its blood trail. Even though the crippled elk lay down frequently and was bleeding heavily, it managed to elude them. They never did find it. The record book bull escaped to die in some far-removed corner of the Granite Creek drainage.

That night as the horses whinnied in alarm, a bull elk rampaged around their camp, crashing through the timber, grunting and bugling. It finally spooked the horses, which ran through camp and down the canyon. In the morning, the stock had to be found and driven back to camp. Then George and the wrangler took two pack horses and rode off to get the dudine's elk, while Cal and the clients headed out on the long ride directly back to town. Arriving in Jackson about four in the afternoon, they dropped the horses off at the Wort's livery stable and their personal gear at the Crabtree Hotel.

"Jackson is a typical frontier town," the dudine wrote, "the life of the place centers in the saloon... at supper that evening, Cal was very, very jovial." Spying a guide friend, Cal walked over and clapped him on the back: " 'Wal,'" he exclaimed, "'if I had brought those heads I saw you a cartin' in, I'd have waited till after dark and crept into town with 'em.'"

The dudine's hunt drew to a close when at seven-thirty the next morning she crawled onto the front seat of a four-horse stagecoach beside the driver and rode away, waving farewells to Cal. The coach would deliver her across Teton Pass to the railhead at Victor. "I was leaving behind me an experience wonderful for a woman to have had, and I felt that better days than those could never be."

Over the course of the physically challenging ten-day hunt, Cal's two clients had shot six bull elk. They had managed to successfully retrieve three of those. Nobody got hurt too badly; everyone appeared on a definite high afterward. The job of deconstructing the camp and bringing in the pack horses, camp gear, and trophy heads fell to George and the wrangler.

The heads would have been turned over to a local taxidermist for mounting. Then the artfully prepared trophies were crated up and hauled by wagon to the Victor railhead. Shipped by railroad freight to the proud owners, the sportsmen rightfully did some big-time bragging about their hunt and the impressive Wyoming trophies occupying their mansion walls.

The guides kept the elk teeth, called "ivories," if the clients didn't want them, which amounted to a nice bonus. There was a ready market for the ivories, up to twenty-dollars a pair. Outfitting and guiding hunters, and the related ancillary activities and businesses, powered the local Jackson Hole economy in those years. More than ranching, the local economy was dependent on the dude business and sport hunting, particularly for elk.

The aspen leaves had begun to appear gloriously golden on the hillsides around Jackson and snow dusted the mountain summits during the night. Cal was planning to return to the Bar BC that day. More hunting clients waited to be outfitted and guided.

Stagecoach that traveled from Jackson over Teton Pass to the railhead at Victor, Idaho, in 1916.
Courtesy JHHSM 2008.0018.012.

13

My God the Count!

In late-summer of 1917, providence provided a dramatically lucky break for Cal, fortuitously transforming his life forever. A countess and heiress to the *Chicago Tribune* fortune, Eleanor "Cissy" Patterson Gizycka, and her eleven year old daughter, Felicia, arrived at the Victor, Idaho, railhead with seven large steamer trunks and a French maid, en route to vacation in Jackson Hole at the Bar BC.[1]

Cissy was restless and her health tenuous after a difficult marital separation from her abusive husband Count Josef Gizycka of the Polish sector of the Russian Empire. She was involved in a continuing and ongoing custody fight over their child, Felicia. The trip west to Jackson Hole was intended to be restorative. Her much publicized divorce trial didn't actually take place until a few years later in Chicago. Count Gizycka was absent from the proceedings.[2]

Cissy, Felicia, and the maid had traveled across the country on the Union Pacific, and then on the recently constructed Oregon Short Line from Ogden, Utah, to Victor. Air conditioning had not yet been invented. The prairie sun relentlessly beat down on the Pullman car. The August heat and dust were nearly unbearable. When windows were opened for relief, smoke from the engine blew in, blackening them and the other passengers with a layer of soot.

The railroad depot at Victor, Idaho, c1920s. Courtesy Library of the Tetons.

Early day Union Pacific Railroad advertisement.
Courtesy American Heritage Center, University of Wyoming.

The Killpack Hotel in Victor, Idaho, c1920s. Courtesy Library of the Tetons.

On the final leg of their journey, between Ashton, Idaho, and Tetonia in Teton Valley, everyone excitedly rushed to the windows to peer into the canyon defile when they crossed the giant eight-hundred-foot span, 155-foot-high Bitch Creek trestle. It was the longest on any Short-Line branch.

That night they boarded at the Killpack Hotel, Victor's "largest and most luxurious hotel," where Felicia remembered "behind a sign saying 'LOBY' was a gathering place for cowpokes who sat chewing tobacco and aiming in the general direction of a row of tall brass spittoons." They found the dinner to be inedible – "as appetizing as boiled slippers"– the rooms filthy, and the beds unmade.[3] For an aristocratic Eastern socialite, Victor's finest accommodations left much to be desired.

Nathaniel Burt maintained, "Victor was the van of progress."[4] But if Victor, Idaho, warranted the title of "vanguard," it gives some indication of the rawness of the conditions in Teton Valley and Jackson Hole back then. For outsiders, it appeared frightfully stark; literally, "the end of the line."

Four-horse team and wagon hauling freight, also referred to as a "stagecoach,"
which traveled Teton Pass. Courtesy Library of the Tetons.

Unlike the dudine from Ardmore the year before, who
traveled by stagecoach to the railhead, the Bar BC sent a team
of horses and a crude ranch wagon to "drag them acrost" Teton
Pass. They had to use a wagon because Cissy's seven steamer
trunks were too much for any stagecoach to haul.

On the steep grades of the pass, fiery-haired Cissy marched
ahead of the laboring team in her custom-made Parisian skirt
and specially made high, lace-up, hobnail boots. Felicia wandered
along behind, bedazzled and entranced by the vistas. The sky
darkened, a mountain storm descended. Their arrival at the Bar
BC that night, soaked from driving-cold rain, and covered with
dirt, is a Jackson Hole legend. Cissy raged when she found out
there was "no electricity, hot bath, soft bed, nor dinner on a tray,"
imperiously announcing she was leaving the next day.[5]

In the morning, the prospect of the long, exhausting and
dirty wagon ride and walk back across Teton Pass, and the
likelihood of an indefinite stay at the Killpack Hotel because of
an infrequent train schedule, gave her pause; as no doubt did the

captivating view of the sky-piercing Tetons. Instead, she sent the French maid and six trunks back and she and Felicia stayed for the rest of the summer and into autumn.

Cissy was led to vacation at the Bar BC by a wealthy Chicago friend, George Porter, who specifically advised her to collar Cal Carrington as her escort and guide. But Cal, it turned out, was off purchasing "gentle squaw ponies" at an Indian Reservation for the Bar BC, most likely at Fort Washakie, near Lander, Wyoming.[6]

His return trip would have involved driving the horses over one-hundred miles, including crossing Togwotee Pass. The pass was named after a Shoshone Indian (meaning "spear thrower") who guided the Jones 1873 government expedition. The craggy mountain road that had been improved by the U.S. Army in 1895, and again in the early 1900s, defined the rugged route. The way was not unfamiliar to Cal, however. He stated in a 1957 interview that he had once ridden bucking horses in Lander. In any case, Cissy's first look at Cal may have been a thrilling one, as likely, he made his entrance with the remuda a dust-filled dramatic moment.

As was common among aristocracy, Cissy was an accomplished and fearless rider and a huntress. Her grandfather Medill, a noted horseman, had taught Cissy to ride when she was a child. She planned on hunting big game while at the Bar BC and had brought along a 6.5mm Mannlicher.[7] The Mannlicher-Schoenauer rifle is considered one of the sweetest handling rifles ever produced. Weighing only 6 ½ pounds, its 160-grain bullets are adequate even for elephants. It was, in fact, a rifle preferred by professional hunters in Africa for a time. Cissy must have brought plenty of ammunition along with her, too, because she occupied herself with target practice until Cal returned.

Arrangements had already been made for Cal to take another party out on a pack trip when he returned, but that all changed. Years later, Felicia disclosed, "Cissy bribed him with a huge bunch of money, the likes of which he had never seen."[8]

The Countess of Flat Creek, Eleanor "Cissy" Patterson. Courtesy JHHSM 1958.3401.001.

On that first hunting trip with Cissy, Cal outfitted and packed them into Soda Fork of the Buffalo Fork of the Snake River deep within today's Teton Wilderness. The Soda Fork originates as a full-blown tributary emanating out of the mountainside as a bubbling spectacular cascade below Crater Lake.

A string of ten pack horses was required to tote, not just camp equipment, but also Cissy's significant amount of baggage. Apparently, just one additional hand served to do the camp tending, wrangling, and cooking. Unlike some of Cal's minimalist trips, this time they appear to have packed wall tents and sheepherder stoves, too.

Crossing the Snake River on Menor's Ferry, or fording near there, they likely rode to Ben Sheffield's Teton Lodge at Moran for a late lunch. Afterward, they rode through remote wilderness for the rest of the day and most of the next, to reach their campsite. In all likelihood, it was at Soda Fork Meadows. Felicia rode behind, sulking along in the dust.

Cal and Cissy would be gone hunting all day, leaving the bored-adolescent Felicia in camp with the painfully shy camp tender who, according to her, "said absolutely nothing all day." It wasn't all bad, however, on September 3, 1917, Felicia had her twelfth birthday while they were camped in the wilderness. Reminiscing years later, she recalled, "She caught twelve fish on her twelfth birthday"– native cutthroat trout.[9]

They were out twenty-two days, subsisting on a spike bull elk Cissy shot for camp meat. She fascinated Cal. When they became snowbound, they huddled around the sheepherder stove in the tent, while she read Tolstoy aloud to them. She was unlike any other woman Cal had ever known, independent and able to both ride and shoot. She bagged a trophy bull elk: "Them fellars [at Ben Sheffield's Teton Lodge in Moran] kidded me about my fancy dude," Cal said, "all right, she done it. Look ... and I showed 'em the [trophy bull elk's] head."[10]

Cissy was impressed with Cal's "tough self-reliance." Their pairing became one of the most glamorous and jawed about "dudine-cowboy affairs" that Jackson Hole and perhaps the West has ever known. Gossip galloped up and down the Hole. Folks would say, "There goes Cal and the Countess." Cal was forty-one years old, Cissy thirty-five.

Cal possessively referred to the Countess and Felicia as my dudes. Cissy would refer to Cal for the rest of her life as "dear old Cal."[11] In her novel *Glass Houses*, Cissy portrayed a connection to her character "Ben" (who is recognizable as Cal) as one that was enduring for all time: "No – never goodbye between us. It wouldn't make any difference if we didn't meet [again] for a hundred years." Nearly a hundred years later, the town of Jackson recalled their romance in Petticoat Rules, a musical comedy about the legendary couple. It played at the Pink Garter Theater in 2000-2001 and at the Center for the Arts in 2009-2010.

At a dance in Jackson, "Cal monopolized Cissy," and, as Felicia described, "cowboys hopped around like grasshoppers on the rough dance floor." In her life, Cissy had danced with princes, dukes, counts, ambassadors, and multimillionaires, but cowboys were something new.

Cal must have put on a dazzling performance. Someone was heard to remark "the Countess was a great lady, but my God, the count!"[12] "My God, the Count!" was a branding Cal was never allowed to forget, it became Jackson folklore. Cowboys enjoy horseplay, greeting Cal with My God, the Count! ranked among the best of boisterous jokes.

Not surprisingly, there was an ornery, self-protective side to Cal. Nathaniel Burt noted: "Cal would openly mock Cissy's suitors, mount them on dangerous horses, spit contemptuously when they tried to shoot, and make slighting references to their virility."[13]

Cissy grew to adore Jackson Hole. For her, it became a restorative place where she could be herself. She loved its natural beauty, eloquently christening it, "a small secret valley which lay like a warm opal set in stone." It was also a place, as her daughter Felicia later penned, "full of [colorful] characters who could be themselves without benefit of psychiatry or interference from the law."[14] People in Jackson Hole had the courage and freedom to live their lives as they wished and they displayed a tolerance for differences in others. In those days, the Hole was occupied by a classless society.

The next summer, in 1918, Cissy returned and rented the entire White Grass Ranch for the season. Cal, hat in hand, regretfully explained to Struthers Burt that he had decided it was his duty to become her foreman and take care of her, saying: "She don't know nothin'... She's a mighty nice woman and someone might get the better of her."[15] Moreover, the job must have paid more than Cal could ever have imagined in his wildest cowboy dreams. Nathaniel Burt later recalled his father, Struthers, was not too pleased at the time.[16]

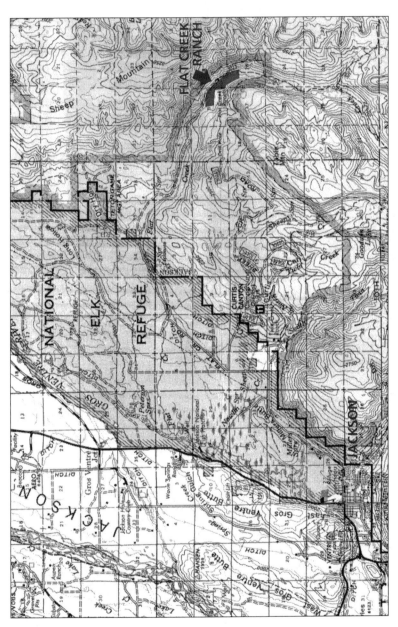

Map of the Flat Creek Ranch location homesteaded by Cal Carrington.

14

A Tale of Two Ranches

Sometime during that summer in 1918, Cal took Cissy on a horseback ride to the outlaw's hideaway in Flat Creek Canyon beneath Sheep Mountain – the place where he had sometimes stayed in the early years when he first came into Jackson Hole, and where he generally stopped over at the meadows with hunting clients on his way to Granite Creek. Cal and Cissy no doubt camped at his favorite place at the meadows on that trip.

According to her biographers, "Cissy thought it was the most perfect spot she had ever seen." Cal may have represented it to her as his, but at that time he did not own it. It was National Forest land.

Histories generally state that Cissy wanted to buy it from Cal, and much to do is made about Cal's "reluctance to sell." According to popular accounts, George Ross, an employee of the Bar BC, who later became a part-time employee and also a big-game guide for Cissy, was finally sent to Cal's homestead in Bates to fetch the deed from his trunk. Another myth was given birth. [1]

Ross's errand needs to be set in chronological context. It would not have happened until about six years after Cissy first saw the canyon. Of course Cal seemed "hesitant, unsure, and smilingly reluctant" at first about selling – he didn't own it. The stories of Cal's hesitancy to sell have been played up in the literature –"Cal was reluctant, highly reluctant."[2] It was pure smoke and mirrors, a myth jokingly created by Cal and Cissy themselves and later perpetuated by naïve journalists.

There can be no doubt, though, from first sight, Cissy was intrigued with Flat Creek Canyon. That spurred Cal, he was driven to please her. Cissy was used to getting what she wanted. Together they schemed how to gain title to the mountain hideaway.

Having worked for the Forest Service, Cal was knowledgeable about a 1906 law allowing homesteading on the National Forest, and furthermore, he knew from experience how to go about it. Unlike the Desert Entry requirements at Bates, which had consumed years of his life, this time he was experienced with the proving-up process. But, even more important, Cissy had the political connections to intimidate and induce cooperation from agency administrators.

Cal proceeded to establish squatter's rights within the isolated and rugged, steep-walled canyon, a scenic spot, but at over 7500-feet in elevation, not a place where homesteading a farm or ranch normally comes to mind. Besides, the 1906 law was intended to apply only to "tillable lands" within the National Forest system. Flat Creek Canyon most certainly did not qualify as tillable or anything close to government defined prime farmland.

During the time period 1918 through 1920, while Cal was engaged in establishing the homestead claim at the Flat Creek location, influenza struck Jackson Hole and Teton Valley. Residents were totally occupied in fighting the devastating sickness. Neighbors took turns feeding each other's livestock in order to free time up to help out with the sick. There were only three automobiles in Jackson Hole and the owners wore their tires out driving back and forth on the rough wagon roads providing assistance for the sick. Death outran the valley's capacity for burial services. The pandemic was personally felt by Cal, when Jim Berger's wife, Dessa, was tragically stricken and died.[3]

Cal had begun cleaning up and "improving" the old cabin

at the Flat Creek Canyon site in 1918, chasing the pack rats out, making it more livable, and adding an outbuilding and corral. He also had the proposed homestead boundaries surveyed. By spring of 1920, he reportedly had taken up residence – albeit sporadic – and cleared some trees.[4]

According to the Flat Creek Ranch's present-day website, "two years later he was running twenty-five cattle and horses." This would have been by permit on the National Forest. The livestock all bore Carrington's brand–"C A L."

More than coincidence, Cal had chosen a "name brand." Large name brands are considered the hardest to alter. But neither the Flat Creek Ranch, nor Cissy, ever registered a brand.[5] In Dwight Stone's 1958 interview, Cal claimed he ran "fifty head of cattle on the National Forest," conceding, "It didn't work out too well."[6]

One has to wonder where the livestock were kept in winter. Livestock drifting down the canyon off the homestead claim or from the adjacent National Forest would have ended up on other homesteads or on the National Elk Refuge, which had begun to be established already in 1912. Locals referred to the Elk Refuge as "the government's ranch."

Hauling enough hay into the isolated and snowbound Flat Creek Ranch, or cutting sufficient quantities from the ranch's streamside sedge meadows, dubbed "beaver meadows," to over winter the cattle and horses would have been an impossible task. Most likely, the ranch – that is, Cissy – paid for leasing over-wintering ground, purchasing hay, and feeding the livestock, on one of the valley's homesteads down below; such as, perhaps, Frank Peterson's on Poverty Flats. Cal did not generally hang around much in the winter months, as should become apparent, he had more interesting fish to fry.

In those years, the road to Kelly was not where it is today. Rather, it took the route of the present-day National Elk Refuge

Frank Petersen's improved homestead cabin. Courtesy Rena Croft.

roadway lying east of the Gros Ventre Hills and going across Dry Hollow and through Long Hollow, passing through homesteads en route. The road to the Flat Creek Ranch branched off from it. It was Cal's habit to stop off at the different homestead ranches and visit with people on the long ride to and from town.

Lifelong Jackson Hole resident, Johnny Ryan, grew up at the location of Jackson Hole's very first homesteads. Situated on Nolin Creek, a tributary to Flat Creek, Johnny's grandfather, Ben Goe, had purchased the homesteads from their original claimants, Carnes and Holland. Ben Goe later became the owner of the Cowboy Bar in downtown Jackson.

The Ryan ranch lay along Cal's route to town. Johnny recalled, when he was a boy "his mother was always talking about Cal Carrington." Whenever he stopped off at their Nolin Creek homestead, "my mother would tell me, 'stay out of the way and don't say nothin'. I always liked to see Cal's horses, because he had good ones. Cal once warned me, 'Kid, don't git behind that horse.'" He said, "Everyone liked Cal."[7]

Historian Wendell Gillette's wife, Bertha, also knew Carrington. Her family once had a homestead located within what is today's National Elk Refuge. She described Cal as "a jolly, lanky, young man, as rigid and sound as a stake of iron and never known to be without a broad smile."[8] Wendell and Bertha later moved to Victor, Idaho, but Bertha may have played a role in influencing her husband, Wendell, to later research and chronicle his account of Carrington.

Frank Petersen's homestead was located on Flat Creek, at the western edge of Poverty Flats within today's National Elk Refuge. Poverty Flats was ground that was known for having a mere skin of grass covering cobble and rock. Frank's son, Charlie, remembered, "Cal a ridin' in with the north wind 'n' snow a blowin', wearing a heavy mackinaw coat. All the buttons was gone from it, and he had a piece of rope – string off a bundle of grain – tied round him to keep it closed."[9]

Petersen family picking cultivated gooseberries at their homestead garden, l-r: Charlie, Martha Anderson, Frankie, Rena, and Leonard. Courtesy of Rena Croft.

The Petersen's kept a little band of elk within a 10-foot high rail enclosure. Petersen's elk were sometimes shipped to states, such as Pennsylvania, that were reintroducing elk. Like many settlers in Jackson Hole in those days, Frank was a hunting guide and they relied on game meat for subsistence. The choice of menu was venison or elk meat, it was all one and the same. Frank was one of the Hole's original old timers. He had ridden with the 1893 Cunningham Ranch citizen posse, and with Jackson's constable, William Manning, in the 1895 Indian War, and notably, he had made the 1898 ascent of the Grand Teton with surveyor Billy Owen and Jackson Hole settler Jack Shive.[10]

Cal and Frank were longtime friends, and at times Cal would overnight with the Petersen's in the comfort of their seven-room log home before going on to town. The two men would sit next to a glowing woodstove discussing hunting and horses, swapping yarns, and reminiscing about early day Jackson Hole.

There was frequent confusion about the spelling of Petersen's name, whether it was spelled ... sen or son. Contributing to this problem was the fact his wife, Rena, who was from Teton Valley, spelled her maiden name Peterson. Frank's son, Charlie Petersen, said, "even the post office couldn't get it right."

On his lengthy horseback rides into town, Cal had time to amuse himself by inventing mischief, so when he was asked, "What are you a doin' up thar at the Countess' place?" he came back with: "I'm a beautifyin' it, makin' it real purdy."

Someone would get curious and take the bait, "How ya doin' that?"

"Well, I'm a buildin' bird houses an' putting them up on posts," Cal would reply with a grin.

Indeed, Bertha Gillette, for one, passed it around. "Cal was beautifying the ranch for the Countess by making and putting birdhouses up on poles, corners of cabins, and on fence posts."[11] It might have been true, but on the other hand, things must have been awfully slow at the ranch if Cal was building birdhouses.

In those years, when Cal rode into Jackson, two odors strongly permeated the town – the fragrance emanating from the livery stables and the aroma of hops from brewing beer. No one found either smell offensive. Hitching rails conveniently lined the streets in front of residences and businesses.

Testimony to the fact Cal was not spending much time in Teton Valley during those years was that from 1918-21, he leased out his Bates ranch. The Thompson family had the lease. Victor resident Grant Thompson's father, Charles Jr., was born there in 1919. Grant remembers a family story of how during those years, "they weren't able to pay the rent because their crops froze out." Cal did not receive his rent money and rode over from Jackson. As he approached the cabin he began angrily shouting: "Charlie, get your wife, kids, horse and ass out of here."[12]

Cal attempted to physically throw Charlie off the place.

"They wrestled around in the yard," and as the family story goes, "suddenly Cal stopped and exclaimed, 'Dammit, I can't whip you, Charlie, I guess you're a stayin'.'" Mounting his horse, Cal rode away cussing and muttering that he would be back for his rent. The Thompson family came up with the rent money the next season.[13]

Christmas rolled around in 1922 and Cal faced the dilemma of what to get Cissy – a person who already had everything. On rides to and from the ranch, and during his travels, he had time to reflect on it. With a hint of devilment he composed and sent a letter to Cissy saying he had given her a cow for Christmas. He would care for it, but it was now her cow. Included with his letter was a bill of sale: "For value received I give to Countice Gizcka one spotted cow four years old branded CAL on left ribes." It was signed C.E. Carrington and witnessed by Gus Graceclose, the 25th day of December.[14]

Built in 1901, the Patterson mansion on Dupont Circle was the place of lavish Washington, D.C. parties and gathering for influential guests—aesthetes, poets, scholars, politicians, dignitaries and wealthy industrialists.

15

Among High Society

When Jackson Hole's interminable winter set in, Cissy would scoot back East to her family estates in Chicago, New York or Washington, D.C.; or sometimes, to southern California. Cal would slip back into his old solitary ways, but with his Bates ranch leased, more often in this time period, he boarded the train at Driggs, traveled the Short Line to Ogden, Utah, and from there rode the Union-Pacific back East or to California to join Cissy, wherever she was at the time.

Among her friends and acquaintances, Cissy was touted as "brilliant, well read, and sophisticated." Scandalously, she paraded Cal around Chicago, Long Island, and Washington in all his frontier essence, delighting in showing him off to her high society friends.

The Patterson Mansion at 15 Dupont Circle (today's Washington Club) was acclaimed as the meeting place for Washington D.C.'s elite and for lavish parties. The mansion sported thirty rooms, ten bathrooms, two libraries and fireplaces throughout.[1] It was enough to awe any cowboy and must have kept Cal busy just wandering around.

Among the influential guests that regularly crossed the mansion's threshold were aesthetes and aristocrats, renowned poets, scholars, and playwrights, wannabe politicians, high-level government officials, foreign dignitaries, wealthy industrialists,

Built in 1889, the 320-meter (1050-feet) Eiffel Tower was at one time the tallest manmade structure in the world. Cal Carrington visited it in 1921.

and get-rich-quick schemers. A guest list might have included the likes of Alger Hiss, Harold Ickes, Gene Tunney, Douglas McArthur, John L. Lewis, J. Edgar Hover and similar others. Cal met many of them. Dupont Circle became a familiar place to him. But as one might guess, not all of Cissy's family was favorably impressed with the cowhand. One well-heeled family member sarcastically questioned Cissy, "Where did you dig him up?"[2]

Cal had learned from guiding wealthy clients at the Bar BC, that they put their pants on the same way he did. Affluent and elite people with luxurious and lavish lifestyles did not intimidate him much. However, his cowboy origins and ways fascinated them. If anything, he may have felt, but wisely did not openly display, contempt for the highfalutin dudes. Instead, he demonstrated intelligent open-mindedness and was a quick study, adept at learning and adapting to whatever was socially expected or required. Responding appropriately to novel situations is considered a mark of intelligence. Cal appears to have epitomized a cowboy version of the Hollywood 1980s movie character *Crocodile Dundee*.

Journalists picked up on something they described as "troubling" for Cissy: Cal didn't particularly like to take baths. They claimed he would say, "Baths weakened the constitution … hot baths robbed you of your manhood." Similarly, Cissy's daughter, Felicia, later wrote, "Cissy could never get used to his wearing clothes that smelled and needed washing. She was forever telling him to 'go wash.'"[3] Cal likely had a Westerner's ambivalence towards water, in his mind it could end drought, but it also caused mud and flooding.

It is true, in the Old West the cold climate and scarcity of hot water did not encourage frequent bathing. But contrary to the above assertions, Cissy confessed in her *Glass Houses* novel that "the smell of leather and harnesses, lathered horses, livery stables, and healthy, strong, unwashed men" was a heady and exciting part of her Western experience.

In 1921-22, Cal traveled abroad with Cissy and Nellie Patterson, Cissy's mother. They visited London, Paris, Berlin and Russian Poland. In Paris, Cissy took Cal to see the Eiffel Tower. Completed in 1889, at 320-meters (1,050-feet) it was the tallest man-made structure in the world at the time. They attended the French Cancan at the *Moulin Rouge* and also joined revelers at the *Le Revue Negre*'s, where Josephine Baker performed her erotic dancing. Known as "the Bronze Venus," Josephine danced and sang nude except for only an ostrich feather. Cal and Cissy spent the Christmas holiday at the *Hotel de Crillon* in Paris.[4]

Ernest Hemingway, F. Scott Fitzgerald, and Gertrude Stein were living in Paris in those years. Aristocratic parties Cal and Cissy may have attended would have had the likes of those expatriates in attendance. The liberal social customs of Europe in the 1920's were literally light years away from the staid Victorian mores of Jackson Hole and Teton Valley.

They sat at Parisian outdoor cafes – Cal in his cowboy hat and best boots and Cissy glowing. Cissy's biographer, Ralph Martin, later penned, "Even the blasé Parisians must have stared as the cowboy and his red-haired lady rode horseback in the *Bois de Boulogne*."[5]

Cissy wrote to Jackson's hotel proprietress, Rose Crabtree, with whom she had become good friends, saying, she and Cal had visited Napoleon's tomb and "both of them cried from the majesty and beauty of the thing."[6] Rose raised an eyebrow at the idea of hard-nosed Cal Carrington weeping at a tomb.

Cal wanted to see Italy, Nellie Patterson did not, so Cal went alone on the overnight train. Imagine the cowboy on a sightseeing excursion to Milan, Venice, Florence, Rome – seeing the Leaning Tower of Pisa, the Pantheon and Coliseum, the Imperial Monument. Cal never stopped being his own man. When he wanted to be with Cissy, he was. When he wanted to go elsewhere, he did. When he took a long time to return, Cissy wrote Rose: "I really have begun to fear something terrible has happened, although I'm sure the old simp is merely having the time of his life and is too busy to write. Or else he's in jail."[7]

The original restored Flat Creek Ranch lodge as it appeared in 2004. Photo by the author.

16
Flat Creek Politics

In March 1922, Cal returned from Europe aboard the French liner *Rochambeau* to New York and then proceeded on to Washington, D.C. by train. Nearly four years had passed since he had taken up squatter's rights and made some "improvements" on the Flat Creek homestead. While they were in London, Cissy had written a letter to Wyoming Senator Francis Warren, who's company it was rumored "she favored while in Washington," asking him to "assist a fellow Wyomingite" in gaining title to the property.[1]

Wearing his Western boots and cowboy hat, and emboldened with a letter of introduction to Cissy's social acquaintance, the powerful Senator Warren, Cal strode into the Washington, D.C. headquarters of the Forest Service. There he swore out a claim, stating: "He had occupied the Flat Creek homestead tract under squatter's rights since 1901."[2] That date was a colossal stretch of the truth that would have made Jackson Hole's renowned teller of tall tales, John Cherry, proud. The date may have reflected the year Cal first rode up into Flat Creek Canyon, or maybe first stayed overnight at the old trapper's cabin, but he could never have "occupied" it beginning with that date in the manner required by the 1906 Forest Homestead Act. He had been much too occupied elsewhere.

Remember, the Forest Homestead Act of 1906 was intended to apply only to "pre-determined tillable lands" within the National

Forest system. And, in order to prove up on those lands, a claimant had to live on the parcel, build a home on it, make improvements, and successfully farm it for three or more years.[3]

A politically overwhelmed forest ranger in Jackson was asked to comment on the application. He fumbled for a reply: "I'm not against the homestead, even though Cal's cultivation has consisted almost entirely of harvesting wild hay [from the streamside beaver meadows]."[4]

The ranger's statement did not take into account the 1906 law's requirements and his response could have been interpreted either way – for or against the application. The ranger's report was dutifully filed away. But Flat Creek Canyon was never among the National Forest lands bona fide as tillable under the Act by the Secretary of Agriculture, and simply cutting wild sedge grass for horse feed was not farming, nor did fixing up the old cabin qualified as a home built by the claimant.

In Cal's and Cissy's time, the valley above the ranch looked different than today. Rather than a lake, a stream cut through it, with beaver dams, willows and sedge meadows bordering it. Cal's description of it was that "there was a meadow up there half a mile long, not quite a quarter mile wide." The meadows would have been resplendent with wild flowers. It was a beautiful setting. The beaver meadows were useable for summer horse pasture and for cutting some wild hay, however, none of it remotely qualified as "tillable agricultural land." The meadows were the holding pasture where rustled stock was rumored to have been kept before Cal's time. The present-day lake was created in the 1950s when ranch caretaker Al Remington dammed the creek and flooded the meadows to create a fishery.

Sometime shortly after filing for the homestead patent in 1922, in a whirlwind of travel, Cal had managed to meet up with Cissy in Santa Barbara, California. Cissy was put off by the particular gathering of people she found herself with and tried to warn Cal away, but he showed up anyway. Cissy condescendingly remarked in one of her letters to Rose that Cal "will probably get mad and run off before we get tired of him."[5] Cal was obviously a very busy man between operating two ranches and becoming an accomplished gadabout socialite.

The initial homestead patent issued for the Flat Creek Ranch, No. 49044, was dated April 12, 1922, but it got hung up in the bureaucracy, perhaps intentionally.[6] The Forest Service was never keen on opening the National Forests to homestead entry in the first place. The Flat Creek application was not only legally questionable, but it also went against the grain of the agency's unwritten policy of preventing the National Forest system from being carved into homesteads. The Forest Service dragged its feet on the application's approval, not wanting a private inholding deep within the National Forest.

Cissy, always used to getting her way, wielded her political power again. To put an end to further delay, she asked for help from her friend, Senator Warren. He personally fired off a letter dated November 15, 1922, to the Department of Interior's General Land Office (GLO) flat out directing them to "expedite the matter" of the Flat Creek approval. After that, the patent application was approved in record time – two days later on November 17. A follow up letter was promptly sent to the senator by the GLO informing him the homestead authorization was completed. In turn, the senator announced the approval to Cissy.[7] The Forest Service had been politically outgunned and overridden.

Cal couldn't contain his ear-to-ear grin when he opened the official looking envelope at the Driggs post office. Inside was the patent document (H.E. 07481) for the Flat Creek homestead. It was approved by President Warren G. Harding on December 4, 1922.[8]

Rather quickly thereafter, in February 1923, Cal overcame his much ballyhooed "reluctance" or "misgivings" and sold the property to Cissy for five-thousand dollars.[9] As the story goes: "Cissy handed Cal a check saying, 'This is for the ranch, now you take it and shut up'." Indeed, we can be certain he took the money. That was the plan. It was a far different transaction than the myths about Cal's "reluctance to sell" had previously led one to believe. If George Ross was, in fact, ever sent to Bates to retrieve the homestead patent from Cal's trunk, as was mentioned earlier, it would have occurred sometime around then, not before.

For whatever reason, Cal did not record the original homestead deed when he received it. The sale transaction to Cissy, however, was recorded in Jackson on February 28, 1923. Later, a warranty deed was also recorded by Cissy on March 10, 1924. Curiously, the 1924 warranty deed was prepared in San Diego, California.[10] Additional evidence that Cal was not in Jackson that winter is that Cissy asked Rose Crabtree to keep an eye on the Flat Creek Ranch for her. Apparently, Cal or Cissy, or both together, spent the winter in or near San Diego that year.

During Carrington's years working to prove up on the Flat Creek Canyon property, while also pulling a salary from Cissy, it seems that few, if anyone, ever thought to ask, knew about, nor apparently even cared about his Desert Entry farm in Teton Valley. However, the law did provide for a person to have both, a Desert Entry tract in addition to claiming a homestead.

It is possible Cissy knew little about his Bates property at the time, as neither Felicia in her writings, nor Cissy in her letters to Rose, make mention of it until sometime after the Flat Creek homestead was patented. Oddly, there is no mention that Cal ever took Cissy to his Bates farm in all their time together either. No doubt, in his mind, the ranch at Bates was his, and he intended to keep it that way.

Most people today still incorrectly believe or have an impression that Cal already owned the Flat Creek Ranch when he first met Cissy. Felicia wrote: "He had homesteaded the Flat Creek Ranch to hide his stolen horses;" Wendell Gillette said, "Cal built a small cabin in Flat Creek Canyon in 1898 and took up squatter's rights, this he held secretly;" and, in 1916, his dudine hunting client from Ardmore, Pennsylvania, recorded that Cal told her, "Here he had homesteaded as a boy."[11]

Homestead application records in the National Archives and deed transfer records in the Jackson Hole courthouse conflict with those traditional stories. Before 1906, too, there were government efforts to remove illegal squatters from the Forest Reserve. Flat Creek horse thievery, indeed. More hanky-panky than just horse stealing went on there. Illusions about horse rustling were entertaining, but also an effective distraction, too. Cal could be guilefully tight-lipped when it counted. He had spent much of his adult life mischievously lampooning greenhorns, dudes and bureaucrats and he must have smiled to himself all the way to the bank after he and Cissy pulled off the Flat Creek caper.

Cissy gushed to Rose with ideas for developing the ranch: "I want a good dance floor in the living room. I want a big brick fireplace in it too – a big, huge one – I want a barn painted red. I want the [access] road to go up the left side [of the creek], to avoid swampy places. I also want a little cabin for myself to write in." And she got all those things, too.[12]

Cal was made foreman of Cissy's Flat Creek Ranch. It took several years to construct the ranch, foremost because of the difficulty of transporting materials to the site. Author Bertha Gillette described Cal in those years as "the Countess's hired man, her horseman, her fixer-upper and tearer down."[13]

The completed ranch structures consisted of a lodge, several cabins, corrals and Cissy's little red barn, styled after Midwestern barns. Compared to historic photographs, the restored ranch looks much the same today as it originally did. It has been well maintained, remaining delightfully unchanged. Only the stream-bottom meadows above the ranch have been modified by the creation of the dam and lake.

Charlie Fox was the building contractor. One of the several carpenters employed was Henry Crabtree, Rose's husband.

Biographer Martin portrayed Cissy as being incredulous at the fact Rose had only known one man in her life, her husband. Cissy made it a point to tease and encourage Rose to have an affair. So while Henry was working up at the ranch, Cissy would write notes to Rose, which she'd have Cal deliver since there was no phone at Flat Creek. Once in Jackson, Cal would stay over at the Crabtree Hotel – to catch Rose up on how things were going at the ranch, perhaps?

Cal and Cissy's relationship grew to become stormy. Felicia wrote that "they would have fights at the ranch that probably loosened the mountains and caused the famous Gros Ventre landslide." After a fight, Cal would saddle his horse and ride down the canyon. He would be gone for long periods, only to return muttering and cussing while he deftly unsaddled his horse.[14]

It is certain Cal used those occasions to ride over Teton Pass and check on his Teton Valley property, which in those years sometimes sat unoccupied for long periods. At one point, word reached Cal that a claim jumper had taken up residence in his place. Bates neighbor, Monte Piquet, said, Cal "rode day and night" getting back. Another neighbor, Oren Furniss, recalled Cal arrived on a lathered horse and found a stranger living in his cabin. Oren remembered an uproarious commotion, punctuated with loud cursing and yelling: "Cal run the trespasser off with his quirt," declared Oren. [15]

A scow of the type that Harry Guleke and his crew piloted on the Salmon River for Cal and Cissy. Guleke is pictured standing in the center. Courtesy Lemhi Historical Society.

17
Famous Hunting Couple

In *The Diary of a Dude Wrangler* Struthers Burt wrote "as a hunter Cal was intuitive, putting himself into the mind of the animal."[1] Cissy, a serious huntress in those years, became Cal's protégé. One guide acknowledged, "She would go anywhere an elk went." Another guide, George Ross, boasted, with her favorite rifle, the 6.5 Mannlicher, "She could hit an elk at four hundred yards."[2] Cal gave her a pair of black angora chaps to keep her warm on their autumn pack trips into the mountains.[3]

Their hunting and adventuring together throughout the West and parts of Canada went on for a number of years around the early 1920s. Cissy wrote and published three articles for *Field and Stream Magazine* in which she recounted some of those experiences. Later, in 1939, the *Saturday Evening Post* would report: "Visitors to [Cissy's] Dupont Circle home were struck by the sight of thirteen heads and pelts which hung on the wall overlooking the grand staircase." These consisted of grizzly bear, moose, elk, deer, bighorn sheep, mountain goat, and wolf. In addition, there was also a large Gobelin hunting scene tapestry. Manufactured in Paris, this type of tapestry was generally made for European royalty.[4]

In 1921, Cissy decided she was going to be the first woman ever to run Idaho's Main Fork of the Salmon River. Known as the River of No Return, it was considered "the wildest boat ride in America." She organized a party of a half-dozen people, including another woman whom she does not name, except as "R.E. Among those was the most experienced river guide available, Harry Guleke.

In her many writings, Cissy customarily gave Cal the pen name "Ben." On the river trip, Cal, dubbed Ben, went along as her "first mate." In her story, *Diary on the Salmon River*, she credits him as being a "philosopher, guide and friend."[5]

Their river guide, Harry, was a big, muscular and likeable fellow, who built and piloted boats known as scows on the Main Fork from 1896 through the 1930s. A giant in Salmon River boating history, he is buried in Salmon, Idaho.[6]

The custom-built wooden scow Harry provided was squared off at both ends, thirty-feet long by eight-feet wide, with three-foot high gunnels, and double hulled. It had two clumsy, over twenty-feet-long, fore and aft sweeps for steering. Cissy labeled the boat an "unlovely, but capable, little scow drawing only six inches of water."[7] At the mercy of the currents and cramped quarters, the ungainly craft was not rowed, only steered. It depended entirely on the skill of the steersmen to make it down the river safely.

Cissy described how, from Salmon to Riggins, Idaho, they ran the river's formidable white water rapids – "shooting clear out of the water [and], sometimes lying flat to avoid the swinging sweeps." Besides reveling in the adventure, there were also discomforts that she disparaged: grilling daytime heat, poor and monotonous food, and at night, sleeping on sandbars with rattlesnakes everywhere.[8]

One has to wonder how at ease Cal was on this powerful river. As a cowboy he had no experience in boating, and once admitted "he never learned to swim because his horse could do it better."[9] Still, Cal was intrigued with the remote ranches along the Salmon River which remained snow-free all winter, compared to the rigors of ranching in Jackson Hole where livestock had to be fed six months of the year. It caused him some wishful daydreaming: "What I want is a place where I can raise peaches and cream and let the rest of the world go by... turn my stock out on them hills where they'll feed themselves year round. Raise plenty of grapes and drown myself in a barrel of wine if it gets too lonesome." [10]

They stopped at Polly Bemis's place on the river. Polly was already a Salmon River legend. More than fifty-years earlier, Mr. Bemis, had been shot and left for dead in a barroom fight in the frontier mining town of Warren, Idaho. Polly nursed him back to health and he married her. "At age sixty-seven," Cissy remarked, "Polly was not much over four-feet tall, neat as pin, wrinkled as a walnut." Polly told Cal and Cissy, "My folks in Hong-Kong, they had no grub, they sells me, a slave girl. Old women she smuggles me into Portland. I cost $2500. Don't looka it now," she chuckled. "Old Chinese man he took me to Warren by horse pack train."[11] Polly Bemis's life story was the subject of the 1991 Hollywood movie, *A Thousand Pieces of Silver*.

Cal and Cissy tried to do some hunting along the way, stalking deer for camp meat. The season of the year and 110-degree temperatures were generally not conducive to hunting. At one point, they spotted four mountain goats. The goats were shedding a tapestry of loose, clinging-white hair. One person in the party argued there were eight goats. Cal allowed how "every time a goat went behind a rock and came out again, [that person] counted it twice." At another place, they saw three bighorn sheep ewes. Cissy remarked, "I killed a young ram in Wyoming a few years ago that would make almost two of these [Salmon River sheep]."[12]

In her boating story, Cissy off-handedly mentions she and Cal had been hunting in the "savage, gloomy Wilson [Creek] Canyon," of the Middle Fork of the Salmon two years earlier. Part of the Frank Church River of No Return Wilderness today, it was a rugged and incredibly wild place. On that trip, Cissy had bagged two mountain goats. They left one of the dead mountain goats lying out over night, intending to retrieve it the next morning;

Cissy in her black angora chaps and Cal with one of the two grizzly bears taken by baiting in Upper Flat Creek above the ranch, c1922. Courtesy JHHSM 2010.0003.001.

instead, a mountain lion stole it.[13]

Cissy wrote in her journal, "The [Salmon River] country is wild, inaccessible and stupendous." Cal agreed, adding, "The white man can never kill [all] the game off here." They finally arrived at Riggins, according to Cissy, "in water-stained, raggedy shirts and breeches, and sunburnt shiny-beet red." They sold the drift boat for lumber; there was no way to get it back to Salmon.[14]

Sometime around 1923, Cal's friend, Frank Petersen, was supposed to have accompanied them as wrangler on a hunting trip into the West Fork of Crystal Creek and Granite Creek in the Gros Ventre Mountains. One of Cal's favorite spots. However, Frank had some critical ranch work that needed tending, so instead he sent Charlie, his inexperienced teenage son. Charlie recalled, "We wuz all gonna sleep under the stars, but then it began rainin'. I crawled under a tree, but Cal, he drug his saddle an' blankets into the tent with Cissy, an' stayed."[15]

Charlie divulged an embarrassment he suffered on that trip: "One night most of the horses got away from me. Cal saddled one of the others and set out after them. He finally caught up with the runaways nearly back at Flat Creek and brought them back to camp – all but one. Said he couldn't catch mine, so I had to walk for the rest of the pack trip. I never let those horses get away again."[16]

Charlie Petersen later went on to become a hunting guide and outfitter himself, guiding renowned clients such as *Outdoor Life*'s gun editor, Jack O'Conner, on moose and bighorn sheep hunts in the Jackson Hole area.[17]

One autumn, Cal killed a neighbor's crippled cow for bear bait above what they called the Upper Meadows in Flat Creek, not too far from the ranch. In her *Field and Stream* story entitled, "Two Bear," Cissy wrote about how she and Cal killed two different grizzly bears that came to feed on the dead cow. She described one bruin as "big, humped-up, and soft black." It took five shots between them to finally bring the huge grizzly down. Cal admired the bear, saying, "He's a fine specimen, he's got awful pretty fur on him."[18]

A week later, the remaining bait, nearly the entire cow disappeared. Cal found it cached beneath debris, uphill some distance away from where it had lain. "He's a bear, and a big one," Cal exclaimed. A neighbor offered Cal the use of a trap —"a heavy contrivance, reminiscent of the Middle Ages," according to Cissy. No longer legal nowadays, a grizzly bear trap was a forty-two-inch long, forty-pound, solid steel device with seriously teethed jaws and an attached heavy chain. Setting it could be a hazardous undertaking requiring large C-clamps to compress the trap's double-long springs and open the trap's powerful jaws.

George Ross accompanied Cal and Cissy the next morning when they went out to check their trap. "Over the top of some fallen logs, a large dark-brown head [of the ensnared bear] appeared. It fixed with congealed attention in our direction. Oh, I think this is horrid. He looks so humble ... bitter and broken like the men I [once] saw in Joliet Prison."[19]

"Well, he ain't," Cal snapped back. "You act like you thought he was a new born lamb tied up with a daisy-chain. He's starting to sway and swayin' bears are just working themselves up for a fight." From a sitting position, resting her elbow on her knee, while controlling her breathing, Cissy "shot the bear neatly through the forehead."[20]

In the 1990s, Cissy's grandniece, Alice Arlen, donated "Cal Carrington's grizzly bear hide" as a raffle prize to raise money for the medical center in Dubois, Wyoming. It was from one of the bears Cal and Cissy had shot in the 1920s. The hide has been restored and is now in the possession of Shane Brazil in Dubois.[21] The other bear hide, recently discovered in storage at the Flat Creek Ranch, has been donated to the Teton Science School in Jackson.

Cissy poses with her 6.5 Mannlicher rifle and her horse, Ranger.
Courtesy JHHSM 1958.0202.001p.

Under Cal's expert tutelage, Cissy graduated from deer, elk and bear to even more elite and challenging big game – Rocky Mountain bighorn sheep. Because of the rugged, high-elevation mountain terrain bighorn sheep inhabit, hunting them can be notoriously difficult. It required, in Cissy's words, "endurance, patience, nerve, and skill."[22]

Earlier Cal had helped Cissy pick out a pony that she named "Ranger." They declared he had been "born with nineteen legs," he was so surefooted. Riding across the steep-mountain slopes Cal would call back over his shoulder: "Loosen up on your [horse's] reins, he ain't a-goin' to fall, he's got four legs and twice as much sense as we have."[23]

They pursued mountain sheep from the Flat Creek Ranch on the boulder-strewn, windblown precipices of Sheep Mountain (Sleeping Indian). They trailed their way up the steep, nearly-impassable mountain with horses. Pushing their luck, until in one mishap, Cal's horse cartwheeled end-over-end and was saved only by the trees below. Together, they also stalked mountain sheep along the high-elevation, rocky ramparts at the head of Jackson Hole's Crystal and Granite Creek, which today is part of the federally designated Gros Ventre Wilderness Area.

Cissy thrived on the challenges. In 1923, their obsession for hunting bighorn sheep took them to the Canadian Rockies in Alberta, in the vicinity of Cathedral Mountain near Banff. On one occasion, within the "dizzying-high rocky walls," they located a large herd of bighorns. Spread out across the rocky terrain were forty-seven rams. Cal and Cissy crawled to within two-hundred yards of a half-dozen large rams led by an exceptional monarch. Afterward, in her *Field and Stream* article, "Sheep Hunting in Alberta," Cissy sensibly wrote: "You experienced hunters know that two-hundred yards is an extremely long shot. The majority of all big game is killed under one-hundred."[24]

Cal was equally as good on foot in the mountains as he was on horseback. On another occasion, while hunting high among

Cal looking for bighorn sheep along the rimrock at the head of Granite Creek in the Gros Ventre Mountains. Courtesy JHHSM 2008.0018.012.

Canadian Rockies Cathedral Mountain near Banff, Alberta, where Cissy and Cal hunted bighorn sheep. Courtesy Lukas Novak.

the crags, Cissy shot a full curl ram across a chasm. The animal tumbled into space and out of sight. She badly wanted the trophy head and implored Cal to retrieve it.

"How you gonna get it?" Cal asked, "I ain't noticed no airplanes around here."

Finally, Cal relented and began climbing down over cliffs and talus, disappearing far below. Four hours later, he reappeared on a lower ledge, radiant and triumphant, carrying the magnificent head. Fortunately, the horns were not damaged by the ram's tumbling fall.[25]

Another source states, "They became known as the famous hunting couple from Jackson Hole."[26] A photograph of Cissy high on a mountain ridge with two full-curl trophy rams attests to their success. While in Canada, Cissy also added a bull moose to her ever-growing collection of trophy mounts.

However, on one Alberta trip, Cal and Cissy had a serious

Cissy with trophy bighorn sheep rams taken in Alberta, Canada, in the 1920s.
Courtesy JHHSM 1958.2183.001.

blow up that apparently eclipsed all others. What caused the falling out may only be guessed. Cissy wrote Rose Crabtree saying, "I really think this will be my last hunt with Cal," vaguely complaining, he had been "a little treacherous and light fingered all his life, [and] he has been both [with me]." She swore she would never trust him again. What had occurred was never explained. That winter when she directed Rose Crabtree to have the ranch's horses taken care of, she specifically stipulated "not in Cal's care."[27]

Cissy may have been fed-up, angry, spiteful, or maybe all of those, because the next summer, in 1924, she brought Elmer Schlesinger – a debonair tennis-playing Harvard man and prominent East Coast attorney – with her to Flat Creek. Turned out, Elmer had actually been courting Cissy for some time. They married in 1925. Elmer's world, however, was New York City; Jackson Hole was a totally alien place to him.[28]

18

Riffs and Rescues

Regardless of Cal and Cissy's falling out and her marriage to Elmer, in what would appear like an awkward arrangement, Cal continued as the Flat Creek Ranch foreman and hunting guide.

Cissy still relied heavily on Cal, but at times tension at the ranch was so palpable you could have forked it like hay. Tempers flared, people were edgy. When Cal misplaced his knife, he asked Cissy if she had seen it. She snapped, "It's in an employee where you stuck it."[1]

Cissy and Elmer always arrived in Jackson with enough cases of liquor to last their stay, especially during prohibition. According to accounts, Schlesinger was always worried about his whiskey bottles getting broken on the rough wagon ride into the ranch. Other new arrivals at the ranch included a pack of poodles that Cissy began bringing along with her, too. Of all her poodles – Toto, Bo, and others – her favorite was Butch, whom she identified with as being "gentle when stroked, fierce when provoked."[2]

Cissy had begun drinking more in those years, and she was a notoriously "mean drunk." Drinking brought out her violent temper. Cal, on the other hand, a ranch employee informed, "got quiet when he drank. You wouldn't know he was drunk until he talked." Years before, Jackson settler Dick Turpin had accused Cal of "being Irish," saying, "Cal would drink anything."[3] Needless

Portrait of Felicia Gizycka as a young woman. Courtesy JHHSM 1958.2468.001.

to say, the boozing contributed to some volatile and explosive altercations at the ranch.[4] Dawn peeping over the scenic canyon walls was frequently overshadowed by monumental hangovers.

The Countess kept a Model T Ford truck at the ranch. If Cal was annoyed or angry when he was driving, which he frequently was in those days, he would speed at twenty-five miles per hour in a reckless fury, bouncing up and down on the rough and narrow wagon road with its precipitous drop-offs. Few today dare to travel the road at that speed, even with modern four-wheel drive vehicles. Somehow he – and those who may have had the misfortune to ride with him – survived.

On one occasion, teenaged Felicia – who Cissy characterized as being "about as easy to drive as a team of young bull moose"– forgot to close a gate, letting all the horses escape. It took Cal until nightfall to find them all and haze them back up the canyon. Totally riled, he notified Cissy when he returned, announcing: "A kid is an expensive proposition."[5]

Later, Cissy fired Rex Ross, George Ross's son, when Cal complained after a cow and calf Rex had unintentionally let out of the corral ran off. Rex denied it was his fault. [6] The Ross's had a homestead at Teton, Wyoming, near where Teton Village is located today. Both Rex and his father also worked for the Bar BC Ranch at times, too.

Sometime around then, in a tantrum, Cissy tried to fire her maid, Aasta, but Felicia intervened. A knockdown drag out fight ensued between Cissy and Felicia with screaming, hair-pulling and clothes tearing. Felicia ended up riding away bareback on her pony that Cal had given her, using tied-together cotton socks for a halter. The incident caused quite a stir in Jackson. The town prattle about Felicia's bareback flight from Flat Creek became a Jackson Hole legend.[7] The same cow pony, some many years later, transported by rail to Maryland, became Felecia's daughter Ellen's horse. It lived out its last days among thoroughbreds at Cissy's Dower House stables in Maryland.[8]

In Jackson, Felicia went to the Crabtree Hotel and lied to Rose Crabtree: "Grandmother is sick and I have to go home." Not easily fooled, Rose asked, "How did you get the message – by Ouija board?"[9]

Felicia pulled her savings from the Jackson Bank, left her horse at the Wort's livery stable in Jackson, took a stagecoach to Victor and caught the train to Salt Lake City, and then disappeared. By chance, in Salt Lake City she ran into Irvin Corse, who had just bought the Bar BC. Felicia confided to him that she was running away to California.

A young reporter from New Jersey, Drew Pearson, who had been a guest at the Flat Creek Ranch that summer, had developed a crush for Felicia. In California, after a few months of washing dishes and waitressing in a San Diego waterfront bar and hash-house, staying in cheap boarding houses, and sharing an apartment with a Navy couple, Felicia began corresponding with Drew.[10]

After Cissy learned of Felicia's whereabouts through Irvin and Drew, she put Cal on a bus to San Diego to track her down and bring her home, not unlike what she might have had him do with stray livestock. It drew quizzical looks when the tall cowboy walked into the waterfront bar in San Diego wearing a big hat and high-heeled boots looking for Felicia, who was waiting tables. "Hey, Little Fellar, your mama sent me to look in on ya."

Once Cal determined Felicia was okay, he didn't try to persuade her to return. Secretly, he may have empathized, remembering when he, too, had run away from abusive circumstances. Moreover, he reckoned, at eighteen years of age, she was a grown woman.

Former director of Jackson Hole's museum, and an acquaintance of Felicia's, Robert Rudd, confirms Felicia was in San Diego around that time, and also that her good friend Dorothy Redmond Hubbard was there, too, attending school. Bill

Redmond, Dorothy's father, was an early homesteader in Jackson Hole who moved up to the Red Rock Ranch in the Gros Ventre in 1916, after selling his Spring Creek homestead to Bert Charter. Redmond thought Jackson had become much too over crowded. Charter, it is believed, had once been a member of Cassidy's Wild Bunch, but had become respectable. According to Rudd, Cal spent time in San Diego at Cissy's bidding serving as a chaperone for the girls.[11]

Off and on, for the rest of his life, Cal would serve as an intermediary in attempting to resolve the frequent warring that went on between Cissy and Felicia. Cal would tell Felecia: "You know, honey, she took a de-spite to your Dad [Count Gizycki], I think that's what all this is about."[12]

Cal was already familiar with San Diego. It was a place early Jackson Holers moved to for retirement. The first settler on the west bank of the river, Bill Menor, who had built and operated Menor's Ferry at Moose, started the trend by retiring to San Diego already in 1918. By the 1930s, so many Jackson Hole residents had moved or retired to there, they were able to hold reunions.[13]

Understandably, Cal was not quick to turn around and head back to Wyoming. The perfection of southern California's climate enticed him to poke around some. Just north of San Diego, next to the ocean beaches at Encinitas, he discovered a 23.72-acre triangular-shaped tract for sale. Historic Highway 101 passed nearby. The live oak, citrus tree, and poppy flower covered property, with its balmy climate, coastal beaches, and magnificent sunsets, contrasted sharply with Idaho and Wyoming's monochromatic winter landscape. Promoters had dubbed the area "the flower capital of the world." The property and its setting translated into a good investment in Cal's mind.

Instinctively, without much deliberation, Cal purchased the Encinitas tract. No doubt he paid cash for it. Mortgages were not the way he did things. And he was not short on greenbacks after

Pack string and riders crossing in front of the Teton Mountains in Jackson Hole. Harrison Crandall photo, courtesy Quinta Pownall, JHHSM 1958.0967.001p.

years working for Cissy and having also sold her the Flat Creek homestead for $5000.

Some time later he acquired another investment property, a lot on the beach next to what is today's Moonlight Beach State Park at Encinitas. Typical of him, he apparently did not record the deeds. For years he told few people, if any, about his southern California beachside properties near San Diego, while their value soared like a raven in a thermal updraft crossing the Tetons.[14]

In the winter of 1924, Cissy wrote Rose, "It always worries me to think of him living alone. I suppose he hibernates like an old bear in his cabin."[15] Her worry was misplaced; going dormant was something Cal never considered.

Journalist Drew Pearson courted Felicia in San Diego and they married in 1925, but divorced in 1928. She lived what one chronicler termed "a life of international frivolity." She ended up marrying and divorcing two more times, all the while pursuing a career in writing. She and Cissy had one thing in common – they were both alcoholics. Through it all, Felicia continued her writing. And she never gave up her friendship with Cal. But Felicia never returned to Jackson again until she was fifty years old.[16]

In 1925, Jackson's newspaper reported a total of six-hundred dudes vacationed in Jackson Hole. Cal continued seasonally as Cissy's foreman, and he guided his share of dudes. From a 1958 interview, we know he took clients not only into the Gros Ventre and Absaroka Mountains, but also into the Tetons for pack trips and day rides.

Cal knew and rode all the high mountain trails in the Tetons, amid the snowbanks and alpine flowering splendor, up Phillips Canyon to Phillips Pass and on to the Teton Crest, past Housetop Mountain to Marion Lake, and north from there to wherever time allowed, finally looping back down the side-canyon trails into Jackson Hole.

Cal once said his "most favorite view of the Tetons was from

Table Mountain." He claimed to have frequently ridden there on horseback.[17] There is a Table Mountain (Table Rock) on the west side of the Tetons, but there is also a Table Mountain in the Gros Ventre Mountains, a few miles southwest of the Flat Creek Ranch. Both provide direct views of the Grand Teton. Locals generally call the mountain on the Teton Valley side Table Rock, so most likely Cal was referring to Table Mountain in the Gros Ventre Mountains.

In the autumn, Cal continued outfitting and guiding hunters for the Flat Creek Ranch and the Bar BC. Head mounts of big game taken by Cal from around this period hung in the Wort Hotel in Jackson up until recent time.[18] In 1926, he took four hunters from Philadelphia (many dudes originated from Pennsylvania in those years due to Struthers Burt's connections there and at Princeton, New Jersey) into a favorite spot on the Soda Fork of the Buffalo River. He also set up another hunting camp for the ranch several miles away.

After dark one evening, Reed Henry, the guide from the other camp, showed up, obviously distraught, looking for Cal. One of his hunters, "a great big strapper from Princeton University," as Cal put it, "had gotten himself lost." Cal went looking for the college football player early the next morning, cut his tracks and trailed him: "I found him sitting under a tree along Blackrock Creek." Word of the wilderness rescue got back to town, elevating Cal's reputation to local hero status.[19]

19

Africa Safari

Cal had often expressed an interest in hunting in Africa. Some say he had saved his money for it, others believe Cissy – the Schlesingers – financed it as a reward for finding the ranch's lost hunter. No doubt there is some truth to both scenarios.

Cal, not surprisingly, was notoriously rude to Elmer. Cissy wrote Rose Crabtree remarking that Elmer would have bought Cal a ticket on any freighter ship "just to get rid of him." In any case, in September 1926, Cal's desire to hunt in Africa became a reality.[1]

In a letter, Cissy informed Rose, Cal was among the one-hundred thousand spectators who attended the famous Dempsey-Tunney fight at the World's Fair in Philadelphia in September 23, 1926. He then traveled to his port of departure and several days later boarded an East Indian freighter going to St. John's, New Brunswick. From there, it crossed the Atlantic bound for Mozambique, British East Africa, by way of the Suez Canal. Cal had his own cabin and a black East Indian youth to attend to his needs. He wrote Cissy, "There was even a porthole to throw his wash water out."[2] It was a voyage in the tradition of nineteenth-century adventurers!

In Africa, Cal had to have been struck by the lustrous-green landscape, bustling outdoor markets, crowded streets, colorful sarongs and glowing black skins – all the sensory delights of tropical Africa. Much of the arid West that he knew was drab in comparison. Cal traveled by train from his port of entry to Nairobi, and then on to Lake Albert where the railroad terminated. There he bought a secondhand "tin-lizzie"– a Model T Ford touring car. The vehicle had three gears, two forward and reverse. It was capable of running on gasoline, kerosene, or ethanol. The factory price on the new Model T in those days was $395.

Alone, Cal toured East Africa, inquiring the way to hunting country and subsisting on game he shot with the 9mm rifle (most likely a 9.63x62 Mauser) Cissy had given him for the trip. With it, he hunted hippos from boats at close range. Cal wrote to Goldie Chismsan, his friend in California, that the natives called him *anakosea-aka!* In Swahili roughly meaning, "he never misses" or "never miss." Struthers Burt wrote, "At night he would close the car windows and go to sleep with lions prowling about."[3]

From there, historian Gillette recorded, he hired a guide and eight porters, and obtained safari supplies and equipment to travel three-hundred miles on foot hunting as he went. Sometimes he met up with other white hunters who joined him. He killed three or four elephants with the 9mm rifle. Once, while out with a tusk hunter from the Barbary Coast, a bull elephant Cal wounded charged him at close range, nearly trampling him before he finally killed it. It had one-hundred-twenty pounds of ivory, which he sold for four dollars a pound, more than covering his one-hundred dollar license fee.[4]

Cal calculated one of the elephants he bagged stood twelve-feet at the shoulder and weighed six-tons or more. An entire village of natives camped next to the carcass until it was totally consumed. Cal commented, "Elephant meat is sweet, but awful coarse and tough."[5]

Cal returned home to Teton Valley around December 1927. Years later, when asked what his best experience in Africa had been, he replied, "Well that's kinda hard, cause something happened pretty near every day."[6]

He had shipped his trophies back from Africa. They eventually arrived without notice and sat on the Victor railroad freight dock. In a letter to his friend, Goldie, Cal wrote, "If I had took the noon train my trophies would of been left in Victor for goodness [k]nows for how long."[7]

For the rest of his life, Cal would spin yarns about Africa. He did not simply tell stories about his experiences, he would put on a one-man show imitating animal sounds such as elephants trumpeting and even pantomiming giraffe's mating.[8]

Cal was gone over a year on the African safari. Once back home in Teton Valley, he resumed his seasonal work for Cissy, wrangling dudes and guiding hunters. He spent part of the winters in California, or sometimes Mountain Home, Idaho, and later, even the Bahamas and Sarasota, Florida.

Compared to Africa, his old life may have seemed a bit tame. So, perhaps, it shouldn't be too surprising that a few years later, the 1930 census somehow recorded Enoch Carrington at two different places: Los Angeles, California and Cape Nome, Alaska.[9] If Cal took a junket to Nome, it must have been to see the storied gold fields, not to labor at placer mining.

Cal Carrington contemplates the globe at Cissy Patterson's Dower House in Maryland.
Jackie Martin Collection Courtesy Syracuse University Library.

20

Tea Cups and Silk Socks

Cal had always tended to roam. This frisky leaning was now fueled by his exposure to possibilities and aided by connections with well-to-do dude clients and friends. He became sort of a social gadabout. As a colorful character, he acquired instant insider status back East. Struthers Burt characterized Cal's excursions as "triumphal."[1]

It was the *Roaring Twenties*. Cissy had introduced Cal to the euphoria. Swept away with the trendy fashions – sports, cigarettes for women, flappers, short-skirts, and gin-soaked jazz-syncopates – major cities, such as New York, Chicago, Berlin, Paris, London, enjoyed unprecedented and sustained economic prosperity. The availability and use of automobiles, telephones, and motion pictures, and leaving the farms for the factories, greatly accelerated. But the wild times and affluence were primarily confined to major metropolitan areas. For the homesteaders and ranchers eking out a living in the rural West, the prosperous trendy times were not a part of their day-to-day lives. Cal on the other hand, managed to straddle both worlds.

In Chicago, Cal reportedly was a "civic institution," falling in with the "Alley Bazaar crowd," frequenting the narrow alleyway's fashionable shops and restaurants along with opera singers, actors, follies girls, and millionaires. Burt said, "When I went through Chicago, all I had to do to introduce myself was to

Cal Carrington and Felicia Gizycka and her daughter Ellen on the street in front of Cissy
Patterson's mansion in Washington, D.C. c1930s.
Courtesy Eugene Downer, Teton Magazine.

mention Carrington's name. Cal was so popular in Chicago that, as he himself expressed, 'he had to make his getaway from that city between sundown and sunup'."[2]

In Philadelphia, Cal went fox hunting with the city's elite equestrians. Never having ridden an English saddle before, he was unseated several times and unceremoniously dumped onto the ground, much to the amusement of his hosts and embarrassment to his cowboy pride. But being stubbornly determined, he soon joined the ranks of "first flight."[3]

One may wonder, while fox hunting, did he wear Western garb, with a stampede strap to keep his hat on and yell "yahoo", like a buckaroo, or did he dress in a traditional red hunting uniform with a black top hat and call out "tally-ho"? Either way, it certainly would have amused his crusty cronies in Jackson Hole had they witnessed any of it.

In New York, he stayed with a famous portrait painter who had been a frequent Bar BC client. His patron gave a dinner in Cal's honor and put him next to a worldly French Countess who was famous for her decadent leanings. Cal thought she was the "nicest, simplest, little woman he had ever become acquainted with." Struthers Burt commented, "Cal had a way with women."[4]

On another occasion, back in Jackson Hole, a famous blond-haired motion picture actress, most likely Mary Miles Minter when she was in Jackson for the filming of *The Cowboy and the Lady,* was being patronizingly gracious to "the dear simple people [of Jackson]." She had picked up on a local greeting and at a gathering, seated next to Cal she bubblingly asked, "How did you winter?" "Fine," he replied, "I wintered in Paris, Berlin, and Rome."[5]

In the 1920s, after Cissy had married Elmer Schlesinger and sometime before his Africa hunting trip, Cal met a woman named Goldie Chisman. Goldie lived at 3765 Fifth Avenue in San Diego. She and Cal carried on a correspondence and friendship for thirty years, up until Cal's passing. At first their letters indicated a romance; later, friendship. Goldie apparently visited Cal at his Bates ranch in Teton Valley.

In one of her letters Goldie wrote, "I remember how beautiful the lilacs and poppies were on the road to your place, one spring." Cal replied from Jackson, July 1928, "I just got your letter so I can go home [to Bates] contented. You did not say you maid it home when we left ... everything was all right when I came back ... I ben so lon som every since, all I live for is to come and see you again."[6]

After Felicia returned to New York, she said, "Cal would take a train east and find his way to my walkup apartment on 35th Street off Park Avenue, simply by remembering the convolutions of the land. I'd hear a knock on the door, and there would be this loveable, silver-haired giant in his cowboy boots and ten-gallon hat. He'd bring elk meat that he'd roast in my apartment fireplace for me and my friends."[7] Felicia would also later have a home at East End Avenue and upstate at Towers, New York, where she was able to keep two horses.

In New York City, Cal marveled at the sky-lined landmark Empire State Building, which in 1931, at 1,454-feet, had replaced the Eiffel Tower as the world's tallest building.

Earlier, Cissy had written about her character Ben, "for all his lithe slimness, he was well along in years."[8] It was true, Cal, by this time he was getting up in years, but he was still a vigorous and active man.

21

Teton Valley Roots

"We believe the entire Jackson Hole should be set aside as a recreation area," was how a 1925 petition signed by ninety-seven Jackson Hole residents read.[1] The petitioners, however, were not as altruistically motivated as it might first seem. Rather they were hopeful the government would buy them out and relieve them of their hardscrabble existence. Charlie Petersen referred to homesteading in Jackson Hole in those years as "a living dug out of the rocks."[2] People were tired of back-breaking labor, sub-zero temperatures, and subsisting on rutabagas and game meat.

But the petitioners hardly represented a unanimous opinion. Throughout the 1920s and into the 1940s Jackson Hole's residents were bitterly divided about which direction the valley's future should take. A Teton National Monument, which included just parts of the mountain range, was proclaimed in 1929. But a number of prominent Wyoming ranchers and residents remained staunchly opposed to any set asides. They enlisted movie actor Wallace Beery on their side and conducted outrageous stunts to gain national attention, like arming themselves and driving cattle through the area they disputed. Moreover, they tried to paint individuals who favored expansion and National Park designation, such as Struthers Burt, Horace Albright, Mardy and Olaus Murie, and the Rockefellers, as extremists – the radical environmentalists of the time.[3] After twenty years of local and legislative attacks opposing it, Grand Teton National Park, as it exists today, was only finally established in 1950.

The late 1920's saw the rise of America's beloved George "Babe" Ruth. He was more popular and better paid than the President of the United States. "What the hell has Hoover got to do with it?", Ruth famously replied when asked why he demanded a better salary ($80,000) than the President's $75,000. "Besides, I had a better year than he did," Ruth quipped.[4] The Babe was best loved in Pennsylvania, the state where many of the Bar BC guests and Cal's hunting clients originated from. No doubt news about the Babe's barnstorming career filtered into the far reaches of the West, but the ranchers were more apt to be occupied with local concerns – Omaha cattle prices, water for their crops, hunting clients – rather than national and sports news.

Over the time period leading into the 1930s, the inevitable winds of change swept through Jackson Hole. Cal's friend and original settler, Frank Peterson, died in 1929, others left or moved on. By the 1930s, many of the homesteads on the National Elk Refuge had already faded from the scene, and the private lands that would eventually comprise the National Park gradually followed over the next few decades, in the end all being acquired by the federal government. Where Cal came down on the issue is not known, he was not directly affected, but likely he was cautious about expressing his opinions.

The Depression of the 1930s and World War II came and went without much change in lifestyle for those who hung on in the Hole. Ranching and squeezing out a subsistence living went on pretty much as before. Old timer Roy Chambers, who was born at Grovont (Mormon Row) north of Jackson, summed it up: "We never realized there was a Depression because we were living on the ranch and had no money anyway. But we always had enough to eat."[5]

Dude ranching and guiding and outfitting hunters remained the primary sources for any hard currency. Budget travelers who visited Jackson Hole, but couldn't afford the top-dollar dude ranches were disparagingly referred to as "tin-can tourists." Cal was in the gravy compared to most in those lean years. While cash was a scarce commodity, he was receiving a year-round monthly stipend from Cissy. Her ranch and personal expenditures were a one-person booster to the local economy. None-the-less, Cissy still frequently lobbied her friend, Forest Supervisor Felix Buckenroth, for the Forest Service to improve the rough road into her ranch "for fire protection" purposes.

Earlier, in 1929, Cissy had shipped furniture to the ranch. A piano, rugs, and other items, including a large couch, were hauled by horse and wagon from the railhead at Victor over Teton Pass, and then up the narrow wagon road to the ranch by ox cart. The skilled wagon crews that accomplished this feat earned their pay, but were happy there was any money to be made at all. Nowadays, Flat Creek Ranch guests look at the piano and couch, which are still in use in the main lodge, and shake their heads in wonderment. The thought of moving them, especially a piano, up the narrow, bumpy road to the ranch by ox-drawn wagon seems like an impossible and heroic feat.

In autumn 1929, Cissy arranged another hunting trip, this time for mountain goat in the Canadian Rockies. Cal did not accompany her. She wrote an article for *Liberty Magazine* about her hunt entitled, "Who's the Goat." The outing turned out to be a life-altering experience for Cissy. She shot "a magnificent specimen of mountain goat." In pursuing the mortally wounded animal, which struggled to elude her while "moaning and emitting sobbing, choking sounds," she discovered she had lost her "former zest for the kill." She wrote, "I felt very sick indeed, the thrill [of the chase] has suddenly quite all gone." Cissy would never hunt big game again. Instead she devoted herself and considerable means to being an advocate for animals and to the prevention of their suffering.[6]

"Black Thursday" hit October 24, 1929, when the stock

Hover Dam the largest manmade structure in existence at the time transformed the South-western United States. Photo by Ansel Adams, National Archives.

market crashed. The Roaring Twenties skidded to an abrupt end overnight. Few Jackson Hole or Teton Valley citizens were directly affected since most farmers and ranchers were not heavily invested in the stock market. Cissy, fortunately, was so conservatively invested that she was hardy affected either. [7]

Long-time Jackson Hole resident Johnny Ryan claimed, "Cal liked to help people out, and in those days there was plenty a needin' help." Johnny recalled one homesteader who was having a hard time, "Cal made it a point to ride out there and tell 'im, 'I got twenty dollars, I don't need it; here, I'll just give it to you.' "[8]

In February of 1929, after a marriage of little over four years, Cissy's husband, Elmer Schesinger, who was only forty-eight years of age, died suddenly of a heart attack at a South Carolina golf course. Although another chapter had closed on Cissy's life, others would open.

Toward the end of this period, Cal reconnected with Teton Valley. He became more involved with farming his 160-acres at Bates, growing hay and ninety-day oats, and in addition running up to twenty-five head of cattle. At one point, he also raised hogs and chickens. When he was gone from Teton Valley, he arranged for his neighbors to look after his place and livestock.[9]

In late winter in 1931, Cal did just that. He left his livestock in care of his neighbors, and he and a friend toured northern Arizona – Prescott, Jerome, Williams, Flagstaff and the Grand Canyon – by automobile. They visited the Hoover Dam site where construction had gotten underway in September 1930. Originally known as Boulder Dam, at 726-feet high and 1,244-feet long, it was one of the largest man-made structures in the world, and at the time, one of the greatest engineering works in history. Taking five years to complete, it transformed the American Southwest. Carrington had a knack for being at historic crossroads and witnessing things for himself.

In the historic cow town of Prescott, they undoubtedly took the opportunity to knock-a-few-back at the Palace Saloon, a

Palace Saloon in Prescott, Arizona, c1934. Courtesy Sharlot Hall Museum.

legendary cowboy watering hole on Whiskey Row. Frontier Prescott once boosted twenty-six saloons along Whiskey Row. Old West characters like Doc Holliday, the Earps, and Big Nose Kate, reportedly hung out there. Scenes for the 1972 Hollywood classic, *Junior Bonner*, about a rodeo cowboy starring Steve McQueen, were filmed in the Palace.

The Arizona trip involved nearly a month. Cal did not return until the first week in April, after most of the snow had receded from the valley.[10] One wonders, did he visit the old Arizona cow camp site, where as a teen-ager he had ended up after running away from his Utah foster family?

In July, after things had settled down from his Southwest tour, Cal wrote Goldie from the Crabtree Hotel in Jackson. "Loks like I wont half to work at all this summer. Movies has gone a way. Just a stray Dude now and a gain. What do you do Sundays now days, tell me so I can doo just the opsit, I believe that is the way the sects [sexes] works." The effects of the depression had reached Jackson Hole's tourist business.[11]

Wrangling dudes and their horses in the heat of summer and horse packing hunters into cold snowy camps in the fall was becoming a job best left to the young bucks. Besides, as former Wyoming Senator Cliff Hansen remembers, "Cissy's good friend, Rose Crabtree, had taken a proprietary interest in the Flat Creek Ranch for her." Cal did not need to be there all that much, and apparently Cissy did not want him there either. Still, Cal continued to remain on her list of employees and receive his monthly check.

Cissy's visits to the ranch had become infrequent. Through Rose Crabtree, Cissy hired Forney (also spelled Farney) Cole to care take the ranch. Jackson Hole historian, Fern Nelson, said that Forney drifted into Jackson Hole in 1917, after his rumored involvement in Wyoming's Johnson County War. Two sheepherders had turned up dead in Johnson County, killed by someone believed to have been hired by cattlemen.

Forney Cole was credited as being a horseman who had a way of getting the best out of horses without the rough handling common for the time. He was also rumored to be one of the toughest men in Jackson and, much to Cissy's disgust, one of the dirtiest and most in need of a bath.

However, local lore indicates he did sometimes wash his clothing. On one occasion, Forney put his clothing in the washing machine at the ranch, then forgetting about them, went into Jackson. The next day when he returned, they were still washing, but only threads and buttons remained.[12]

While at the ranch Forney gained national notoriety by fighting off a bear attack with a club. The club Forney used, and a newspaper article detailing how he beat the bruin off of him, are framed and still displayed at Dornan's Bar in Moose, Wyoming.

Regardless, Cal continued to seasonally make random trips over to the Flat Creek Ranch to check on things, satisfying himself that everything at the ranch was in good order. Cissy's biographer Ralph Martin dramatized the two men "bristling at each other," and

Forney Cole served as caretaker of Flat Creek Ranch from the late 1920s-1946. The club on the table was used by Forney to fight off a bear attack.
Courtesy JHHSM 1958.0200.001.

that in a showdown, Forney told Cal, "By God, one of us better go, and it hain't a gonna be me." Forney had a speech impediment, so he probably did not articulate it as neatly as Martin penned it. Martin stated, "Cal laughed, but left."[13]

Other sources tell it differently, reporting Cal, in fact, assisted Rose Crabtree in hiring Forney. Cal's own related version in a July 1931 letter to Goldie is a bit different, too: "The countes had a lot of foundations put under her cabans, and I went up thaire and got teh men all sore at me, but believe they got through quicker. The watchman said he was going to quit." The "watchman" was probably caretaker Forney Cole.

Back at his Bates ranch, although electricity was widely available in Teton Valley after 1923 from a plant located in the Teton River Canyon, Cal lived mostly without benefit of modern conveniences. He used kerosene lamps and candles for light. He had no indoor plumbing; his domestic water came from a rain barrel and a spring or shallow well he had dug near the cabin. If he was there in winter weather, he melted snow. It was Spartan like, but simple and cheap.

Cal heated the cabin with a woodstove, which also served for cooking. If he needed a telephone, he went over to the Furniss homestead next door. His Mormon neighbors in Teton Valley, for whom family was all-important, thought of Cal "as alone in the world without anyone to depend on" – "a lone man;" "a solitary man;" "a hermit;" and some might add, a character of sorts.[14]

Cal would turn heads by going into Driggs wearing chaps and spurs.[15] At one time, cowboy regalia wasn't even noticed in Teton Valley, and in Jackson it still didn't attract a second glance, but among the bib-overall clothed servants of the soil in Teton Valley, it caused sidelong glances. Still, in that community of by then second and third-generation ranchers and farmers, Cal received the unconditional respect granted to old timers. After all, he had come into the Valley when it was still raw frontier. His generation was cherished as proof of the pioneering past.

At some point, Cal had a Model T Ford at Bates, but to his disgust the ornery mechanical contraption would rarely start. It was frustratingly temperamental. To get it running, Cal swore he would "crank it till she boiled."

He would drive around on his property purposely running over and flattening the willow bushes claiming "it keeps them down."[16] At times, no doubt, Cal would clatter into Driggs on the dusty streets, parking beside other spoke-wheeled vehicles and horses tied to hitching posts.

When Mormon men went into Driggs, they generally did not carouse in a bar, instead they visited the barbershop. The local blather got passed around there. Cal generally dropped in on the barbershop when he was in town, entertaining everyone with his yarns.

The barbershop crowd would try to get him to talk about the Countess, straining forward for tasty morsels like tethered hounds at feeding time.[17] However, while Cal expounded on farming, hunting, rodeo, horses, and places he had traveled, he remained unforthcoming about Cissy. He felt it was none of their damn business. Besides some of the stories he could have told about wealthy life styles may have seemed mighty far-fetched and quite possibly would have garnered resentment.

Like other men looking for entertainment and news in Driggs, besides the barber shop, Cal made the rounds at the harness store, livery stable, and pool hall, too.

George Furniss had the homestead immediately north of Carrington's, and Cal would go over to the Furniss farm occasionally to get milk and eggs. Oren Furniss, George's son, was a stereotypical farm boy, complete with straw hat, overalls, and chewing on a stalk of timothy. Cal was a deep curiosity to him, fueled no doubt from overhearing the adult chatter about their bachelor neighbor. Oren and Cal became good friends.[18]

On occasion, Cal invited the neighbor children – Oren Furniss, Farrell Buxton, Monte Piquet, Laren Piquet, the Spencer boys, and others – into his cabin to see his African souvenirs and hear his tales. "I liked to listen to his stories," Oren said, "and he had all kinds of trinkets to show us."

Cal, ever the consummate raconteur, took pleasure in telling his stories, delighting in the entertained and wide-eyed astonishment he could engender among the local farm kids: "He had a rhinoceros horn mounted on a board;" and best of all, "He'd swat flies with a swatter made from an elephant's tail while he talked."[19]

Cal employed Oren to help him cultivate his fields. Commonly, he planted ninety-day oats. Oren would drive a team of horses pulling a wagon up and down the field while Cal sat in the back with a tub of loose grain between his knees and broadcast the seed by hand. Oren emphasized, "Cal was a strict taskmaster. Everything had to be done exactly as he wanted, especially keeping the rows straight. For a day's work, Cal paid me one dollar."[20]

One time, Oren was across the ditch, where Cal couldn't see him, when a rooster crowed. Oren remembered Cal shouting at the rooster, "What in the hell do you have to crow about?"

As Oren got older and was working in his family's fields plowing and cultivating, he fondly recalled: "Cal would step outside his cabin at exactly 11:30 and wave a white flag, signaling lunch was ready. Then I'd go have lunch with him."[21]

Cal must have gotten electricity installed into his cabin at some point, because he purchased what he called "talking furniture" – a radio. But when he went to use his "radio setup," he said it would "only growl at him." Next his "word machine" (typewriter) gummed up. Ever resourceful, he used coal oil (kerosene) to clean it.[22] For awhile afterward his letters reeked as if they had originated from a petroleum refinery.

It did get lonely at the Bates Ranch sometimes. In January 1938, Cal wrote Goldie, "Thanks for the Xmas card. Why didn't you tell me how many bows [beaus] you have and stur me up a little. I haven't had a girl smile at me for so long, I wouldn't believe it was me if they did. Coming down [to San Diego] to see you some day soon.[23]

Any loneliness Cal experienced was short lived, however. He was enjoying opposing life styles. When he was not masquerading as a poor dirt farmer and one of the good ol' boys, he was off on some incredible escapade, such as to Ringling Brother's Circus' private parties, the Bahamas, or the beaches in Encinitas, near San Diego, California. Sprees his cronies, and especially not his Mormon neighbors in Teton Valley, would never have believed.

In 1941, before the country was plunged into World War II, Cissy, at age fifty-nine, began retreating to tropical Sarasota, Florida, and exclusive Lyford Cay at Nassau in the Bahamas, for the winter. There she would lease luxurious accommodations and hop around the Caribbean. Today Lyford Cay is considered one of the wealthiest and most elite neighborhoods in the world. By the 1940s, there were commercial DC-3 flights from Miami to Nassau, but Cissy probably chartered her own plane and yachts. It turned into an opportunity for more exotic travel for Cal.

In January 1946, Cissy purchased what was considered "the show place of Sarasota"– seventeen-acres of empty, very private beach at Siesta Key, with a grand beach home. Each room in the beachfront manor was modeled after a different Hollywood motion picture set. The light chandelier in the living room came from Tara in Gone with the Wind. [24] In those years, one source claims, Cissy had six different estate properties scattered across the country, totaling ninety-rooms and requiring 1,300 employees. Cal still continued to remain on that employee list over all the years.[25]

Cal and Felicia were invited to visit Cissy in Sarasota. Cissy chartered a cruiser – a motor yacht with a permanent crew and comfortable living spaces. They cruised the Caribbean to Spanish Wells, a small, laid-back village on St. George's Cay in the Bahamas known for its lobster fishing. Cal was again put into the uncomfortable role of serving as intermediary between warring mother and daughter. [26]

Sarasota was the hub of circus activity and the winter headquarters for the Ringling Brothers' and Barnum & Bailey Circus. More than just saw-dust kicking, at John Ringling North's mansion, there were magnificent private parties where glamorous young cosmopolites were entertained with the newest circus acts. North's extravagant living room was sixty-five by fifty feet in size and three-stories high, where the performers were always pleased to be able to show off their latest costumes and acts. At one of North's circus parties, Cal allegedly found himself "a new admirer"– a woman trapeze artist.[27] It strains belief, the aging cowboy and a circus aerialist? It is probably not a story Cal was inclined to share in the Driggs barber or saddle shop.

22

Hard Knocks

Cal rightfully took pride in his horsemanship, so when a cranky little horse he was riding at his Bates ranch – a pony he had disparagingly named "Scrubby" because of its size – began bucking for whatever reason, Cal stubbornly stayed with him. Cal, however, was in his late sixties and no longer an agile young cowboy. Before it was over, Scrubby, with crow-hopping and sunfishing maneuvers the infamous bucking horse, Steamboat, would have admired, managed to pitch Cal violently catty-wampus onto the saddlehorn.[1]

In that painful hoofed incident the self-esteem from a lifetime of working with dangerous stock without serious injury was ruefully besmirched by the little horse. Remounting Scrubby, while operatically cursing him, Cal struggled back to his cabin and refused to see a doctor. Oren Furniss recalled, "Cal was down for ten days recovering from the injury, while neighbors looked in on him and helped out."[2]

Then another accident followed a few years later while gathering his winter supply of firewood. Firewood was an annual necessity, involving a lot of labor – hitching up and driving a horse-drawn wagon into the forest; using a single-buck, cross-cut saw and double-bit axe to fell and cut the trees into lengths; then loading the wood onto the wagon and hauling it down the mountain. It was honest hard work and Cal had been doing it for years – an accustomed autumn chore in the high-mountain valleys surrounding the Tetons. But sometimes even experienced hands have accidents and working alone makes it more risky. Anyone in Teton Valley who has ever heard of Cal Carrington generally knows the story of his near fatal wood-hauling mishap.[3]

Cal had cut a large wagonload of wood in October of 1943. It was late in the day when he started down out of the Big Hole Mountains' Middle Twin Creek with it. Sitting sideways on the load, he was driving his old bay horse teamed with a new horse he had recently purchased from Frank Moss, the local forest ranger at Driggs. Perhaps Cal's mind wandered, but suddenly on a steep downgrade, the new horse picked up his gait and the bay followed. Sitting sideways on the load, Cal found himself unable to gain any purchase to check them. As the horses ran down the mountain trail, the wagon hit a chuck hole, bouncing and pitching Cal forward. He slipped down between the wagon tongue and the horses; the wheels of the heavily loaded wagon ran over him, badly breaking his left arm and right leg.

It was a serious situation. He was alone. The bone protruded through the flesh of his arm, his leg was numb and useless. It was one-and-a-half miles down the wagon road to the closest neighbor (over five miles from his own cabin), night was coming on, the temperature was dropping, and the horses and wagon were gone. Cal had experienced serious challenges before in his life, he did not panic. He rolled to the center of the road and onto his left side, and with the help of his right arm, began crawling down the canyon road.

After an interminable length of time he reached the National Forest boundary where the gate had stopped the team. It was all he could do to open the gate and he realized he would not be able to get himself up onto the wagon or handle the reins. But it occurred to him that he could turn the team loose and send them down the canyon. Maybe someone seeing the unhitched team would know there had been trouble and come up to investigate.

Straining with difficulty, he crawled and struggled around under the horses until he was able to get the traces undone. Then wiggling out to the side of the new horse, he smacked it on the rump. The team moved off but only went a short way down the road before turning off into the trees.

There was no alternative but to continue seesawing on his side to make his way down the road. His badly broken arm kept getting in the way of his good one. He managed to get a piece of barbed wire loose from a fence and improvise a sling by twisting it around the wrist of the helpless arm and hooking the other end through his shirt collar.

In this manner, foot by exhausting and pain-filled foot, he crawled and worked his way down the road until around 1:00 a.m., when he reached neighbor Fred Bowen's barnyard. It was dark in Bowen's small rough-built log house, but with all the strength he could muster, Cal called out, "Fred, come and get me."

The Bowens heard someone calling as they lay in bed. They figured a drunk must be outside raising a commotion. Reluctantly rousted out, Fred took his time dressing. When he finally went outside in the darkness and turned a light onto the person lying in the barnyard muck, he recognized Cal Carrington.

Cal was a big man and it was impossible for Fred to move him out of the muck and into the house alone. He sent his wife, Rula, to get a neighbor. Between them, they finally managed to get Cal into the house. They cleaned the dirt and barnyard muck off of him and attended to him the rest of the night. Cal was not in shock and did not complain.

There was no 911 or MEDVAC in those days. Early in the morning Merlin Christensen and Cal's neighbor, George Furniss, responding to a phone call, arrived with a car. With all of them working in concert, they managed to load Cal up and drive him to the hospital at Idaho Falls.

Cal's postscript to it all was that he refused to be taken to the hospital until, with assistance, he had shaved, bathed and was dressed in borrowed clothes: "I wasn't a-goin' to let no pretty young Mormon nurses see me in no shape like that," he said. Struthers Burt later commented, "Cowboys can be vain."[4]

After three weeks, they could not make him stay in the hospital any longer. Within four months, he was back at work. Remarkable for a man of any age and Cal was seventy! As historian Gillette put it, "The incredible man, Carrington, was repaired with no noticeable impairments." Fred Bowen remarked: "Cal was rugged, tough and determined, both mentally and physically."

However, the accidents with Scrubby and wood-hauling must have caused Cal to reflect on his mortality, because on October 13, 1941, he made out and recorded a warranty deed in Driggs for the sale of his Bates property to "Eleanor Patterson for one dollar."[5] He never told Cissy or anyone about it, but it was there in the record book for when he died. He must have figured he'd die before Cissy, who was six years younger, but this wasn't how the stars would align.

Why would he have deeded his property over to Cissy? The curious conveyance of his property outside of a Will was typical of the unconventional way he had conducted business most of his life. It almost makes one smile. He no doubt chuckled to himself while doing it, picturing Cissy's annoyance when, after his death, she would learn about it. It also says something about their long-term relationship and his feelings of indebtedness towards her, too. No doubt he intended it as a grand gesture of reciprocity; recognition for all she had done for him. As Struthers Burt had observed years earlier, Cal was "sensitive to obligation."[6]

Cal Carrington with poddle, tea cup, and silk socks at Cissy's birthday party at the Dower House in early 1940s. Jackie Martin photo, courtesy of Joe Arnold and family.

23

Cissy's Passing

Over the years, Cal continued to be invited to special events, birthday parties, and weddings at Dupont Circle in Washington, D.C. Cal was characterized by Cissy's biographer A.A. Hoge in those years as "an aging, mangy fixture at Cissy's country houses... a grouchy old character, who snarled at servants and guests ...but who was an ancient and loyal friend."

On May 28, 1944, a birthday party was held for Cissy at the Waldorf Hotel in New York City, and a banquet followed at the Dower House in Maryland, both of which Cal attended. The Dower House was only about an hour's drive from Dupont Circle. Some of the guests snootily observed it was the cowboy's first encounter with an elevator.[1]

In writing about Jackson Hole, Cissy once confided, "I have seen taller mountains and larger lakes, but the people I love."[2] In 1948, while in residence at her Dower Estate, she knew her health was failing and asked for a private railroad car to be prepared to take her to Jackson Hole one last time. She had named her luxury Pullman car "The Ranger," after the horse Cal had given her years before. The Pullman Ranger had three bedrooms, three baths, an observation platform, and cost $100,000. It also was estimated to cost $50,000 a year to maintain it and pay the associated employees.[3]

Cissy never made that final trip west. She passed away in her sleep on July 24, 1948. Her maid recalled the poodles set up a terrific howl.[4] Fourteen years had gone by since she had last visited Jackson. During that time, she had been consumed by a demanding lifestyle involving non-stop social events, high-level politics, and the stressful demands of running a publishing empire. Her estate at the time of her death was conservatively valued (for tax purposes) at more than seventeen-million dollars. While that dollar amount today does not seem so large, it was truly a fortune back then. The comparative value today adjusted for inflation is roughly $167 million.

In her heyday as a newspaper and publishing giant, she had gained a reputation for her volatile temperament. At times, she had been variously labeled "willful, headstrong, perverse, flighty, petulant, sulky, spoiled, domineering, malicious, catty," and "the mercurial matriarch." One wag wrote, "The list of her lovers was exceeded only by her enemies." On the other hand, she received accolades for being "full-blooded and vibrant" and "one of the greatest newspaper editors this country has produced."[5]

Cissy had continued correspondence with her good friend Rose Crabtree over the years. Rose was said to be the only woman in Jackson with diamond earrings, a gift from Cissy. Once she arranged for Rose and Henry to visit her in Washington. She asked Rose what she'd like to see. Rose half-jokingly replied, "I'd like to meet the president." Cissy arranged it and Rose met President William Taft, a friend of the Patterson family. [6]

When Rose learned of Cissy's death, she cried. Cal had taken a trip over to the Salmon River two weeks earlier and had another mishap, a narrow escape. Falling asleep while driving home, he had run off the road and rolled his vehicle, barely avoiding serious injury. As it was, he was hospitalized with bruises and broken ribs: "sore and sorry," as he put it.

News of Cissy's passing reached him the day before he got out of the hospital. He was struck quiet and then he muttered sadly, "If only we could have had one more trip together."[7] A fine old friendship, a cinch that wouldn't bust, was suddenly gone. He later wrote Goldie: "I certainley feal the loss of the Countis."[8]

Cissy's passing unsettled him. Following her death, it was not a coincidence that he became embroiled in a number of quarrelsome issues. He didn't dwell on his feelings, that's just the way things were; but in truth, in his grief, he may have grown cantankerous and become a bit morose.

Cissy had originally bequeathed the entire Flat Creek Ranch property to her brother Joe, but he had deceased first. In the end, the ranch went to her niece Josephine Patterson Albright (Joe's daughter). Josephine, however, found the Flat Creek Ranch much too remote for her liking and consigned it to caretakers and renters.

Felicia contested parts of Cissy's Will and the nasty legal maneuvering continued for many years. Cal was among those called to testify. As late as, September 16, 1951, in a letter to Goldie, Cal wrote, "... they are having more trouble over Mrs. Patterson's estate. So I came to show up again [in New York], it is not very pleasant."

Cal was troubled, too, that Cissy had not willed him any part of the Flat Creek Ranch. It tormented him. After all, the Flat Creek Canyon had been part of his life for many years, going back to 1901. Cal believed it had been his doings that had gotten a homestead title to the property in the first place. He must have also felt somewhat betrayed, since, after all, in what he imagined was a conspiratorial pact of reciprocity, he had deeded over his Bates ranch to her if he should have died first.[9]

It is frequently noted in the literature that Cal was mentioned in Cissy's Will, but it begs the question, which Will and in what manner? Cissy had seven different Wills going back to 1924, the most recent being 1946. Some believe Cal was mentioned in the 1946 Will in the context of her employee's who were to receive continuing pensions for life: "annuities to continue to friends as indicated by my books." Rose Crabtree, who had been Cissy's close friend and helpmate over the years, was not listed as an employee, and simply received a flat sum of $3000. [10]

On lonely nights, while winds shrilled in the stovepipe and gloom crept down from the Big Hole Mountains behind his darkened cabin, Cal obsessed about the fact that Cissy used to call the old Flat Creek Canyon cabin, where he had often stayed in the early years, "his cabin." Rummaging around in his trunk, under shadowy light cast by a kerosene lamp, he may have found an old letter where she had off-handedly referred to it in that manner – "his cabin."[11]

It was evidence enough for Cal. It proved to him Cissy intended the cabin and six acres, as they may have once talked about, to be his. The fact she hadn't mentioned it in her recent Will – well, that was mere oversight in his mind.

Cal sought legal assistance to initiate a lawsuit. In building his case, he retrieved his 1922 Flat Creek homestead patent from his trunk where he had kept it all those years. He finally recorded the title in Jackson on July 24, 1953, long after the fact. Perhaps he figured it would strengthen his case.[12] His legal wrangling went cussedly slow, and in the end, it went nowhere.

At one point, when he traveled back to New York, according to Felicia, he sought to enlist her help on his lawsuit. By this time, he had worked himself into a self-righteous wrath. He exclaimed to Felicia, coming down hard on the last word, "The cabin and six acres, they're mine!" She wisely put him off, telling him, "We'll talk about it in the morning."[13] Felicia was deeply embroiled in her own legal battles over Cissy's Will. She continued to be for years.[14]

Not easily deterred, Cal returned to Jackson and moved into the old Flat Creek cabin, obstinately taking up residence, working old tricks: adverse possession, squatter's rights, claim jumping, bluffing and blustering. Cal was of the school that believed possession was proof of ownership, an opinion born from his frontier years.

Al Remington's patience, to whom Josephine was leasing the ranch, grew thin from repeated and quarrelsome run-ins with Cal. Remington called the sheriff out to the ranch and Cal was evicted. "It was the only time in my life," Cal fumed, "that a sheriff ever caught up with me."[15]

Afterward, in a letter further indicating he believed he had a legal interest in the cabin property, Cal wrote Josephine Patterson Albright:

> "Dear Friend, Mr. Remington... got the sheriff and run me off; broke in [to the cabin] and took possession... If i sew him for rent, would it inter fear with your plans, he sais he would have a damage suit against you... I want one hundred dollars a month [rent] during the life of his leas... he is doing no good up theair."[16]

Times had changed in Jackson Hole. The frontier code wherein a man could have whatever he wanted as long as he was strong enough to take it no longer prevailed. In spite of all the legal fighting and the eventual final settlement of Cissy's Will, Cal stubbornly held onto the belief that she had wanted him to have the cabin and six acres. He willfully continued to visit and stay at the Flat Creek cabin. In fact, his last time there was in May of 1959, only seven months before his death. Perhaps he visited there out of nostalgia, it took the old cowboy wistfully back in time. It gave him comfort to recall those times and the people he had known long ago.

Around this same time, Cal also became caught up in water right disputes with his Teton Valley neighbors. If someone is looking to pick a fight in the West, water rights are always a good starting place. As Mark Twain said, "Whiskey is for drinkin'; water is for fightin'." Teton Valley native Farrell Buxton, who recalls Cal's remonstrations says, "As a youngster, I tried to avoid the frequent meetings and long arguments about water that went on."[17]

Driggs Idaho   Aug   5/1952

Mrs, Allbright
Dear Friend

The U.S.Destrict Cort
in Washington,D,C,

Alowed Me A cabin and a few acers on
Flat Creek Medows,not deaded but as
a Intrest,
Mr ,Remington your Baser got the sherif
and run me off, broke in and took poshen
If i sew him for rent would inter fear
with your plans,he sais he would have a
damage suit a ganst you,
If you dont claim my Cabin ,it looks to
me he wouldent get verey for,
I would like your Lowyer-lety--to take
my cace on a comishen forwhat he colects.
I want one hundred dallars a month during
the life of his leas,
he is dooing no good up theair,taks his
doods up a fishing,Killed of all the Beavers
this last year,
I was theair a while in July,saw no in
provements what so ever,more harm than good,
If you and your Lowyer dont like my butting
in pleas tell me,
Eney advice I would like to have it,from
you, I stick a round Worts Hotel when in
Jackson,look me up when you are theair,
        As ever your Friend,
                        CCarrington
                Driggs Idaho

Cal Carrington's 1952 letter to Josephine (Patterson Reeve) Albright regarding the disposition of the Flat Creek Ranch. Courtesy Flat Creek Ranch.

Cal had a recorded water right on Mahogany Creek in Teton Valley, filed on May 26, 1900 and again in 1901, but he sometimes had trouble getting his share of the water. "First in time, first in right" was the decree. But in practice, by the time those above him took off water in late summer, little reached his place since he was fourth in line near the bottom end of the ditch. Water coming down the ditch was required to be "divided in the field," which meant cooperation among neighbors.

Neighborly cooperation on water generally was not forthcoming from Cal in those years. Teton Valley rancher Art Mackley said, "Carrington enjoyed being an authoritative know-it-all and tried to assert himself over others with threats, bluffs, and deceptive mannerisms to gain the upper hand."[18] Conversely, his neighbor Oren Furniss's wife, Eva, expressed appreciation for Cal's efforts which assisted them in obtaining water they too needed for their farm.[19]

Cal fomented on the water issue, deciding he was going to single-handedly resolve the situation. But the problem of his disputed water right became even more complicated. Any early established right which had not been used for more than five years was subject to preemption by a "prescriptive right filing." A neighboring rancher made such a claim on Cal's rights, hiring attorney Harold Forbush to prepare the filing, giving Cal notice by a hand delivered letter.[20] Cal finally ended up in court over his water, but was able to recover only half of his original right.[21]

Cal also resurrected an old grievance with the Crabtree's. Rose had the angora chaps he had long ago given to Cissy. Nobody wore angora chaps anymore and Cal could not have possibly had any use for them; they would never have fit him. He wanted them back for sentimental reasons. They were a tangible part of his past. Once again, Cal asked – "pesticated" as he called it – Felicia to intervene for him, insisting Cissy had wanted him to have the chaps. "They're mine!" he'd complain.

Cal Carrington in Jackson, Wyoming, at age 82. Courtesy JHHSM 1958.0022.001p.

Rose responded pithily: "Tell him if he's real good, I'll bury him in them."[22]

Today, the chaps are part of the Jackson Hole Museum's collections.

Next, the County sent Teton Valley resident Russell Stone and his crew to contour an embankment along Cal's property line for a road and a fence location. Cal distrusted their ability to do a good job and carefully monitored the progress. However, he liked the completed work. It was a hot and dusty day, so Cal brought out a case of cold beer to share. Russell and his men, all devout Mormons, refused the beer. Cal was offended. Russell said, "He walked away and never spoke to me again, not ever."[23] The incident recalls how Struthers Burt once described Cal's anger: "without a word of explanation... sharp as moonlight, cold as a knife."[24]

"Cal," Felicia finally said to him, "why don't you quit that foolishness about suing everyone and fighting with your neighbors?" He was quiet for a while, then burst out, "Girl, I'm too old to ride in any more rodeos. I can't steal no more horses. Your Mama is gone. My God, I've got to find something that is entertainin'."[25]

Moonlight Beach at Encinitas, California, in the 1940s, where Cal acquired property and maintained a winter residence. Courtesy of Encinitas Historical Society.

24

The Jeep and Encinitas

Sometime after World War II, Cal bought a green Willys Jeep. He purchased the Army surplus vehicle in California and drove it back to Bates. First, though, he paid the car salesman to drive the jeep and himself through the heavier traffic to the city limits.[1] Once outside of the city, he felt safer driving. California's rural highways and the long lonely stretches through Nevada and southeast Idaho were less worrisome for him.

After he got home, he would bounce across Teton Pass to Jackson in the jeep. It took him no time, compared to the long and arduous trips over the pass by horseback or wagon in the early years. Although, roads in Jackson Hole and Teton Valley were still dirt surface – billowing dust or gumbo mud – through the 1940s, they continued to be upgraded and improved.

Unlike his earlier hot-headed and reckless driving with the Countess's Ford truck, now instead, he would occupy the middle of the road with his jeep holding everyone up. Passengers who rode with him would joke and complain: "Hey, go over that bump again, my head ain't come off yet."[2] Jackson resident Bonnie Budge and her husband once encountered a slow moving vehicle blocking their laboring truck on the "dugout hill" beyond Moose. When they finally managed to go around, Bonnie's husband exclaimed: "Oh, that's that darn Cal Carrington."[3]

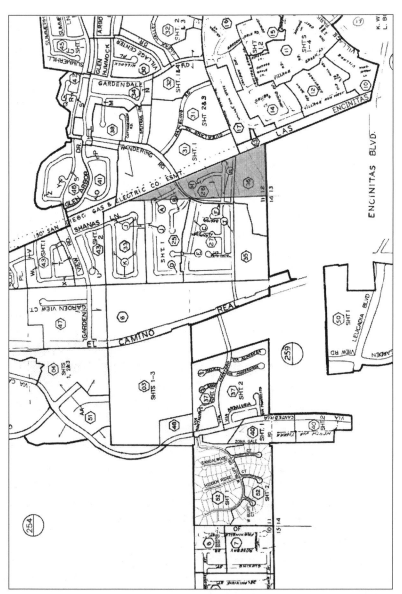

The shaded area shows where Cal Carrington's twenty-four acre parcel was located in Encinitas, California.

Cal and his neighbor, George Furniss, would drive over to the Salmon River to fish for Chinook salmon and be gone several days. They would return with salmon that "stretched clear across the hood of the jeep"; other times they would go to Jackson Lake ice fishing.[4] Cal had more than a few close calls with the jeep. One time while trying to repair a flat tire, the jack kicked back knocking him flat. Rumor claims Cal never bothered with getting a driver's license in his later years.[5]

Even though Cal had the jeep, and before that the Model T, he still kept and used horses, too. A life-long horseman did not give up horses overnight, in spite of motor cars and other mechanized contraptions. Old timers like Cal had a distrust of mechanical things. "Horses," they'd say, "started more dependably than engines." At some point, though, Cal rarely stayed in Teton Valley during the winter. Rather than continue to hire someone to care for his horses and livestock while he was gone, he gave up having any at all.

When winter was approaching and snow was beginning to drift around his cabin, he would take a Greyhound bus from Driggs to his Encinitas, California, beachside property. He would stay there until spring, when the snow in the valley had receded. Cal had become a California snowbird.[6] He was not alone. His friend Jess Wort was also spending winters in southern California during that same time period, too.

When Cal applied for a permit to build on his Encinitas property it was rejected. The house he proposed to construct was too small under the zoning requirements. After mulling it over, he cleverly resubmitted a plan to instead build a "garage." The story goes, Cal put up and lived in what was permitted as a garage within the exclusive Encinitas resort neighborhood.[7]

In September 1952, Cal wrote Goldie from New York, where he was visiting Felicia, "Hope to be along [to Encinitas] some tim[e] this fall and get out of the coald."[8]

Cal's colorful personality and eccentricities attracted people's attention. Teton Valley native Farrell Buxton recalled, "Cal worried someone would vandalize his cabin in Bates when he was gone, so he'd rig up a booby trap which released a spear toward the door when it was opened." No one as far as is known, was ever impaled attempting to enter his cabin.[9] But Cal, as it turned out, did have reason to worry.

Sometimes, when he was going to be gone from the valley, he took his trunk and guns over to Jim Berger's in Victor for safe keeping.[10] Locally, it was rumored he had money hidden somewhere in his cabin. His lifestyle, stories, guns and African trophies coveted attention. He became a burglary victim: his guns and other personal property were stolen.

It is not certain if Cal filed a complaint with the Sheriff's Department, but it is known that he gave the gun serial numbers to the Driggs sporting goods store owner to be on the lookout for them. Cal had carved his brand –CAL– into his gunstocks, and it is rumored the thieves crudely altered the markings. The elephant rifle Cissy had given him was one of the guns taken. The looters were never charged or punished nor were the guns ever recovered. [11]

25

Felicia Returns to Jackson

Imagine what Cal must have thought about the contrast between revved-up southern California in the 1950s and Teton Valley, where some claim he still did not even have electricity and the outhouse was out back.[1] A place Felicia claimed, "He lived so poorly, he'd wear his clothing until it fell off him." Simply put, Cal chose to live alone in relative squalor at Bates, rather than spend any of his savings.

When he returned from California after the winter, one of the barbershop crowd in Driggs quipped, "It must be spring, the sandhill cranes and Cal Carrington are back." The witticism became a favorite around Driggs; locals still recall it.[2]

Felicia's self-imposed exile from Jackson Hole lasted until she was fifty-years old. She had developed an alcohol problem, which she finally had gained control over. Cissy had been gone for many years. Cal was about seventy-nine years old and Felicia admitted, she "felt doubt and hesitation about returning," but Rose Crabtree wired her saying: "You are as welcome as the flowers in spring."[3]

Jackson was no longer a frontier town with hitching posts, livery stables, and the jingling of spurs and clomping of cowboy boots on wooden boardwalks. Trees and grass had been planted in the dusty square in the 1940s and the first elk antler arch was erected by 1953. John and Jess Wort's luxury hotel catering to well-heeled guests had been built in 1941 on ground where the Wort Livery Barn and Stables and a speakeasy had previously stood. Many Jackson residents wrongly predicted the Wort Hotel was doomed for failure because they felt Jackson Hole was too much of a backwater to attract wealthy tourists.[4]

Cal had told Felicia about the changes in Jackson Hole over the years when he visited New York: "There's a park where the square used to be; big paved roads where motor cars kin go; and the Park Service has people stayin' in camps and motels where they can't git lost. You can git to town without gettin' tangled in sagebrush and they's got all kinda lookin' people in big crowds on the streets and all kinda new fangled things in them new stores."[5]

When Felicia arrived in Jackson, Cal rented some gentle horses from the Wort's and they rode up Cache Creek. Then on another day, John Wort trucked their horses over to Flat Creek. John outdid himself with some fancy cursing while he cinched the horses up for them. Cussing, while working with horses was a much admired and practiced art, a Western horseman's tradition. Felicia wrote they rode up the old wagon road into the canyon toward the ranch until they came to a fence with a padlocked gate. Cal dismounted saying, "'Here, hold my horse.' "[6]

Still resentful about the disposition of the Flat Creek Ranch property, and in spite of Felicia's protests, Cal proceeded to break down the fence. The ranch was leased to Al Remington, who was also the owner of the Wagon Wheel Hotel in Jackson. Cal wasn't about to be locked out of the place which he had considered his for many years, a part of which he still felt belonged to him. When they encountered Remington, he took Cal aside, threatening: "If you ever come back I'll get the sheriff and have you jailed."[7]

They continued on their ride, Cal taking Felicia and the horses straight up the old trail towards Sheep Mountain, the same way he and Cissy used to ride decades before. Felicia said, "Cal was muttering to himself and shaking his fist the whole time. All he was thinking about was that Remington wouldn't let him go back to his cabin and six acres."[8]

Amazingly, though, at that age, Cal apparently still retained his skills in the mountains, the same ability Struthers Burt had admired years before. Felicia recorded: "He got back [to the horse trailer] the way an animal gets home – straight through the country, right on target."

There was lots of contemplating the past to be done in those years. Cal's friend Struthers Burt passed away in 1952. That same year, too, the Crabtree's sold their hotel, which they had operated for more than forty years, and moved back to the Midwest. It caused Cal to thoughtfully remark: "The excitement of life is a wonderful thing, but when the beauty of youth has went, there's no more excitement in it."[9]

Al Remington hired Joe Madden to help manage the Flat Creek Ranch from about 1952-56. Joe had at one time worked a homestead at the bottom of Flat Creek Canyon. Madden and Cal were friends, so when Remington wasn't around, Madden had no problem with Cal showing up at the ranch. The Madden's also boarded and guided hunters at the Flat Creek Ranch in those years. [10]

Cal spent time at the Flat Creek cabin in early spring 1951. He wrote Goldie about it: "I took a stroal to the upper end of the field and I bumped into a big black bear." And again in the spring of 1959, when he wrote Felicia: "[I] locked it up and naild a sine on [the] door, 'Keep Out.'"[11] That was the last mention of anyone seeing the old cabin. Whatever became of the it after that, no one today knows. It was either accidentally or purposely burned down.

Current ranch operator Joe Albright reported, "There are remnants of an old cabin that burned some unknown time in the past. In the dirt at that location we found pieces of an iron stove with a mid-1800s date."[12]

In trying to reconstruct the outlaw's holding pasture story, the present location of the gate at the Flat Creek Ranch property boundary was probably not the same spot used by horse thieves to shut the canyon off more than a century ago. More likely, it would have been down at the bottom end of the meadows, where the canyon narrows into a bottleneck. And the old cabin was located above there on the left, according to Charlie Peterson, before getting to the ranch.

Cal's last horse pack trip was taken with Felicia to Two Ocean Pass on the Continental Divide, deep within what is today's Teton Wilderness. John and Jess Wort outfitted them. This was country where Cal used to outfit and guide hunters and he knew it well. He confided to Felicia that they were close to where he had taken Cissy on their first hunting trip over forty years before.[13]

Anyone who has made the trip into Two Ocean Pass knows it is a long and demanding horseback ride. Incredibly, Cal was eighty-three years old. Felicia says, "He still rode magnificently, and around camp still moved with a grace that an Eastern man never has."[14] On the trail, it recalled an earlier time when Cal would call over his shoulder to those following behind him: "For God's sake, kick that horse of yours, and come on!"

Cal Carrington, c1958.
Courtesy Karl C. Allan papers, Box 7, American Heritage Center, University of Wyoming.

26

A Cowboy's Last Years

Cal leased out his tillable farmland in Bates in the 1950s and generally retired to Encinitas in the winters. Orville "Jack" Buxton was a lessee for several years in the 1950s; and later, Jack Spencer and his boys had the ground. Farrell and Jaydell Buxton remember putting up hay in Cal's field. Farrell said, "We used side delivery rakes and baled the hay, then sold it to a feed lot at Sugar City, Idaho."[1]

Jack Buxton, and Farrell and Jaydell, would go over to Cal's cabin and visit with him. Farrell recalls, he and his cousin Jaydell would sit on the edge of Cal's rough-built bunk, fascinated, while "Cal spun yarns about Africa." Like Oren Furniss, Farrell also remembered Cal's rhinoceros horn mounted on a board and Cal swatting flies with the "elephant's tail," while moving about like an actor on stage telling his tales. No doubt Cal did the same with the Spencer boys. Invariably, when he told his Africa stories he would show the wide-eyed farm boys his 9mm elephant gun. Africa was an unimaginably distant place to Teton Valley farmers in those days.

Farrell's younger sister, Shirley, was present on occasion. "Why don't you come along home with me, I need a cook," Cal would tease. She would cringe, frightened by the old man.

Farrell recalled one time when he was approaching Cal's cabin, Cal was trying to comb his hair flat, but "he had a rooster-tail that kept sticking up. Cal didn't know I was there and he was cussing up a blue thunderbolt."[2]

Other neighbor youngsters, Monte and Laren Piquet, who lived at the mouth of Mahogany Creek Canyon used ride over to Cal's and listen to his stories all afternoon. They would help him with chores, too, and he would cook dinner for them.

"God he used to be dirty," Laren recalled. "He'd have mouse traps set around the cabin and to prevent the caught rodents from dragging his traps off, he attached a large iron nut on a string to the trap. His fishing pole, made from a willow, was rigged with bailing wire for guides. And there were clippings of cartoons he fancied tacked to his kitchen wall. He had a buffalo robe coat hanging in the cabin and his elephant gun, which he liked to show us. It had a hexagon barrel."[3]

At times Cal would go over to the Piquet's for dinner and afterward they would all sit on the porch, while Cal told stories about his travels and old time cattle drives. Monte remarked "Cal was a tough old guy."[4]

There is no doubt, Cal was an original character. Those who met him did not forget him. There is evidence that points to him being more than a bit ornery, too, especially in his later years. Many mention him as being a rough customer. Interestingly, Cissy was considered to be something of a misanthrope in her later years as well. In some ways, Cal and Cissy were a matched pair. Local lore claims she, like Cal, was accomplished at the art of cussing. One teamster on Teton Pass, who considered himself very practiced in the art, claimed, "Cissy was the only other person he let talk to his horses when they needed talking to."[5] She could "talk like she came right out of an alley."[6]

Old timers who had lived through having to make every meager bit count just to get by, sometimes revert to the same parsimonious behavior in their later years, whether they need to or not. Such was the case with Cal. Maybe, too, it was what the strict Mormon elder had ingrained into Cal as a child. In any case, Farrell remembered Cal would get a pitchfork and go around the field complaining and scatter-raking up the small amounts of missed hay. Farrell recalled, "It was hard to please Cal."

In those days, saloons were more than just watering holes, they were places where the local news and gossip got circulated. When Cal was in Jackson he would invariably go to the Wort Hotel to visit his old sidekicks and share stories. It was a gathering place for the town characters. As Cal put it, "I stick around Wort's Hotel when in Jackson."[7] Whenever Cal walked through the bar past the card players he'd routinely observe, "Still a doin' it?"[8] Cal was also a member of the Elk's Club in those years.

After Wyoming Governor Millward Simpson shut down the gambling in 1956, Cal said, "Jackson became a dead town."[9] Perhaps, but not entirely. The gambling operations were merely moved out of sight to the Wort Hotel basement, where the action was continued for a select crowd.

When the basement gambling came under scrutiny, the gaming operation was moved to the remote Flat Creek Ranch. Potential high rollers were hauled fifteen miles up the rough road to be relieved of their cash at the ranch's "casino room."[10] The dance floor Cissy had long ago visualized for her lodge became a set up place for card tables and roulette wheels. Flat Creek Canyon became a kind of hideaway once again, this time for questionable characters of a different stripe.

In his old age, Cal enjoyed celebrity status in Jackson. Trail Creek Ranch manager Margaret "Muggs" Shultz remembers being at the Jackson Hole Rodeo in the early 1950s when Cal was introduced to the crowd. Muggs said, "He appeared tall and carried himself very erect when he walked into the arena. After the customary tipping of his hat to the crowd and applause, he went behind the chutes."[11]

Felicia wrote, "In the last summers of his life, Cal would

come over from Driggs and stay at the Elbo," a small dude ranch, which also offered cottage cabins, a roadside store, and gas station. Located on Ditch Creek north of Jackson, the Elbo had a large sign at the entrance proclaiming it the "Home of the Hollywood Cowboy." Felicia's friend Katie Starret from California operated the ranch through a lease arrangement in those years. Felicia wrote, "We'd all try to get Cal to take a bath," and he'd say, "Don't send my clothes to the laundry, they steal everything."[12]

Jackson Hole locals remember Felicia from that time period as "a tall woman with a low and cultured voice;" also, as someone who wore English riding boots, jodhpur pants, and floppy felt hats, not western clothing.[13]

According to Felicia, during Cal's last years, "The cabin in Driggs [Bates] was a hovel that was never cleaned."[14] It is no doubt true, since Cal generally put off spring cleaning until he got around to it. He had once written Goldie: "I havent cleand the hous yet, I don't think I will. It has more dirt in side than thear is outside, so I gess I will just clean the farm insted."[15]

Cal's cabin contained a curious and eclectic collection of items: a home-built bunk, a captain's chair, a large trunk with personal items, a wood-burning cook stove, his "talking furniture"(radio), a "word machine"(typewriter), African trophies, guns, home-made fishing poles, saddles and horse harnesses dangling from the wall, cartoon clippings tacked to the kitchen wall, and a closet containing formal suits next to tattered Western work clothes and a buffalo robe coat.[16]

Still, even in his eighties, Cal epitomized the Western image. There was an unpretentious aura of the true Westerner about him. He was willing to let Felicia buy him new shirts and trousers, and "with his great silver mane, like Buffalo Bill's," Felica observed, "he'd cause such a sensation in Jackson, she and Katie Starret felt they were out with a movie star."[17]

In the last years of Cal's life, a brother, Zeneiph J. Julin, and two sisters, all in advanced age by then, located him. The brother traveled to Driggs to see Cal and tell him that the family had reached Salt Lake City, and that the parents were buried there. For years they had all tried to find him. Cal's response was: "It's only because the grass is green and tall on my place that you're a'comin' round now."[18] Meaning, he felt they were only interested in his money.

Felicia tried to convince Cal he should forgive them: "Your parents did you a good turn, when you really look at it. If you'd stayed with them, you'd never had this wonderful life. You'd never met mama and me."

Thinking it over, he agreed, "That's true." Felicia thought she had convinced him, however, she should have known better. "But it weren't no doin' of theirs," he concluded.[19]

Cal did not let it rest there. He followed up on his bitter life-long resentment against his family. In his Last Will and Testament, he included a section specifying: "I recite that in my lifetime a certain person or persons have sought to claim blood relationship with me, for the purpose, I presume, of inheriting my property. However, I herewith renounce and disclaim any such relationship, and declare that no part of my estate should go to such person, but as herein above mentioned should be distributed to those persons who have proved to be my friends, and who have given me comfort and companionship in my life."[20]

On January 14, 1956, Cal filed suit in Teton County, Idaho, District Court against "Eleanor Patterson, if alive, and/or if dead, and all unknown heirs" obtaining a decree quieting and regaining full title to his Bates property.

In his last years, people recognized Cal as a link to bygone eras and a living Jackson Hole legend. In 1957, prior to his election as Wyoming governor, Jackson Hole rancher Cliff Hansen drove Cal to the University at Laramie. They conducted and recorded an oral interview with Cal in the presence of history department faculty.

Instrument #54230 ✓ ✗   IN THE DISTRICT COURT OF THE NINTH JUDICIAL DISTRICT OF THE
STATE OF IDAHO, IN AND FOR TETON COUNTY

E. C. CARRINGTON sometimes known as)
ENOCK C. CARRINGTON,)
        Plaintiff)
)
    vs.)
)
ELEANOR PATTERSON sometimes known as)
CISSY PATTERSON, if alive, and/or if)
dead ALL UNKNOWN HEIRS AND DEVISEES OF ELEANOR)   DECREE QUIETING TITLE
PATTERSON, and ALL UNKNOWN OWNERS OF Lots 1 & 2 of)
Section 6, Township 4, N. Range 45 EBM, Teton County,)
Idaho; and also E½SE¼ Section 31 Township 5, N. Range)
45 EBM, Teton County, Idaho; and also: NE½SW¼ and)
the NW½SE¼ Section 32, Township 5, N Range 45 EBM,)
Teton County, Idaho.)
        Defendants)

This cause came on for hearing this 13 day of January 1956, before his honor Henry S. Martin, sitting without a jury; the plaintiff appearing by counsel A. A. Merrill and the defendants did not appear either in person or by counsel, and it appearing to the court that due proof was submitted and each and all of the defendants were duly served with summons by publication as required by law and that each of said defendants have defaulted in said cause; that none thereof have answered or appeared herein within the time allowed by law after service of summons as aforesaid or at all, and upon motion of counsel for the plaintiff default of the defendants was duly filed and was by the court ordered entered and was entered.

Whereupon the court proceeded to hear the proofs submitted in plaintiff's complaint from which it appears:

1. That the court has jurisdiction over the subject matter of this suit and over the parties hereto and the right to grant the relief prayed for in plaintiff's complaint.

2. That all material allegations of the plaintiff's complaint are true and were duly proven.

3. That the plaintiff is entitled to have the title to the real estate described in plaintiff's complaint quieted in him.

WHEREFORE, IT IS ORDERED, ADJUDGED AND DECREED:

That the defendants and neither of them have any right, title, interest or estate whatsoever in and to the said land and property hereinafter described.

That the title of plaintiff in and to the said hereinafter described premises is good and valid and the title of the plaintiff herein is adjudged to be quieted against all claims of all of the defendants and that said defendants and each of them and all persons claiming through or under them and all unknown heirs and devisees of Eleanor Patterson, if deceased, and all unknown owners of the property hereinafter described are hereby debarred from asserting any right, title or interest in or to said land and premises or any part thereof adverse to the plaintiff.

That the said premises are bounded and described as follows to-wit:

Lots 1 and 2 of Section 6, Township 4, North Range 45 EBM, Teton County, Idaho; and also: E½SE¼ Section 31 Township 5, North Range 45 EBM, Teton County, Idaho; and also: NE½SW¼ and the NW½SE¼ Section 32, Township 5, North Range 45 EBM, Teton County, Idaho

Dated this 13th day of January, 1956.

        Henry S. Martin
        Henry S. Martin
        District Judge

Filed for record at 15 minutes past 11 o'clock A.M. this 14 day of January 1956 and recorded in book 83 of Judgments, page 1, records of Teton County, State of Idaho.
        Dwight C. Stone, Recorder
        By Beth Zohner, Deputy

Decree to recover title to his Bates Ranch in 1956 after Cal had deeded it to Eleanor Patterson in 1941.

Gene M. Gressley, who was a faculty member at the university, recalls Cal put on an unforgettable performance that had everyone laughing so hard they had to stop the interview at times. At one point in his grandstanding, Cal, dressed in western shirt with a bolo tie, stood up on the table and did his well-practiced African routine – mimicking animals and their sounds, including elephants trumpeting and giraffes mating.[21]

Cal seized the opportunity to give his unabashed opinions on, and associate his name with, historic figures A.A. Anderson, Hiram Chittenden, Teton Jackson, "Beaver Tooth" Neal, Charlie Russell, and many more. Dwight Stone's recorded interview of Cal, arranged by Harold Forbush, in Teton Valley followed a year later. Interestingly, during Stone's interview, Cal appeared to dodge questions similar to those he had answered at the University of Wyoming about his early cowboy years, saying, "None of your damn business."

In the autumn of 1959, Cal didn't leave for Encinitas. Not feeling well, he was having difficulty managing alone at his cabin in Bates. He submitted to an examination by Jackson's Dr. Larsen in September who simply noted: "Very bad breathing." Cal's health continued to deteriorate that autumn, and he was diagnosed and recorded as having "pneumonia followed by two heart attacks and stomach ulcers."

Cal allowed himself to be hospitalized in Jackson. A few days later, a "preacher" walked into his room and piously asked, "Are you ready to join the Church and commit to God?" Cal angrily struggled out of bed, cursing all the while he wrestled into his clothing. Then he walked out of the hospital and drove back across the pass. Back in Driggs, he checked into the hospital there, only to indignantly stomp out again when they forgot to bring him breakfast.

In desperation, Cal tried sweat baths and electrical shock treatments with a healer in St. Anthony. When he returned home after a week, a friend took one look at him and told him flat out: "You look like hell." Cal checked into the Driggs hospital once again.[22] Old cowboys can be independent cusses.

Two years earlier, Russia's Sputnik had ushered in the space age, and it would only be four more years until men walked on the moon, but in Teton Valley, Cal was still living as if it were an earlier era. His cabin had not been modernized – it had only the old woodstove for heat and cooking; some believe he had no electricity or running water; nor was there indoor plumbing, just an outhouse and chamber pot. It would have been challenging for even a healthy young person to have lived there under those conditions during Teton Valley's rigorous winters.

Cal fought a good last fight. Although he tried to stay at his cabin, in the end it was too much for him. He finally moved into Driggs, renting a cabin at the Harris' Cabins Motel. The motel proprietors, Clarence, known by his middle name, Earl, and his wife, Sadie, worried about Cal and looked after him. Earl was eighty-years old himself, at the time; Sadie was seventy-three. Both Earle and Sadie had originally come from Utah. Sadie, who had been a school teacher in Driggs, had grown up at Summit, Utah – the same settlement where Cal had lived in his youth with his Mormon foster family. After a lifetime of being close-mouthed about his childhood and personal life, Cal opened up with Earl and Sadie, who listened to his reminiscences and amazing stories.[23]

Cal went back into the Driggs hospital in December, but did not improve. Realizing his condition was serious, he had a woman friend, Karli Johnson, in Jackson notify Felicia: "He's awfully sick and says he wants you to know about his property." The friend rattled off a list of real property and financial assets to Felicia over the phone – a fortune beyond belief for an old cowboy like Cal.

Felicia thought Cal must be delusional, her response was, "He certainly is sick; his mind is gone."[24] Felicia, who was then living in Washington, D.C. immediately made arrangements and traveled to Driggs.

Shirala Franz was one of Cal's nurses at the Driggs Hospital. She was ninety-four years old in 2008, but remembered him well, remarking: "He was a very good patient." Teton Valley neighbors, such as Laren Piquet would stop in and visit Cal. Laren commented, "He sure liked them Mormon nurses." Cal was conscious and still rational when Felicia arrived. He said to her, "You look tired, Little Fellar, come sit down on the bed." She had brought him slippers and he protested, "You ain't a gonna' start dudin' me up now."[25]

While she was in Driggs, Felicia learned about Cal's early life from the Harris's and Cal's neighbors in Bates. She had been one of Cal's closest friends for many years, yet she had not even known his real name was Enoch Julin or that his family had given him up to Mormon missionaries. Felica only learned those things from the Harris's and his neighbors in Teton Valley, and also perhaps from Cal himself, near the very end of his life.[26]

Cal had always cultivated dual identities – a glamorous Wild West Jackson Hole persona and a Teton Valley farmer. Jackson Hole folks apparently knew little about Cal's life as a Teton Valley farmer and California snowbird. They only recalled colorful images and myths of an outlaw, cowboy, hunting guide, and dude wrangler.[27]

An exception was his friend Struthers Burt, with whom Cal had been inclined to selectively share some of his life history, albeit somewhat embellished. In Teton Valley, most were unimpressed or put-off with the flashy Jackson Hole stories. They judged Cal more as a neighbor and on his down-to-earth lifestyle. His two personas reflected place as well as personality. And it is unlikely his cowboy cronies ever got told the details of his time spent among the wealthy and famous.

Cal Carrington died from pneumonia at 10 a.m. on December 22, 1959, without his boots on, in a clean hospital bed. He was eighty-six years old. Earl Harris was present at his passing. In Cal's heyday, life expectancy for a man was about forty-nine years. Cal had managed to live a rugged, active and long life – in spite of his having engaged in risky outdoor endeavors and bronc busting – that far exceeded every expectation for the time. His was a life that in many ways stretches the imagination.

For burial, Felicia dressed him in his "best checked wool shirt, his favorite bolo-tie and his least worn out pants."[28] He made the familiar trip over Teton Pass and down the mountain switchbacks into Jackson Hole one last time. A long procession of chained-up vehicles followed in the fresh snow that had fallen that morning. His old friend Jim Berger was undoubtedly in the cavalcade, as no doubt were Buxtons, Furnisses, Gillettes, Harrises, Piquets, Thompsons and others. Teton Pass was a far different place from when Cal had first crossed it on horseback more than sixty years before. The trip across the pass into Jackson was made in less than an hour.

After a service and reading of the twenty-third Psalm – "He maketh me to lie down in green pastures and leadeth me beside the still water"– Cal was returned to the familiar earth among old friends in Jackson's Aspen Cemetery on Christmas Eve. At the large gathering of friends and neighbors from both Teton Valley and Jackson Hole, Felicia sadly noted, "Their tears were as genuine as mine."[29] A colorful living link to the Old West was gone.

The old buckaroo had witnessed incredible changes over his lifetime. He had known the freedom of the West's unsettled open range, and had lived the hard and romantic life of a cowboy on long cattle drives. When he first came into the Teton country in 1897, it was still wild, mostly unsettled frontier. He had known, lived and worked among the outlaws and the original homesteaders who settled Jackson Hole and Teton Valley. The town of Jackson did not exist then; he witnessed its beginnings and participated in its growth. He worked for the Forest Service and Yellowstone National Park in their historical infancy. He saw cattle drives, horses, hitching racks and livery stables give way to the arrival of the railroad, spoke-wheeled cars, modern highways, tourism, and the space age, all in the course of his lifetime.[27] And, along the way, he had also been invited into the realm of the very wealthy and had experienced a taste of their opulent lifestyles.

Felicia passed away in 1999. She also lived to see tremendous changes in Jackson Hole, including a K-mart and McDonald's fast-food restaurant, as compared to the wide-open country she first experienced in 1916 at age eleven. A time she fondly described as, "when [she and her friends] could race bareback, galloping across the sage, with only one rule – be home in time for dinner." She is buried next to Cal in the Aspen Cemetery. The inscription on her monument reads: "Life Long Friend of Cal Carrington."

THURSDAY, DEC. 24, 1959

Cal Carrington Dead; Funeral Thursday

Last rites will be held Thursday, December 24 at 10:30 at the Elks Club for Cal Carrington, 86, who died Tuesday at the Driggs hospital. Cal was a member of B.P.O.E. 1712.

He first came to Jackson Hole in 1889, and lived here for many years. He later bought a ranch in Teton Valley, Idaho, which has been his home since, although he still visited often over here.

In 1927 he went on a big game hunt in Africa, where he brought down three elephants and several species of other game animals. Some of the heads adorn the walls of the Silver Dollar Bar at the Wort Hotel and always attract interest, especially among outsiders.

Cal was the subject of a story in Readers Digest some years ago by Struthers Burt, "The Most Unforgettable Character I Ever Knew."

He was widely known in our valley, and very well-liked by all.

A telephone call from Felicia Macgruder, Tuesday, said that he passed away quietly. She had flown from Washington a few days ago to be at his bedside. For many years Cal worked for Felicia's mother on "The Countess' Ranch" on upper Flat Creek, and the two had been friends since Felicia was a little girl.

Further information about this fine old gentleman will appear next week.

LAST RITES HELD THURSDAY FOR "CAL" CARRINGTON, EARLY PIONEER

Funeral services were held at 10:30 a.m. Thursday for Enoch C. Carrington at the Elks Lodge with burial in the Jackson Cemetery.

Enoch C. Carrington, "Cal" as his friends knew him, passed away peacefully at the Teton Valley Hospital at Driggs, Tuesday morning, December 22 of complications incident to old age. He was 86 years old.

Born in Sweden February 10, 1873 he came to the United States at the age of five and grew up in southern Utah. Carrington never married and the names of his parents are unknown.

He came to Jackson Hole in 1889 and lived here for many years. In 1898 he took out a homestead desert claim in Idaho, where he wintered during later years. Mr. Carrington was one of the first forest rangers in Jackson Hole, where he spent the major part of his life.

He worked as a cattle drover, driving from the southwest to Canada, and in 1914 began working as a guide, a work for which he later became quite famed throughout the United States.

Carrington was considered one of the greatest guides and big-game hunters in the west, a trait which helped considerably during a two year stint in Africa hunting big game.

One of the great originals of the old west, Carrington was a man by himself. His colorful personality, marked by eccentricities marked him an ideal subject for writers. Katherine Burt wrote a novel about him and Struthers Burt wrote an article, "The Most Unforgettable Character I Have Met" for Readers Digest.

The Jackson Hole Courier obituary
Thursday, December 31, 1959

CAL CARRINGTON DIED DEC. 22

Funeral services were held in Jackson at the Elks Lodge Thursday Dec. 24 at 10:30 a.m. for Cal Carrington, long time resident of Jackson Hole and Teton Basin.

Enoch C. Carrington, "Cal" as his friends knew him, passed away peacefully at the Teton valley Hospital, Tuesday morning, December 22 of complications incident to age. He was 86 years old.

Born February 10, 1873 he came to the United States at the age of five andgrew up in southern Utah. Carrington never married and the names of his parents are unknown. He is thought to have been born in Sweden.

He came to Teton Valley in April 1898, took out a homestead desert entry claim, where he frequently wintered during later years. Mr. Carrington was one of the first forest rangers in the Jackson Hole where he spent the major part of his life.

He worked as a cattle drover, driving from the southwest to Canada and in 1914 began working as a guide, a work for which he later became quite famed throughout the United States.

In 1914 he started work as a guide on a dude ranch in the Jackson Hole area. He became a guide for Mrs. Eleanor Patterson. She subsequently bought a ranch of his at Jackson Hole. He traveled extensively in Europe and did some big game hunting there.

Several articles have been written about the colorful life of Mr. Carrington. He was a member of the Elks Lodge in Jackson.

One of the great originals of the Old West, Carrington was a man by himself. His colorful personality marked by eccentricities mark him (sic) an ideal subject for writers. Katherine Burt wrote a novel about him and Struthers Burt an article "The Most Unforgettable Character I have Met" for Readers Digest.

Carrington was considered one of the greatest guides and big game hunters in the West, a trait which helped considerably during a two year stint in Africa hunting big game.

Teton Valley News obituary
Thursday, December 24, 1959

Funeral services will be held at 10:30 a.m. today (Thursday) for Enoch C. Carrington at the Elks Lodge in Jackson, Wyoming.

Enoch C. Carrington, "Cal" as his friends knew him, passed away peacefully at the Teton Valley Hospital, Tuesday morning, December 22 of complications incident to old age. He was 56 years old.

Born in Sweden February 10, 1873, he came to the United States at the age of five and grew up in southern Utah. Carrington never married and the names of his parents is unknown.

He came into the valley in April 1898, took out a homestead desert claim, where he frequently wintered during later years. Mr. Carrington was one of the first forest rangers in the Jackson Hole where he spent the major part of his life.

He worked as a cattle drover, driving from the southwest to Canada, and in 1914 began working as a guide, a work for which he later became quite famed throughout the United States.

One of the great originals of the old West, Carrington was a man by himself. His colorful personality, marked by eccentricities made him an ideal subject for writers. Katherine Burt wrote a novel about him and Struthers Burt wrote an article, The Most Unforgettable Character I have Met for Readers Digest.

Carrington was considered one of the greatest guides and big game hunters in the West, a trait which helped considerably during a two year sting in Africa hunting big game.

Burial will be in the Jackson cemetery under the direction of teh Robert Bean Funeral Home of Driggs.

27

Looters, Unexplained Doings,
and Raised Eyebrows

On his deathbed, Felecia said, Cal told her "he kept fifty dollars stashed in his boot" and directed her to retrieve it from his cabin when he was gone. But what all may have actually been discussed between them regarding the disposition of Cal's personal possessions and estate, there is no way to really know?

Sometime afterward, Felicia and Pearl Johnson, who Felicia referred to as "her friend," looked through the cabin. It was probably not by chance that Felicia chose Pearl to accompany her, since Pearl had at one time been Jackson's sheriff. Felicia later wrote, "they found the boot and the hidden fifty dollars."

"Pearl told her, 'you don't know these old timers.'" Felicia said, at Pearl's urging, they searched further uncovering a cache where Cal had hidden "a handgun, field glasses and a pair of brass knuckles."[1] However, again, what all they actually found or were looking for, we will really never know.

While doing research for Cissy Patterson's biography, Amada Smith found personal correspondence of Carrington's in the possession of Felecia Cameron and Ellen Pearson Arnold, Felicia's granddaughter and daughter, in San Diego. The letters and material would have been obtained from Felicia's estate and could only have come from Carrington's trunk when Felica and Pearl searched Cal's cabin in December 1959.[2] Notably missing in the collection was any correspondence from Cissy.

Years after Cal's passing, historian Wendell Gillette disclosed to Jackson resident Bob Rudd that he had visited Carrington's cabin right after Cal's death and discovered an unlocked trunk in the cabin's attic containing personal belongings, including a pair of matched pearl-handled pistols lying side-by-side right on top. Gillette confided that he left the items where they were, but when he returned later to photograph the cabin, the trunk and its contents were mysteriously gone.[3] Since Felicia did not mention the trunk or its contents in her writings, it was previously assumed someone had absconded with it before she and Pearl Johnson had a chance to search the cabin. The papers discovered in the possession of Ellen and Felicia Cameron in San Diego suggest otherwise. What intriguing secrets and stories Carrington's trunk contents may have revealed we can only guess, there is no way to know.

Another puzzle was where did Carrington's guns disappear to, for example, the prized rifle that Cissy had given him for his African hunt? It is known Cal had carved his brand –CAL– into his gun stocks making them identifiable and to discourage their theft; and he had recorded the serial numbers, too.

The gun riddle was solved when several Teton Valley residents independently divulged to this author that the weapons were stolen by local vandals; young adults who, in fact, had known Cal and may have been among those, who years earlier, he had entertained with his stories. Like altering a livestock brand with a running iron, one thief crudely changed CAL to read similar to his own first name.[4] It is believed the thieves sold the guns, but where and in who's possession they finally ended up is unknown.

The rifle theft allegedly occurred before Cal's passing, possibly while he was traveling outside of the valley in winter. One can imagine how distressing it was for him. Cal had a lot of memories attached to his possessions. His worries about vandalism and burglary had been grounded in more than just an old man's eccentricities and mistrust. There had been good reason for him to store his trunk and other possessions at Jim Berger's home at times when he was gone.

After Cal's death, Gillette photographed the inside of the cabin and remarked on its "sad condition." He recorded, "An old white suit hung in the closet, I bet it had made Cal look classy when in New York," but otherwise he noted, "There was very little left of an active cowboy's life."

The guns had been stolen by then, but where had items like the buffalo coat and his African souvenirs gone? Gillette did not mention them, only confiding about the trunk's disappearance. It is pretty certain that Cal's cabin was ransacked, perhaps repeatedly, for anything of value around the time immediately before and after his death; the interval of time between when Gillette first visited the cabin and when he returned again to photograph it.

The valley's treasure seekers didn't stop there. After whisperings circulated of Cal Carrington's financial worth, his cabin, which stands alone in the center of the 160-acre homestead parcel, was over the years repeatedly scoured by hooligans hoping to find hidden money or something of value. Even Cal's old cook stove was removed. Rumors persist to this day that the old buckaroo had hidden money and valuables in his cabin.[5]

Who would believe an old time buckaroo would have had much more than his saddle or the old horse harnesses hanging in his shack to leave to anyone? But when attorney Harold Forbush probated Cal's Last Will and Testament, it was punctuated with a low whistle and eyebrows rose!

While the origins of Cal's financial wealth may be attributable to Cissy in large part, Cal also had an uncanny aptitude for picking good investments. Moreover, he rarely spent any money on himself. In fact, he was more than frugal, at Bates he chose to live in relative destitution.

Attorney Forbush totaled it up: Cal had been receiving an annuity of one-hundred dollars a month for life from the time he began working for Cissy, and he spent little of it. He had accounts in four different banks; a 23.72-acre coastal beach property and another beachfront lot next to Moonlight State Park in Encinitas, California; the 160-acre ranch, cabin, and outbuildings at Bates; stock in Greyhound Bus Lines, Coeur d'Alene mines and A.J. Industries; and his Willys Jeep. The worth of his estate in terms of today's dollar and real estate values was well into the millions.[6]

His will, probated and recorded in Driggs January 29, 1960, bequeathed all his real and personal property in Idaho to Felicia. His will probated in San Diego on February 3, 1961, left the money in his First National Bank of San Diego account to Felicia, while his real property in California was given to Mary Ake. Felicia later wrote that, "Mary Ake, a schoolteacher and Cal's childhood sweetheart, received half of Cal's estate."[7]

There must be a lot more to the Mary Ake story. In his will Cal referred to her as "an old pal since a kid." But there is little recorded about her or Cal's relationship with her. By the time of Cal's passing she was an old woman in poor health living in Mountain Home, Idaho. In her later years, she appears to have also resided with her sister, Mrs. Paul Montgomery, in Seattle.

Mary, also know as, "Mamie," was fourteen years younger than Cal.[8] In his 1958 interview, Cal said, "After I quit cowboying [open range cattle drives], I was down in the Boise Valley country." But he did not elaborate further. Obviously, Mountain Home is a chapter in his life about which little is known. Years later, in 1941, Cal spent part of the winter at Mountain Home, staying at the Hotel Mellen. He wrote, "My friends hear was all glad to see me, after [my] being gone nine years." It suggests Cal returned to Mountain Home from time-to-time to visit friends over the years. [9]

Cal, true to himself to the end, did not leave one-cent to his family, not even the customary one dollar.[10]

Felicia sold Cal's 160.29-acre Bates property to Oren Furniss – the neighbor boy who Cal befriended and used to entertain with his stories – on January 18, 1962, for $21,000. And she eventually

Cal's friend and neighbor Oren Furniss in 2007, at age 89, on his horse, Chip.
Photo by the author

donated the black angora chaps Rose had – those Cal had long ago given to Cissy – to the Jackson Hole Historical Society and Museum. Likely, the museum's other accoutrements of Cal's came from Felicia, too. The chaps were displayed in a showcase at the Jackson play, *Petticoat Rules*, in 2001.

Today, more than fifty years after his death, Cal's stout old cabin still stands, but the inside has been trashed by the elements and looters. The old cook stove and harnesses shown in Gillette's 1959 photographs are gone, only the nailed-down rough built bunk in the corner of the cabin, where the farm boys would sit to hear Cal's yarns, remains. In 2004, an old beat-up wooden captain's chair laid on its side next to the bunk. It was easy to imagine Cal sitting in it holding court, dispensing his stories. When this author returned to the cabin a few years later, even the captain's chair had vanished.

28

Mysteries

Cal Carrington's earliest years in Jackson Hole will always remain a controversial and contradictory story, part of the myths and legends surrounding him and early-day Jackson Hole. Despite all evidence to the contrary, some folks continue to cling to and repeat the outlaw myths. They are reluctant to give up on the cherished wild and woolly notion that Cal drove stolen horses into Jackson Hole and hid them in Flat Creek Canyon, insisting: "All the horse thieves were caught except Cal." There is no doubt it would make Cal grin, it is how he would want to be remembered.

Cal is not recorded in any early U.S. Census. The first he shows up is in 1930. Nor does he appear in Social Security records. In contemporary language he was "off the grid." Combined with his use of multiple names, if one does not dig deeper, it does leave an impression that maybe he was concealing something and hiding from his past. Based on this author's research, however, it is unlikely. Fiercely independent old timers often viewed those things as a government intrusion and avoided them. One thing for certain, though, Cal went out of his way not to mention anything about his birth family to anyone.

When Cal finally does show up in the 1930 U.S. Census, it only raises more questions. How could he have been recorded at both Los Angeles and Cape Nome, Alaska? And what was he doing in Nome? Perhaps this was somehow a prank, more playing with the truth.

There is some evidence that, although he never married, Cal may have had children. Cissy's biographer Ralph Martin alludes to this, but does not tell all: "Before Cissy, women had been transients in his life. He had even refused to marry the woman who had borne his child." It leaves one to wonder, who was this woman and what more did Martin know?[1]

In correspondence with Felicia in the 1920s, Cissy jealously derided Cal for "having a baby" with Mary Ake.[2] Was this merely one of Cissy's "neatly poisoned arrows shot into the air," or was it true? Could this have been the reason for Cal and Cissy's falling out while hunting in Canada around 1926? But Mary Ake's obituary makes no mention of her having any children.

Similarly, hand-written notes at the Jackson Hole Historical Society from Wendell Gillette's interview with Felicia point to Cal having an affair with a married woman in Jackson and a son having been born from that relationship. The annotation indicates it may have been with a woman from an esteemed family in Jackson's history.[3] It is an intriguing clue left for posterity, but there is no longer any way to trace who it might actually have been.

Not much could be learned about Mary Frances Ake or "Mamie" as she was known by her family and friends. Social Security records, an obituary, and the recorded settlement of Cal's estate prove there was a Mary Ake who resided at Mountain Home, Idaho. She was the daughter of Frank and Laura Ake, a prominent Mountain Home pioneer ranching family. It appears Cal may have worked for a time on the Ake ranch after his stint as an open range cowboy. Was "Mary," in Cissy's novel *Glass Houses*, a composite of Mamie? Cissy wrote, "As soon as Mary was old enough to walk, she followed him [Cal] around her father's ranch."

Mary's obituary states she held a college degree from the University of Washington at Seattle and was a member of the Tri-Delta sorority. Obviously, it would seem she was more than just "an old pal" to Cal, since he bequeathed half of his estate to her.

Felicia wrote that Mamie was Cal's "childhood sweetheart"

The bronze plaque Felicia Gizycka had made for Cal's grave marker which is warehoused at the Jackson Hole Historical Society and Museum.

who had nursed him when he was sick and taught him to read and write. Records show she was fourteen years younger than Cal. She died in February 1967, at age seventy-six, and is buried at Mountain Home. It is curious that no correspondence has ever been recovered between Cal and Mamie, since Cal generally kept the letters he received from friends. It seems they would have corresponded if, as he testified, she was an "old pal since childhood."

Another of Cal's paramours about whom we know little was Goldie Chisman of San Diego. He carried on a long-distance relationship and correspondence with her for over thirty years. From letters in the *Felicia Gizycka Collection* in San Diego, it is apparent Goldie may have been a well-to-do businesswoman. She drove a Buick and helped Cal with real estate endeavors in southern California. But she was not above visiting Cal's cabin at Bates and wrote fondly of it. Record of their correspondence begins in 1928, after Cal returns from Africa, but it begs the question: how, when, and where did they meet, and what was the nature of their relationship?

When Cal died, for a monument Felicia's friends helped find a large boulder that looked like the Grand Teton. Another friend in the East, a sculptor, made an impressive bronze plaque of a horse standing with an empty saddle, the reins dropped to the ground. It was to be attached to the boulder resembling the Grand; an impressive monument. Felicia phoned Rose Crabtree and told her about it. "You've done fine," Rose said, trying to conceal she was crying, "a ground-tied horse means a horse thief. And that's just what the old fool was."[4]

But today, Cal's grave is marked only by a simple footstone reading: "Cal E. Carrington." What became of the elaborate monument and plaque? Jackson historian and *Teton Magazine* publisher Eugene Downer thought it was removed from the cemetery because it was feared someone would steal it. Biographer Ralph Martin states, "The plaque was stolen." Actually, it turns out, the plaque is among items being stored by the Jackson Hole Museum, but no one seems to know what became of the rock to which it was supposed to be attached. The plaque was never installed as intended as evidenced by it never having been drilled.

Confusion over Cal's real name followed him to the grave. His headstone marker reads: "Cal E. Carrington." Likewise, the bronze plaque bears the same inscription, putting his nickname before his given name initial E (Enoch).

In the early 1960s, a curious message accompanied by a drawing of an angry, bearded, old man carrying a scythe appeared in the Jackson Hole newspaper. It read: "Notice to the person who stole the flowers from my grave, I will see you soon. Signed – Cal Carrington." Had Cal returned from the grave? Actually, the cemetery caretaker placed the notice after perennials he had planted at Cal's and Felicia's grave sites were stolen.[5]

The Flat Creek Ranch caretakers Forney Cole, Bob Stanton, and George Ryter, always claimed the ranch was haunted. At times things would shake and rattle as if spirits possessed them. Stanton said, "There's ghosts, I saw and felt plenty." Ryter independently confirmed that "It sounded and felt as if all hell had torn loose."[6] Today, it is known the ranch is located on a seismically active fault and occasional quakes rattle the property. It must have been terrifying for the caretakers who did not understand what was happening.

Rumors of the ranch being haunted continue, however. Not too long ago, members of the Jackson Hole Land Trust swear they saw an aura in Cissy's recently restored cabin. They were not the first to confide they witnessed supernatural phenomenon associated with Cissy. Jackie Martin, Cissy's photographer and art director, and also Felicia and others, in separate instances, claimed to have encountered her haunting presence. Cal and Cissy were both strong personalities, their spirits will always haunt the Flat Creek Ranch and windswept precipices of Sheep Mountain.

Whatever became of the old cabin in Flat Creek Canyon and where exactly was it located? No one remembers for sure. Charlie Peterson Sr. recalled that "as you topped out, it sat on the left side of the road before you got to the other cabins." That is where present day ranch operator Joe Albright found charred remnants.[7] The cabin where outlaws of old were rumored to have once hidden out is gone. It has become another of Jackson Hole's legends.

A final puzzlement for people visiting the Flat Creek Ranch is the grand old piano in the lodge. Cissy had it taken into the ranch in 1929. It continues to mystify people how an ox cart crew ever accomplished moving it from the Victor rail terminal to the ranch in one piece.

In the end, chronicling Cal's life history was an endeavor similar to putting together an old jigsaw puzzle where many of the pieces have been lost over time, and other pieces that somehow got into the box may not really belong there at all.

29

Legacy

Cal Carrington left a legacy of stories handed down through literature and oral tradition that figure richly in the mythos and legends surrounding Jackson Hole, Teton Valley, and the West.

Today, what had been Cal's Encinitas coastal beach property is part of Village Park, a residential subdivision. Only three-and-a-half acres of his original 24.72-acre tract remain undeveloped, set aside for open space. The main street in the subdivision is named "Recluse Lane," after a retiring old cowboy who once hung out there, perhaps? Felicia remarked, "Cal lived in squalor there, just as he had in Driggs."[1]

In summer 2004, the ground at Cal's old homestead in Bates was planted with barley. His rustic cabin, weathered by more than a century, sat lonely and abandoned in the center of the grain field. After the grain crop was harvested, flocks of migrating sandhill cranes staged in the fields about the old shack. A few of today's old timers in Teton Valley know this was Cal Carrington's homestead, but otherwise most people passing by it on the Bates road have no idea that the cabin is steeped in Western lore, nor that its original owner was a celebrated early day Jackson Hole figure.

The beautifully restored Flat Creek Guest Ranch is a monument to Cal Carrington and Cissy Patterson. Nearly a century later those legendary original owners still hold dominion over the ranch. The ranch enjoys an incomparable wilderness setting, little changed from the time of Cal and Cissy. It remains as Cissy described in a 1944 letter: "Never anywhere in my life have I seen anything lovelier."[2] Today, it is a place where guests can learn firsthand about Jackson Hole, what the valley was like in the past and experience what it's become.

The ranch is listed on the National Register of Historic Places, ironically, not because of the history surrounding it, but for the type of log work found in the original structures. Regardless, whatever served to qualify the ranch for listing, history justifies it.

Cissy's great-grandchildren, through Felicia and Drew Pearson's marriage and their daughter Ellen's family, Drew and Joe Arnold and their families at Laramie, Wyoming, closed a circle by becoming modern-day Jackson Hole skiers and skilled mountain climbers, creating a climbing and backpacking school they call "Solid Rock." Joe Arnold is also an artist and author specializing in plein air mountainscapes. The Arnolds have had a continuing attachment to Jackson Hole through a recreational property lease with the Forest Service at Turpin Meadows near Moran, which Felicia assisted them in obtaining.

Joe Albright, Cissy's grandnephew, became the custodian of the Flat Creek Ranch in 1996. A Conservation Easement donated by Josephine Patterson Reeve, and held by the Jackson Hole Land Trust, protects the property. The Cissy Patterson Trust supports its stewardship, in part. The canyon hideaway where legend has it that stolen horses were once hidden, where a spirited red-headed Countess found solace, and where an orphaned cowboy's life took an astonishing turn, is today preserved in perpetuity.

It is fitting that Cal's final resting place overlooks much more than the changed and burgeoning town of Jackson. The sweeping view up the valley takes in the open grasslands on the National Elk Refuge, where Cal may have boarded with Dick Turpin and John Holland when he first came into the valley and where his friend's homestead, Frank Petersen, was once located, north to Miller's

Butte, Flat Creek Canyon, Sheep Mountain, and the Grand Teton – all storied Jackson Hole places and ground intimately familiar to Cal. And thanks to conservation-minded individuals, its view still looks much the same today as when Cal first rode into Jackson Hole more than a century ago.

good luck

Cal

Source Notes

Prologue

1   Stanza by Mike Hurwitz, Western songwriter, Alta, WY, 2005.

Chapter 1

1   Several sources: The International Genological Index, U.S. Census Records, Ancestry.Com, through the assistance of Kathy Hodges, Research Specialist, Idaho Historical Society, Boise. It's reasonably certain that Cal knew and remembered his Swedish shoemaker family origins as is evidenced by Felicia Gizcka's 1965 "Reminiscence" story in *Teton Magazine*. Cal's WWI draft card gives his birth date as February 10, 1875, but this may be another case of his playing loose with facts when filling out government forms.

2   Notes hand written on the back of an envelope in 1959 by Felicia Gizycka after talking with Driggs Motel owners, Earl and Sadie Harris, where Cal was staying in his last days, and perhaps also, what Cal himself told Felicia in his last days, while in the Driggs Hospital. The notes and other material were discovered by the research of Cissy Patterson's biographer, Amanda Smith, at the home of Felecia's daughter, Ellen, in San Diego in 2008, and were photographed and mailed to the author. The notes state that a younger brother had traveled in company with Cal to the United States and that the brother had died shortly after arrival in Utah and was buried in the Salt Lake cemetery.

3   Forbush, H. 2000. *Tales of the Big Hole Mountains*. Idaho Falls, ID, pp115-116, is the first to make the connection to the Apostle Albert Carrington. Carrington was one of the intellectual leaders in the Mormon movement. He had a distinguished involving setting up the provisional government of Utah, territorial attorney general, presiding authority over the European Mission, one of the Twelve Apostles, President of the Perpetual Immigration Fund, Church historian, and counselor to Brigham Young. He was also a polygamist with many wives. For his involvement with another man's wife, he was excommunicated from the Church "for crimes of lewd and lascivious conduct and adultery. http://www.media.utah.edu/UHE/c/Carrington,Albert.html.

4   Gizycka, F. 1965. "Jackson Hole, 1916-65: A Reminiscence." *Vogue*, April 1, pp200-203.

5   Olsson, N.W. 1984. "Emigrant Traffic on the North Sea." http://www.genealogi.se/roots/hull.htm. The Wilson Line of Hull was particularly known for steamships with cramped and poor accommodations.

6   Jensen, L.J. "Perpetual Emigrating Fund Company."*Utah History Encyclopedia*. http://historytogo.utah.gov/utah_chapters/pioneers/perpetualemigratingfund.html.

7   Woods, F.E. 2011. "The Arrival of Nineteenth Century Mormon Emigrants in Salt Lake City." Religious Study Center, Provo Utah (on the World Wide Web).

8   "Law of Adoption" at http://en.wikipedia.org/wiki/Law_of_adoption.

9   Gizycka, F. 1977. "Cissy Paterson: The Countess of Flat Creek." *Teton Magazine*, Vol. 10, pp37-48.

10   Utah Death Records.

11   Enoch Carrington's 1901 "Declaration of Intention to Become a Citizen of the United States." Teton County, Idaho, Court House Records and also the National Archives.

12 Burt, S. 1924. *The Dairy of a Dude Wrangler.* Charles Scribner's Sons, p306; also in: Healy, P.F. 1966. *Cissy: A Biography of Eleanor Cissy Patterson.*

13 Gizycka, 1965. op.cit. There is conflicting evidence whether Cal grew up with a foster family in Smithfield, Utah, or whether it was in the Boise Valley. Cal did spend time at Mt. Home, Idaho, in his early years. Struthers Burt wrote, "at age 8 Cal was adopted by a couple with a ranch in Idaho. Whereas Forbush says, Cal's foster family was at Logan (Smithfield).

14 University of Wyoming 1957 recorded interview transcription by Bonney and Bonney. Personal files of Lorraine Bonney, Kelly, WY, 33p.

15 Stone, D. 1958 Recorded interview arranged by Harold Forbush in Driggs. Tape is on file at the Teton County, Idaho, Historical Society.

16 Cal told this to the Harris's at their motel where he was staying near the end of his life. They passed the story along to Felicia Gizycka, who included it her 1965 *Reminiscence* article. Struthers Burt also recorded it in his *Reader's Digest* story, "The Most Unforgettable Character..."

17 Several sources mention Cal's temper and his "hatred for the human race."

18 University of Wyoming 1957 Interview, op.cit.

Chapter 2

1 University of Wyoming. 1957. Cal Carrington oral interview transcribed by Bonney and Bonney. (personal files of Lorraine Bonney, Kelly, WY.)

2 Burt, S. 1948. "The Most Unforgettable Character I've Met." *Reader's Digest* (Oct.), pp83-86.

3 Ibid. Burt has Cal cowboying for about twenty years, but this doesn't mesh with his date of arrival in Teton Basin and what is known about his other activities. His early years saddle

tramping, working as a drover, and bronc busting appear more like eight years.

4   Stone, D. 1958. Recorded oral interview with Cal Carrington. Teton Valley Historical Society, Driggs, ID. Also transcribed and on file at JHHS, Jackson, WY. In the Dwight Stone 1958 interview in Driggs, Cal, for whatever reason, refused to talk about his early cowboy days or where he had been before coming into the Tetons, telling the interviewer, "That's none of your damn business," or "Let's not talk about that." The U. of Wyoming interview provides information on years that previously were pretty much a mystery or question as to Cal's whereabouts and activities. Of course, there is always the issue of whether Cal's stories were true happenings and how much was simply passed around cowboy lore.

5   University of Wyoming interview, 1957, op.cit. Two-dot Satchell's cow camp outfit is described in L.A. Huffman "The Last Bustin' at the Bow-Gun." *Scribner's Magazine*, Vol. 42(8), pp78-87.

6   Ibid.

7   Ibid

8   This remark by Cal in the U. of Wyoming interview in reference to some of his wilder cowboy years contradicts those who like to believe he was an outlaw in those times.

9   University of Wyoming interview, 1957, op.cit.

10   Ibid.

Chapter 3

1   Healy, P.F. 1966. *Cissy: A Biography of Eleanor M. "Cissy" Patterson*. Doubleday, NY.

2   Burt, S. 1924. *The Diary of a Dude Wrangler*. Charles Scribner's Sons, NY.

3   Burt, N. 1983. *Jackson Hole Journal*. University of Oklahoma Press, Norman.

4   Burt, S. "The Most Unforgettable Character... ",1948, op.cit.

5   Martin, R.G. 1979. *The Extraodinary Life of Eleanor Medill Patterson*. Simon and Shuster, NY.

6   Burt, N. 1983. *Jackson Hole Journal...* op.cit.

7   Burt, S. *Diary...* 1948, op. cit. Burt says, "Cal taught himself to read and write at age twenty-one."

8   His friend Felicia Gizycka stated he learned to read and write from Mary Ake (*Teton Magazine*, Vol. 10, 1948). Felicia stated Cal "was barely literate." This is a relative judgment. Felicia was well educated and a writer. For the place and time, comparing him to many contemporaries, he was not illiterate. The author has seen a good number of letters written by him, which demonstrated his capability to read, write and carry on a correspondence (see the *Felicia Gizycka Collection*). Spelling was not his forté. Cal's literacy is not accurately represented by his 1952 typewritten letter to Josephine Albright alone. Early archival documents bear Cal's well-practiced Enoch Carrington signature, but in later personal correspondence, he'd simply sign as "Cal" with an artful flourish.

9   Forbush, H. Pers. Comm. 2004.

10 Burt, N. 1983, *Jackson Hole Journal...* op.cit.

11 Gillette, B. 1992. *Homesteading with the Elk*. Jackson Printing, Jackson, WY. Bertha witnessed Cal's cowboy gallantry when he would stop off at their homestead to visit.

12 Hoge, A.A.1966. *Cissy Patterson: The Life of Eleanor Medill Patterson Publisher and Editor of the Washington Times-Herald*. Random House, NY.

13 University of Wyoming 1957 interview transcription by Bonney and Bonney.

14 Stone, D. Recorded oral interview, 1958. op. cit.

Chapter 4

1   Gillette, W. "The Memorable Character – Cal Carrington." *Snake River Echoes,* A Quarterly of Idaho History. Teton Co. Ed., Vol.8, No. 3: 54-62. A water right filing by Cal in April 1897, on record in the Teton County, Idaho, courthouse substantiates this arrival date for Teton Valley. Also see "History of James Henry Berger," Mimeo, Cascade, Idaho, 2p

2   Gillette and Berger History, op.cit.

3   Stone, D. Recorded oral interview with Cal Carrington, Teton Valley Historical Society, Driggs, 1958. Some have suspiciously viewed Cal and Berger's arrival in Teton Valley, trying to say the two men were partners engaged in rustling. All evidence is to the contrary. Both men were looking for land to homestead in Teton Valley. Both men took up land. Berger put his energy into making settlement, he married, raised a family, and became recognized as being among early upstanding Mormon pioneers in the area. He is buried in the Victor cemetery.

4   Stone, D. Oral interview, 1958. op.cit. and Berger history, op.cit.

5   Forbush, H. 1956. Oral interview with E.G. Adams. *Voices from the Past,* No.163. Bringham Young University, Rexburg, Idaho.

6   Gillette, W. *The Memorable Character...* 1979. op.cit.

7   History of James Berger, op.cit.

8   Ibid.

9   Driggs, B.W. 1970 ed., *History of Teton Valley,* Arnold Agency, Rexburg, Idaho.

10 Stone interview, op. cit.

11 The Desert News quoted in Moss, W. "The Avenues of Driggs Tell a Story," *Teton Valley Top to Bottom Magazine.* (Summer 2006): pp 50-55.

12 Owen, W. 1892. Bill Barlow's Budget, 9 June 1886. Reprinted in *JHHS&M Chronicle*, Fall 2006.

13 Thompson, Edith M.S. and William Leigh Thompson. 1982. Beaver Dick: *The Honor and the Heartbreak*. Jelm Mt. Press, Laramie, WY.

14 Moss, W. "The Avenues of Driggs..." 2006. op.cit.

15 Berger history, op. cit.

16 Gillette, W. "The Memorable Character..." 1979; and also, Stone interview, 1958.

17 BLM GLO National Archives (accessed through: http://www.glorecords.blm.gov/) Berger chose a Homestead Act entry, while Cal took up land under the Desert Land Act. Record of the claim for excess water from Holland's spring is found in the Teton County, Idaho, courthouse.

18 Teton County Courthouse records.

19 GLO records, op.cit.

20 Berger, op.cit.

21 Ibid.

22 Stone, op.cit.

23 Ibid. Interestingly, Nathaniel Langford with the 1872 Hayden Expedition made a similar observation about Teton Valley's prairies, remarking they were "carpeted with the heaviest and largest bunchgrass he had ever seen."

Chapter 5

1 Driggs, B.W. 1970 ed. *History of Teton Valley*. Arnold Agency, Rexburg, ID.

2 Land and patent records, Teton County, Idaho, courthouse. The records at Blackfoot and Oasis were later moved to Driggs after Teton County, Idaho, was created.

3 National Archives, BLM-GLO, Desert Land case no. 3116.

4 Piquet, L. Pers. Comm. 2013. See also Chapter 22.

5   Land and patent records, Teton County, Idaho courthouse; also the National Archives records. It is believed Cal purposely misrepresented his country of origin.

6   National Archives, op.cit.

7   Ibid.

8   Layser, E. 2012. *The Jackson Hole Settlement Chronicles,* Daning Pine Publishing, Alta, WY, 237 p. John Holland's life history is profiled.

9   Ibid.

10 Stone interview, 1958, op.cit.; also O.H. Bonney and L.G. Bonney. *Bonney's Guide: Grand Teton National Park and Jackson Hole.* Houston, TX, (Trip 12, 1972), pp 122-23. Bonney and Bonney refer to Cal as "a crony" of John Holland. Evidence indicates they were good friends.

11 The BLM states, "95% of the early Desert Land Act claims were bogus" (see: http://www.reference.com/ browse/wiki/ Desert-Land Act)

12 National Archives, BLM-GLO case no. 3116, op.cit.

13 Ibid.

14 Ibid.

15 Platts, D. 1991. *John Cherry: His Lies, Life and Legend.* Bearpaw Press, Jackson, WY.

16 It's doubtful that Cal spent many winters at Bates or in Jackson Hole. More likely he rode over to Rexburg and took the train into warmer climes or he went over to the Boise valley, where the author speculates he may have been employed sometime or another at the Frank Ake Ranch in Mountain Home. He would return to Bates in spring to work on his Desert Entry claim, after which he'd go over to Jackson Hole for seasonal ranch work and wrangling and packing for Yellowstone Park or the Forest Service--a man on the move.

Chapter 6

1 Stone 1958 interview; also, Gillette, W. "The Memorable Character... "1979.

2 Ibid. Cal used this line frequently in his later years in response to questions he did not want to answer directly. It was recorded by several authors and also in his 1957 University of Wyoming interview. Interestingly, he doesn't use the complete saying, which was generally spoken as, "... didn't have nothing but a long rope and a running iron."

3 Holmes, B.M. "Victor, Idaho, 1889-1989." Mimeo on file at the Valley of the Tetons Library, Victor, Idaho (1989).

4 Daugherty, J. 1999. *A Place Called Jackson Hole*. National Park Service, Moose, pp 180-82.

5 Wards hotel and store in Daugherty, J. *A Place Called Jackson Hole* (1999): p 209. The Pass road in those days mostly went straight up or down without switchbacks. See McDaniel, L.T. "Dorus Harvey and Lenora...Tyler: Their Ancestry and Their Posterity." (2001), pp 56-60

6 Daugherty, op.cit.

7 Wilson, C. 1985. *The Return of the White Indian*. Fenske Printing, Inc., Rapid City, SD, pp 151-375. Wilson provides a detailed account of the dangers and difficulties of early day crossing of the Snake River at Wilson.

8 Ibid; also Daugherty, op.cit.

9 University of Wyoming interview, 1957.

10 Bonney, O.H. and L.G. Bonney. 1972. *Bonney's Guide: Grand Teton National Park and Jackson's Hole*. Houston, TX (Trip 13), pp 122-23. (The material the Bonney's cite appears to come from Cal's 1957 University of Wyoming interview).

11 Charles Wilson claims anyone who came into the Hole before 1915 was considered an old timer (in *Return of the White Indian,* 1985). However, the original old timers settled in the

1880s–see Layser, 2012, op.cit.

12 University of Wyoming interview, 1957; see also Bonney and Bonney, 1972. Cal claimed Holland let Dick Turpin off because he was a member of the Jackson Hole brotherhood.

13 University of Wyoming interview, 1957.

14 Platts, D. 2003. *Robert Miller: An Enigma.* Wilson, WY. A newspaper story that Platts uncovered quotes outlaw Teton Jackson as saying: "Miller and Holland were providing him and his men supplies." Similar undocumented allegations are mentioned in other sources as well.

15 Gillette, W. "The Memorable Character–Cal Carrington." op.cit.

16 Dyke, J.C. 1962. *The West of the Texas Kid, 1881-1910: Recollections of Thomas E. Crawford.* Univ. of Oklahoma Press, Norman.

17 Betts, R.B. 1978. *Along the Ramparts of the Tetons.* Colorado Assoc. Univ. Press, Boulder.

18 University of Wyoming interview, 1957.

19 Stone interview, 1958.

20 Brown, D. 1991. *Wondrous Times on the Frontier.* August House Publishers. Little Rock, AR. Brown describes and analyzes the Westerner's practice of "stringing greeners." Like Cal, Cissy was very adept at creating and modifying stories, substituting characters and putting Cal into those tales, for example see her novel *Glass Houses.*

21 Burt, N. *Jackson Hole Journal...* 1983, op.cit.

22 Petersen, C. pers. interviews by the author, 2004/2005.

23 Gizycka, F. "Jackson Hole, 1916-65: A Reminiscence." *Vogue* (April 1, 1965): p 209.

24 Cissy's biographers Martin, Hoge and Healy all repeat these same stories about Cal. The tales appear to have been taken from Cissy's novel, *Glass Houses,* pp200-201.

They undoubtedly originated from Cal's yarns, but were embellished or modified to fit her story line. For example, in his 1957 interview, Cal told a story about Ed Hunter, who was arrested and brought in for trail for poaching. The court recessed, as Cal told it, and they took Hunter into a saloon with them. While they were having a drink, Hunter walked out the back door and lit out, swam the river and escaped. The lawmen declined to cross the river after him. In *Glass Houses,* Cissy writes it was Cal (Ben) who escaped the posse by swimming the river. The Hunter episode appears to be the source for the story of Cal swimming the ice-swollen Snake River to escape a posse. It was later picked up and passed along by journalists as fact.

25 University of Wyoming interview, 1957.

26 Ibid.

27 Burt, S. "The Most Unforgetable Character..." 1948, op.cit.

28 Burt, S. 1924. *The Diary of a Dude Wrangler.* Charles Scribner's Sons, p 305.

29 Clay Taylor, pers. comm. w/author, 2013.

30 Gillette, 1979, op. cit. see also the Flat Creek Ranch's history website.

31. Huyler, J. 2003. *And That's the Way it Was in Jackson Hole,* Jackson Hole Hist. Soc. & Museum, Jackson, WY. Playing with names was a common practice in those days. Changing one's name might mean there was something to hide, but on the other hand, for example, Cissy was known by multiple names too: Cissy Patterson, Eleanor Patterson, Eleanor Medill Gizycka, Countess Eleanor, the Countess, the Countess of Flat Creek, etc.

32 Healy, P.F. 1966. *Cissy: A Biography of Eleanor M. "Cissy" Patterson.* Doubleday, NY.

33 Gillette, 1979, op.cit. It's interesting that Gillette, who was a local historian, would not catch the inconsistencies in the

dates of Cal's alleged "horse thieving ring," especially in respect to the 1920s date when Cal actually took up squatters rights on the Flat Creek Ranch. Gillette claimed, "All the rustlers were caught except Cal," but there is no record of anyone ever being apprehended for rustling around that time. This was also a story Rose Crabtree told about Cal, too, before Gillette picked it up. It's repeated in Adare, S. 1997, *Jackson Hole Uncovered*; the Flat Creek Ranch website; and by others.

34   Martin, R.G. 1979, Cissy, op.cit; also in Gillette, 1979; and the Flat Creek Ranch website, et al.

35   Platts, D. 1992. "The Cunningham Ranch Incident". Wilson, WY; also in Betts, R.B. *Along the Ramparts...* 1978; and, Anderson, M. *"Last of Jackson's Hole Horse Thieves."* The *Westerner* (Aug. 24, 1929). Anderson states, as this author also concludes after much research, that the last days of any organized or significant horse rustling in and around Jackson Hole occurred in the early 1890s. The 1892 Cunningham Cabin incident appears to have marked the end of it.

36   The Flat Creek Ranch website, Rose Crabtree, et.al. claim Cal belonged to these "gangs" and that they were a part of organized rustling in the Jackson Hole area in the early twentieth century. In actuality, as explained in Chapter 7, these cliques existed for other purposes or reasons near the end of the nineteenth century and were pretty much before Cal's time in Jackson Hole. Yet they are frequently recalled in myths about Cal rustling horses, e.g.: "Cal belonged to a gang of six [rustlers] identified by the red bandanas they wore, all the outlaws were captured except Cal."

Chapter 7

1   Moss, W. "Friend or Faux." *Teton Valley Top-to-Bottom Magazine.* (Summer 2003): pp 62-67. See also C. Wilson. *The Return of the White Indian,* 1985.

2 Ibid.

3 Dyke, J. 1962 *The West Texas Kid, 1881-1910: Recollections of Thomas E. Crawford*. Univ. Oklahoma Press, Norman.

4 Platts, D. 1991. *John Cherry: His Lies, Life and Legend*. Bearprint Press, Jackson, WY.

5 Ibid.

6 Brandegee, T.S. *Annual Report, U.S. Geol. Survey, 1878-98 of the Teton Forest Reserve*. General Land Office, Washington, D.C. See also: Layser, 2012, op.cit.

7 University of Wyoming interview, 1957.

8 Martin, R.G. 1979, Cissy: *The Extraordinary Life of Eleanor Medill Patterson*. Simon and Schuster. NY. See also Flat Creek Ranch history website.

9 Bonney, O.H. and L.G. Bonney, 1972 (Trip 12), op.cit, pp 122-23.

10 Calkins, F. *Jackson Hole*. Alfred A. Knopf, NY, 1973.

11 Ibid.

12 Ibid. One wonders where John Carnes was that winter since sources say he and Holland settled in Jackson Hole in 1884.

13 Platts, D. 2003. *Robert Miller: An Enigma*. Wilson, WY (see letter quoting Teton Jackson re. supplies).

14 An old photograph (c 1908-1909) of Cal as a young man posing with four other men (one is John Holland) is sometimes pointed to as part of the "gang of six." However, Felicia Gizycka in a *Teton Magazine* article identifies the photograph as being an antelope hunting party. No doubt it's the same early antelope hunting trip Struthers Burt writes about in *Diary of a Dude Wrangler* and Cal also talks about in his 1957 interview. The people in the photograph have nothing to do with the gang of six.

15 Driggs, B.W. 1970 ed. *History of Teton Valley, Idaho*.

16 Wister, O. 1902. *The Virginian*. Macmillan Co.

17 Platts, D. 1992. The *Cunningham Ranch Incident.* Self published. Wilson, WY.

18 USF&WS Natl. Elk Refuge, *"Timeline of the Miller Ranch,"* National Elk Refuge history pamphlet, Jackson, WY.

19 Platts, *Cunningham Ranch Incident*; Betts, *Along the Ramparts...*; Mumey, N. *The Teton Mountains: Their History and Tradition*; et al.

21 Wilson, C. *The Return of the White Indian,* 1985, op.cit.

22 In Platts, D. *The Cunningham Ranch Incident,* 1992, op.cit.

23 Bonney, O.H. and L.G. Bonney.1972. *Bonney's Guide: Grand Teton National Park and Jackson's Hole.* Houston, TX, (Trip 12): pp 122-23.

24 Stone interview, 1958.

25 See: D. Platts, *The Cunningham Ranch Incident* and *Robert Miller, An Enigma*; R. Betts, *Along the Ramparts of the Tetons*; F. Caulkins, *Jackson Hole*; B.W. Driggs, *History of Teton Valley*; C Wilson, *Return of the White Indian*; M. Anderson, *"Last of Jackson's Hole Horse Thieves."* These authors, and this author as well, searched primary sources for any organized rustling incidents in and around Jackson Hole after the early 1890s, there are none recorded. *Helena's Daily Independent* reported on and sensationalized the rustling events that occurred in the early 1890s. Montana rancher John Chapman was one of the hired regulators. He had a personal axe to grind, after having lost a large number of valuable horses and tracking them to Jackson Hole. The regulators with the unknowing local posse at Cunningham Cabin; George Parker's (aka Butch Cassidy) capture at Star Valley; Sylvester Summers capture at Wolverine, Idaho; and Jack Bliss and Kid Collier's demise at the hands of range detectives all occurred around this time as a result of a Montana stock grower's organized dragnet.

Chapter 8

1   University of Wyoming interview, 1957. Bonney transcription.

2   National Archives, GLO Special Agent Brighton's 1907 letter.

3   University of Wyoming interview proceedings described to the author by retired history professor, G.M. Gressley, 2007. The Dwight Stone interview was conducted at Driggs a year later.

4   University of Wyoming, 1957 interview. Bonney transcription. YNP surveys in the Lamar Valley may have been going on at that time and were mentioned by historian Lee H. Whittlesey in a 2007 phone conversation.

5   Ibid.

6   Ibid. For more on Charles Neal see: Fern Nelson, 1994, *This Was Jackson's Hole*, pp258-267.

7   Ibid.

8   Ibid.

9   Anderson, A.A. 1933. *Experiences and Impressions: The Autobiography of Colonel A.A. Anderson*. McMillan Company, NY, pp 89-116. The survey of Forest Reserve corresponds with the date when Cal was hired by Anderson. The survey required a good number of wranglers and large numbers of pack stock.

10 University of Wyoming interview, 1957. John Holland is generally said to have sold his Nowlin Creek homestead and left Jackson before 1900. He already had a Desert Entry Patent on 160 acres on Horseshoe Creek in Teton Valley in 1889 and followed up with an adjacent 160-acre homestead purchase there in 1900 (GLO records). See Layser 2012, op.cit. for Holland's activities and dates.

11 Ibid.

12 Ibid.

13 Daugherty, J. 1999. *A Place Called Jackson Hole*, op.cit. p 295.

14 University of Wyoming 1957 interview.

15 Ibid. A.A. Anderson also describes this incident and gives the name of the sheepman as Jacob.

16 Anderson, A.A. op.cit.

17 Ibid.

18 University of Wyoming 1957 interview; also, A.A. Anderson, op.cit.

19 National archives and Teton Valley, Idaho, courthouse records, Sworn Declaration of Intention. Although Cal's naturalization certification gives England as his birthplace or place of origin, evidence shows he was born in Sweden and immigrated to the United States through England (see Chapter 1). There have been numerous instances giving his birthplace as England, or even Norway (e.g., see the Flat Creek Ranch website). Cal purposely misrepresented his birthplace because of the bad feelings he harbored towards his family.

20 National Archives. Enoch Carrington's 1905 USDA Forest Service Certificate of Appointment as Assistant Forest Ranger.

21 Layser, E.F. "Lone Rangers." *Teton Valley Top to Bottom.* (Winter, 2001): pp 52-57.

22 Marsh, S. "Abandoned Trails" in *Stories of the Wild*, White Willow Publishing, Jackson, WY (2001): pp 237-243.

23 Martin, R.G. 1979, op.cit.

24 Layser, 2012, op.cit.; also, Daugherty, J. 1999, op.cit. Anderson, A.A. 1933, op.cit.

26 National Archives. Patent approval letter by authority of Theodore Roosevelt, 1907.

27 Cissy's biographers R.G. Martin and A.A. Hoge both record Cal was in San Francisco during the 1906 earthquake.

28 National Archives, GLO July 22, 1907 report by Inspector Brighton, Salt Lake City, Utah.

29 University of Wyoming 1957 interview. It's likely Cal may

have been stationed on the Plumas National Forest at Quincy. He named his pack mare Quincy. The horse that as he told Felicia, "came along in the dark of the night."

30 Martin, R.G. 1979, op.cit., p157.

31 Approval of Cal's Bates Desert Entry and his return from California shortly afterward coincide in respect to the date.

Chapter 9

1   Smith, B., E. Cole and D. Dobkin. 2004. *Imperfect Pasture.* USF&WS and Teton Nat. History Assoc., Moose, WY.

2   Thompson, E.M.S. and W.L.Thompson.1982. *Beaver Dick: The Honor and the Heartbreak*, op.cit.

3   Calkins, F. *Jackson Hole*, op.cit.

4   University of Wyoming 1957 interview.

5   Daugherty, J. A 1999, op.cit.

6   Mumey, N. *The Teton Mountains: Their History and Tradition,* 1948, op.cit.

7   *Jackson Hole Courier* newspaper.

8   Daugherty, op.cit.

9   Ibid, p139; also Layser, op.cit.

10 Layser, 2012, op.cit.

11 Layser, op.cit

12 National Archives, *Affidavit of Witness*, June 5, 1901.

13 Layser, op.cit and University of Wyoming 1957 interview.

14 University of Wyoming 1957 interview.

15 Ibid. Holland was fifty-one years old, much younger than Cal stated.

16 John Carnes Obituary, July 16, 1931. Owen Collection (Lorraine Bonney files, Kelly, Wy).

17 Bonney and Bonney, op. cit., pp122-23; Grazing association records cited in Daugherty,1999.

18 Ibid.

19 Layser, 2012, op.cit.

20 Petersen, C. Sr. Pers. comm. w/author, 2005; see also:*Teton Views*, Vol. 2 (30), Oct. 27, 1998; and "Last of the Old West" interview series taped by Jo Ann Byrd, JHHSM, Jackson. Jay Lawson in *Men to Match our Mountains*, (p100) says Billy Bierer and Albert Nelson built a Flat Creek cabin in 1894 when they were trapping the Jackson Hole country. This is consistent with Charlie Peterson also attributing the cabin to Bierer. This cabin was near the mouth of Flat Creek Canyon and would not have been the same cabin Cal used up in the canyon.

21 A number of authors — Martin, Healy, Gillette, Felicia, and others — have passed along the myth that Flat Creek Canyon was used by Cal to hide stolen horses. Presumably, Cal and his outlaw associates lived in the cabin.

22 Gizycka, F. "Forgiveness at Flat Creek." *Teton Magazine* (Vol. 20, 1988): p 27. The pack mare Quincy was probably named after the town or area where Cal was stationed when he worked for the Forest Service (Plumas National Forest) in California. While it's a good story, it's unlikely Quincy was actually stolen by Cal.

23 Stone interview, 1958 and also University of Wyoming 1957 interview.

24 Thompson, G. Pers. comm. w/author, 2004.

25 Furniss, O. Pers. comm. w/author, 2004.

26 Daugherty, 1999, p 192.

27 The closest law officer was at Evanston, 250-miles on horseback, which encouraged Jackson Holers to take care of any problems themselves. The local brand of justice was called Mountain Law.

28 Platts, D. *John Cherry: His Lies, Life and Legend.* Bearprint Press, Jackson, 1991.

Chapter 10

1 University of Wyoming 1957 interview.

2 Ibid.

3 Ibid.

4 Ibid.

5 Ibid.

6 Bonney and Bonney 1972, op.cit.

7 Berger, G. Pers. Comm., 2013; also Gillette, W. "The Memorable Character..." 1979.

8 James H. Berger History, op.cit.

9 University of Wyoming interview, 1957.

10 Dwight Stone interview, 1958.

11 McBride, M. 1896. "My Diary". Mimeo. Jackson Hole Historical Society, Jackson, WY.

12 Nelson, F. 1994, op.cit.

13 University of Wyoming interview, 1957.

14 Moss, W.F. "Those Were The Days My Friend." *Teton Valley Top to Bottom.* (Winter 2005): pp 56-61.

15 Baily, E.H. 1916. "The Dairy of a Dudine," unpublished MS, Jackson Hole Historical Society. 28p.

16 University of Wyoming interview, 1957.

17 Buchan, D. "Ties to the Past." *Teton Valley Magazine.* (Winter 2007-08): pp 74-83.

18 Hansen, C. Pers. Comm. 2008.

19 Burt, S. "The Most Unforgetable Character I've Met." *Reader's Digest.* (Oct 1948): 83-86.

20 Burt, S. 1924. *The Diary of a Dude Wrangler*, op.cit.

Chapter 11

1 Daugherty, J. 1999, *A Place Called Jackson Hole...* p 225.

2   University of Wyoming 1957 interview.

3   Burt, S. 1948, The Most Unforgettable Character... ; also, Gizycka, F. "Forgiveness at Flat Creek." *Teton Magazine*, Vol. 20 (1988): pp 8-9, 26-32.

4   Cal is frequently credited with having made this statement, implying that he had retired from being an outlaw, but in fact, he had already been guiding dudes with John Holland for a number of years before he went to work for Burt and had been working for Burt as ranch foremen.

5   University of Wyoming 1957 interview.

6   Burt, N. 1983, *Jackson Hole Journal*. University of Oklahoma Press, Norman.

7   Burt, S. 1948, op.cit.

8   Burt, N. 1983, op.cit. In *Glass Houses* (p262), Cissy states you could hear everyone snore through the hotel's "flimsy room partitions." *Jackson Hole Courier* articles on Fourth of July rodeo entries were searched around this time period, but none listed Carrington as a rider, perhaps indicating by that time he had quit rodeo and bronc riding.

9   Hank Crabtree interview, from Ralph Martin's research assistant notes, Ralph Marten Collection, Boston University, Box 213, F4 (Courtesy Amanda Smith).

Chapter 12

1   This chapter is based on Edith H. Baily's 1916 unpublished manuscript entitled, "The Diary of a Dudine", Ardmore, Pennsylvania, 28 pages plus photographs. The manuscript is archived at the Jackson Hole Historical Society and Museum. The quotes are taken from her writings. I have added interpretations and information to assist and improve the reading. Shooting distance estimates, night travel, the number of sighted and elk wounded, and other such descriptions, are those as told by Baily. Further evidence of Cal's propensity to

tell dudes made-up stories about Flat Creek Canyon, etc. is what Edith recorded he told them: "He had homesteaded and grown up there as a child, but got too lonely and had to leave." Note the names of horses, too –Cal's pack mare, Quincy; use of Menor's Ferry; staying at the Crabtree Hotel; and a stagecoach to Victor from Jackson. Baily's story supportively ties a lot of things together.

2 Daugherty, 1999, op.cit. and also other local histories of Kelly.

3 Back, J. 1959. *Horses, Hitches and Rocky Trails*, The Swallow Press, Chicago, 117p. An authentic reference work on guiding outfitting and horsepacking.

Chapter 13

1 Gizycka, F. 1977. "Cissy Patterson: The Countess of Flat Creek." *Teton Magazine* (Vol.10): pp 37-48.

2 Smith, A. 2011. *Newspaper Titan: The Infamous Life and Monumental Times of Cissy Patterson.* Alfred A. Knopf, NY. 696 p.

3 Gizycka, F. 1977, "Cissy Patterson: The Countess..." op.cit. For additional information on early day Victor, see also: Holmes, B. M. 1989. "Victor, Idaho, 1889-1989." Bound mimeo, Valley of the Tetons Library, Victor, ID.

4 Burt, N. 1983, *Jackson Hole Journal.* op.cit.

5 Gizycka, F. 1977, "Cissy... ", op.cit.

6 Ibid. p 40

7 Martin, R.G. 1979. "Letters to Rose," op.cit.; see also *Teton Magazine* (Vol. 12, 1979): pp 8-11, 27-28, 44-62.

8 Gizycka, F. 1977, op.cit.

9 Ibid.

10 Gizycka, F. 1988. "Forgiveness at Flat Creek." *Teton Magazine* (Vol. 20): p 27.

11 A frequently asked question about Cal and Cissy's relationship

is "was it ever consummated?" The only doubt comes from Felicia's and her daughter Ellen's spin in later years. For whatever reason, Felicia and Ellen strongly denied that there was ever anything physical between Cal and Cissy: "They loved each other, but not in that way...Cal was too dirty and smelly." That was certainly not true in their early years together. Both Cal and Cissy were very physical and attractive people. Cissy possessed a sophisticated or liberal attitude about men and relationships, and according to her biographers, was involved in numerous love affairs. Cal was considered a ladies' man. Cissy has been described by other writers as "the wildest woman in Jackson Hole" and Cal as a "wild man." They were one of the most celebrated "dude affairs" in Jackson Hole's history, which another writer called a "passionate love affair." Cissy sought out romantic adventure and always had many suitors. Until their falling out and Cissy's marriage to Elmer Schlesinger in 1924, for about eight years, while on hunting trips, Cal and Cissy slept together in tents. Charlie Peterson, in an interview, said, "Cal drug his saddle in her tent and stayed." Cal and Cissy attended parties together, built the Flat Creek Ranch together, traveled abroad together, attended events such as Josephine Baker performing in the nude in Paris. In *Glass Houses*, Cissy writes about the smell of "strong, healthy and unwashed men," indicating she did not find it offensive, but rather an exciting part of her Western experience. Based on all that, readers should be able to pretty much make up their own minds on the question whether the relationship was ever "consummated." The real question is: Why did Felicia and Ellen feel it necessary to persuade people into believing otherwise?

12 Martin, R.G. 1979, *Cissy*...op.cit. p 159.

13 Burt, N. 1983. *Jackson Hole Journal*, op.cit.

14 The "small secret valley..." quote is from Cissy's 1926 *Glass Houses*; "without psychiatry..." is quoted from Gizycka, F.

"*Cissy...*" 1977, op.cit.

15 Burt, S. 1948, op.cit.

16 Burt, S. 1983, op.cit.

Chapter 14

1 Martin, R.G. 1979 *Cissy...* op.cit. Cal's "reluctance to sell" is a frequently repeated story in the literature. It is a myth created by Cal and Cissy themselves. As soon as Cal actually did gain title, he sold. Cissy's opinion of the Flat Creek Ranch's beauty never changed over the years. In a 1944 letter to he brother, Joseph Patterson, Cissy wrote, "Never in my life anywhere have I seen anything lovelier than this place." (*Patterson Family Papers*, Lake Forest College, IL).

2 Martin, R.G. 1979 *Cissy...* op.cit.

3 James H. Berger History, op.cit.

4 Flat Creek Ranch website describes Cal's improvements based on statements he submitted to the GLO (see National Archive records).

5 The Jackson Hole Historical Society and Museum has Cal's artistically made branding iron, Object No. 1958.700.1. No brand is known to have ever been registered for the Flat Creek Ranch or for Cissy.

6 Stone interview, 1958. Twenty-five head of livestock were reported to the GLO (National Archive records). Cal stated fifty head in the interview.

7 Ryan, J. Pers. comm. w/author, 2004.

8 Gillette, B. 1992. *Homesteading with the Elk.* Jackson Printing, Jackson, WY.

9 Petersen, C. Sr. Pers. comm. w/author, 2004.

10 Layser, 2012, op.cit.

11 Gillette, B. 1992, *Homesteading...* op.cit.

12 December 27, 1922 Letter from Cal Carrington to Eleanor

Gizycka, *Patterson Family Papers*, Late Forest College, Il. (Courtesy of Amanda Smith).

13   Thompson, G. Pers. comm. w/author, 2004.

14   Ibid.

Chapter 15

1   Martin, R.G. 1979, op.cit. The remark is attributed to Joe Patterson (*Patterson Papers*, Lake Forest, IL). The website www.culturaltourism.org/dch pictures and describes the mansion.

2   Martin, R.G. 1979, op.cit. This issue in Cissy and Cal's relationship appears to have been overstated by Cissy's biographers and Felicia. Photographs of Cal in Washington, D.C. and the Dower House in Maryland show him formally dressed in suits. In his final years in Driggs, though, Cal tended to be more unkempt and disheveled in appearance, thus allowing Cissy's biographer's and Felicia some credibility on this issue, perhaps. To put it in proper perspective, in *Glass Houses* (p255), Cissy writes about the smell of "strong, healthy and unwashed men" and is clearly not offended by those odors.

3   Martin, R.G. 1979, op.cit. All of Cissy's biographers detail this European trip with Cal.

4   Ibid.

5   Ibid.

6   Ibid.

7   Ibid.

Chapter 16

1   Martin, R.G., 1979, op.cit.

2   Flat Creek Ranch website. Primary source was a National Archive GLO document. (The ranch's website is updated

occasionally, adding new information or different interpretation.)

3   Requirements of the National Forest Homestead Act 1906 and 1912 Amendment.

4   Flat Creek website information obtained from National Archives GLO document.

5   Martin, R.G. 1979. "Letters to Rose." *Teton Magazine* (Vol. 12): pp 8-11, 27-28, 44-62.

6   National Archives GLO material posted at the Flat Creek Ranch history website.

7   Ibid. See BLM-GLO website.

8   Ibid.

9   Teton County, Wyoming, Courthouse Deed and Patent Records bill of sale lists the amount and date. But the story passed on by locals and others has been of Cal's great reluctance and hand wringing to sell, with pressure having to be put on him by Cissy, and with Cissy finally sending George Ross to Bates to retrieve the deed from Cal's trunk. See: F. Gizycka "Forgiveness at Flat Creek," 1988, where this myth originates.

10 Teton County, Wyoming, Courthouse Deed and Patent records.

11 Gizycka, F. 1988. "Forgiveness at Flat Creek." *Teton Magazine.* (Vol. 20): p27; Gillete, 1979, "The Memorable...", op.cit.

12 Martin, 1979, Cissy...1979, op cit.

13 Gillette, B. 1992, *Homesteading with the Elk.* Jackson Printing, op.cit.

14 Gizycka, F. 1988, "Forgiveness...", op.cit.

15 Furniss, O. 2004 and Monte Piquet 2008, Pers. comm. w/ author.

Chapter 17

1   Burt, S. 1948, "The Most Unforgettable Character I've Met."

Reader's Digest (Oct): pp 83-86.

2   Martin, R.G. 1979 "Letters to Rose." *Teton Magazine.* (Vol. 12): pp 8-11, 27-28, 44-62.

3   Felicia donated the angora chaps to the Jackson Hole Museum.

4   Martin, R.G. 1979, *Cissy*...op.cit.

5   Gizycka, F. 1991. "Diary on the Salmon River." *Teton Magazine.* (Vol. 23 & 24): pp11-12, 34-40. Perhaps unknown to Felicia, Cissy also published her river trip diary in *Field and Stream* in May/June 1923. The pen name "Ben" in "Cissy's Salmon River Diary" is also used for Cal in her novel *Glass Houses*.

6   The history of boating on the Salmon River maybe found at a number of websites, e.g.: www.idahoptv.org/outdoors/shows/riverofnoreturn/scows/cfm and www.findagrave.com (for Guleke's life history).

7   Gizycka, E. 1923, "Diary on the Salmon River." *Field and Stream*, June 1923.

8   Ibid.

9   Burt, S. 1948, "The Most Unforgettable..." op.cit.

10   Gizycka, E. 1923,"Diary on the Salmon..." op.cit. This is also mentioned in *Glass Houses* by Cissy.

11   Ibid. Cissy confirms the taking of mountain goats in *Glass Houses*, p70. She also mentions moose and bighorn sheep from Canada and deer and elk from Wyoming, all of which she had trophy heads mounted and hung on her wall at the Dupont Circle mansion.

12   Ibid.

13   Gizycka, E. (c1923), "Two Bear," *Field and Stream*, pp596-598.

14   Ibid.

15   Petersen, C. Sr. Pers. comm. w/author, 2004. Interview in which he showed the author the articles by O'Conner in

Outdoor Life magazine.

16 Ibid.

17 Rena Croft, Pers. Comm. w/author, 2012.

18 Gizycka, E. "Two Bear," op.cit.

19 Ibid.

20 Ibid.

21 Amy Brazil, Pers. Comm. w/author, 2013.

22 Gizycka, E. 1925. "Sheep Hunting in Alberta," *Field and Stream* (July); pp14–15, 57.

23 Martin, R.G. *Cissy...* 1979, op.cit. Martin confuses mountain goat and bighorn sheep as one and thre same. Burt, S. 1948 "The Most Unforgetable..." op.cit. re. "loosening up on reins."

24 Gizycka, E. 1925, "Sheep..." op.cit.

25 Martin, R.G. 1979, *Cissy...*op.cit. Also in *Glass Houses*, op.cit. pp 190-195.

26 Hoge, A.A. 1966. *Cissy Patterson: The Life of Eleanor Medill Patterson, Publisher and Editor of the Washington Times-Herald,* Random House, p 63.

27 Martin, R.G. 1979 "Letters to Rose...", op.cit.

28 Martin, R.G. 1979, Cissy... op.cit.

Chapter 18

1 Gizycka, F. 1965. "Jackson Hole, 1916-65: A Reminiscence." *Vogue,* (April 1): p 203.

2 Martin, R.G. 1979, op.cit.

3 University of Wyoming interview, 1957.

4 Martin, R.G. 1979, Cissy... op.cit.

5 Gizycka, F. 1988,"Forgiveness at Flat Creek." *Teton Magazine* (Vol.20): p 29.

6 Ibid.

7   Gizycka, F. 1965, "Jackson Hole, 1916-65..." op.cit; and, Gizycka, F. 1977, "Cissy Patterson: The Countess of Flat Creek." *Teton Magazine* (Vol.10): p 43 and 206

8   *Jackie Martin Collection,* Syracuse University, NY.

9   Gizycka, F. 1977, op.cit.

10 Gizycka, F. 1977, Ibid, pp17-18 and Gizycka, F. 1988 "Forgiveness at Flat Creek." *Teton Magazine* (Vol.20):p 29.

11 Rudd, R. Pers. comm. w/author, 2004 (Rudd was a personal acquaintance of Felicia).

12 Martin, R.G. 1979, *Cissy...*, op.cit.

13 Daugherty, J. 1999, op.cit.

14 In 2005, Chief of Assessor Records, Brian Salmon, searched the San Diego County records from 1914-30 and found no record of Cal's ownership or purchase for his Encinitas property. There was a fire that destroyed some records from that time period. However, a 1961 distribution order of the real property inherited by Mary Ake was found that described the properties. Either Cal purchased the properties after 1930 or he never recorded the purchase or deed. Knowing how Cal did business, it's likely the property transfers were never recorded. Goldie Chisman may have played a role in assisting Cal in the purchase of his California properties (see letters in the *Felicia Gizycka Collection*).

15 Martin, R.G. 1979 Cissy...p 215; also "Letters to Rose", op.cit.

16 Gizycka, F. 1965, "Jackson Hole, 1916-65..." p206. See: Dannatt, A. 1999, "Obituary: Countess Felicia Gizycka." *The Independent*, London, for details on Felicia's life.

17 Stone, D. 1958 interview, op.cit.

18 *Jackson Hole Guide*, "Cal Carrington Obituary," December 24, 1959. Jay Lawson, *Men to Match our Mountains* (p53), points out that it took something exceptional to stand out as a hunter in the early twentieth century, since nearly everyone in rural Wyoming hunted for at least a portion of their subsistence.

19 Stone, D. 1958 interview.

Chapter 19

1   Martin, R.G. 1979,"Letters to Rose," *Teton Magazine* (Vol. 12), pp: 8-11, 27-28, 44-62. Elmer Schlesinger was happy to have him gone because Cal was reportedly obnoxiously rude to Elmer.

2   Ibid.

3   Burt, S. 1948 "The Most Unforgettable..." op.cit. Also letter Cal wrote to Goldie Chisman about his Africa hunting and said the Natives had called him "never-miss." He also described his excitement about hunting in Africa and shooting hippos from boats at close range (letter in the *Felicia Gizycka Colletion*, San Diego).

4   Gillette, W. 1979 "The Memorable Character...op.cit Gillette provides additional narrative regarding Cal's Africa hunt about the natives gorging themselves on elephant meat after a kill, etc. (taken from the 1958 Stone interview), which has not been included here.

5   Stone, 1958 interview.

6   A letter by Cal from Jackson (in the *Felicia Gizycka Collection*) to Goldie is dated January 7, 1928; in it he writes about retrieving his African trophies at the Victor train station. Previously published accounts say Cal was in Africa for two years, but it could have actually only been a little over a year based on his letter's date and depending on when he actually departed in 1927.

7   *Felicia Gizycka Collection.*

8   Gressley, G. Pers. Comm. w/author, 2007. Also others interviewed in Teton valley who told of listening to Cal's African tales and a January 7, 1928, letter to Goldie Chisman in the *Felicia Gizycka Collection.*

9   U.S. Census 1930. Ancestry.com.

Chapter 20

1   Burt, S. 1924, "The Diary..." op.cit.

2   Ibid.

3   Ibid.

4   Ibid.

5   Ibid.

6   The *Felicia Gizycka Collection*, San Diego.

7   Gizycka, F. 1977 "Cissy Patterson: The Countess of Flat Creek." *Teton Magazine* (Vol. 10): p 44.

8   Gizycka, E. 1926, *Glass Houses*: p 146.

Chapter 21

1   Daugherty, 1999, op.cit.

2   Peterson, C. Sr. transcribed interview on file at Jackson Hole Historical Society.

3   Wilkinson, T. 2005. "Gov Made Poor Pick for G&F Commission." Jackson Hole News and Guide, (March 9): p 6A

4   "The Longest Shot." *Mountain Home Magazine* (Oct.) 2007.

5   Chambers, R. Pers. comm. w/author, 2004.

6   Martin, R.G. 1979 Cissy...op.cit.

7   Ibid.   .

8   Ryan, J. Pers. comm. w/author, 2004.

9   Furniss, O. Pers. comm. w/author, 2004.

10 Hansen, C. Pers. comm. w/author, 2004.

11 *Felicia Gizycka Collection*: April 25, 1931 letter to Goldie.

12 Rudd, R. Pers. comm. w/author, 2004.

13 Martin, R.G. 1979, *Cissy*... op.cit. I have presented Cal checking on the ranch as told by Martin. It's a good tale. But Martin's friction between Forney and Cal is contradicted by other accounts, which say Cal helped Rose Crabtree hire

Forney. In a July 1931 letter to Goldie, Cal himself gives his own version about going up to the ranch: "The Countes had a lot of foundations put under her cabans, and I went up thair and got the men all sore at me...but believe they got through quicker. the Watchman [however,] said he was a going quit..." (*Felicia Gizycka Collection*). The watchman Cal refers to was likely Forney Cole.

14   Furniss, O. Pers. comm.w/author, 2004. Cal was referred to sympathetically as "all alone" by several of the LDS people interviewed in Teton Valley.

15   Thompson, G. Pers. comm. w/author, 2004.

16   Piquet, M. Pers. comm. w/ author, 2008.

17   Breckenridge, D. Pers. comm. w/author, 2004.

18   Furniss, O. Pers. comm. w/author, 2004.

19   Furniss, O., F. Buxton, and M. Piquet, Pers. comm. w/author, 2004 and 2008. Cal apparently liked to grandstand by killing flies with a swatter made from a rhino or elephant's tail while telling his stories about Africa to visiting children.

20   Furniss, O. Pers. comm. w/author, 2004.

21   Ibid.

22   April 27, 1941, Carrington letter to Goldie, *Felicia Gizycka Collection.*

23   January 18, 1938, letter to Goldie, *Felicia Gizycka Collection.*

24   Sarasota newspapers contain several articles regarding Cissy Patterson's purchase of the Siesta Key estates and her residency: *Sarasota Herald Tribune*, January 8, 1946; *Sarasota Herald Tribune*, October 7, 2010; *Sarasota Journal*, May 1, 1975. What was her property is now part of the Gulf and Bay Club.

25   Martin, R.G. 1979, Cissy... op.cit. p420.

26   Martin, op.cit. p421.

27   Ibid, p422. How often Cal made winter visits to Sarasota isn't

known, but Martin's statements implies it was more than just once. After Cissy's passing, Cal regularly began retreating to his Encinitas property in winter.

Chapter 22

1   Furniss, O. Pers. comm. w/author, 2004.

2   Ibid.

3   Both W. Gillette, "The Memorable Character..." 1979, and S. Burt, "The Most Unforgettable Character..." 1948 record the incident in detail. Gillette interviewed Teton Valley residents who were involved. Burt's version was told to him by Cal. The story of the accident is condensed here.

4   Burt, S. 1948, op.cit. p84.

5   On file at Teton Idaho County Courthouse, *Deed and Patent Records.* Cal recorded a warranty deed for his Bates property sale for one-dollar to Eleanor Patterson on October 31, 1941.

6   Burt, S. 1924, *The Diary...*op.cit.

Chapter 23

1   Smith, A. 2011, *Newspaper Titan...* op.cit.

2   Betts, R.B. 1978, *Along the Ramparts of the Tetons,* Colorado Assoc. Univ. Press, Boulder, CO.

3   Martin, *Cissy...* op.cit. According to biographer Amanda Smith, the circumstances of Cissy's death may not have been as straightforward as earlier biographers have described. Martin's story of Cissy's illness and her asking to have her Pullman prepared to take her to Jackson one last time may be just that–a good story. No doubt, though, she did at times wish or long to return to those earlier times. Cissy had already sold the Ranger, but rented or leased other Pullman cars.

4   Ibid

5   Walker, S. "Cissy is a Newspaper Lady," *The Saturday Evening Post*, May 6, 1939, pp22-23, 55, 62. The list of lovers quotation is from journalist Richard Norton Smith.

6   Martin, "Letters to Rose." *Teton Magazine...* op.cit. Martin does not say which President Rose met, but most likely it was Taft, since he was a friend of the Patterson family.

7   Ibid, also: Gizycka, F. 1968, "Reminiscence ...", op.cit. p208.. Cal apparently showed Felicia one of Cissy's letters at one point in which the phrase "his cabin" was used ("The Countess of Flat Creek. *Teton Magazine*, Vol. 10: p 45.) Such a letter, however, as far as the author knows, does not appear to be in the San Diego *Felicia Gizycka Collection*.

Felicia's story about Cal's contentious claim for six acres and the cabin may be a projection of her own mood and legal involvements. She doesn't mention her own acrimonious contesting of Cissy's Will and the fact that the reason Cal was back East several times around then was because he was summoned for deposition or hearings. It isn't known for sure, the hearing records became "lost," but Cal's testimony may have been in regard to Cissy's mental condition.

In a September 16, 1951, letter to Goldie, Cal writes, "... they are having more trouble over Mrs. Patterson's estate. So I came to show up again [in Washington, D.C.], it is not very pleasant." (*Felicia Gizycka Collection*). In short, if Cal did strongly express that six acres and the cabin were his to Felicia, it may well have been within the context of her ongoing contesting of Cissy's will, too. And his travel East, "to ask Felicia for assistance in the matter," as she describes, in reality, may not have been solely for that reason, but rather because he was summoned to appear, perhaps, on her behalf.

8   May 1948 letter to Goldie, *Felicia Gizycka Collection*.

9   Teton County, Idaho, Deed and Patent Records, op.cit.

10   Smith, A. op.cit. and Martin, R.G. *Cissy*...op. cit.

11 Gizycka, F. *Jackson Hole*, 1916-65... (1965): 206.

12 Teton County, Wyoming, Deed and Patent Records.

13 Gizycka, F. 1965. "Jackson Hole, 1916-65..." op.cit., p206.

14 Smith, A. op.cit.

15 Gizycka, F. 1977, "Cissy Patterson; The Countess of Flat Creek." *Teton Magazine* (Vol. 10): p 45.

16 Cal Carrington, 5 Aug 1952, letter to Josephine Albright.

    A June 17, 1959, letter by Cal to Felicia states, "I was up to the cabin on Flat Creek about a month ago and locked it up..." (*Felicia Gizycka Collection*). The circumstances that had Cal believe he had a claim to the cabin and six acres may have in actuality been more substantial than what we have earlier been led to believe, but it's impossible to prove at this point.

17 Buxton, F. Pers. comm w/author, 2004.

18 Unpublished draft of "Tales of the Big Hole Mountains" compiled by H. Forbush.

19 Furniss, E. Pers. comm. w/author, 2007.

20 Forbush, H. Pers. comm. w/author, 2004.

21 Piquet, L. Pers. comm. w/ author, 2013. The neighbor was the Dustins. Their original water right went back as far as Cal's.

22 Gizycka, F. 1965 "Jackson Hole, 1916-65...": p 206.

23 Stone, R. Pers. comm. w/author, 2004.

24 Burt, S. *Diary of a Dude Wrangler*...op. cit.

25 Gizycka, F. "Jackson Hole, 1916-65..." op.cit. p 206.

Chapter 24

1 Piquet, M. Pers. comm. w/author, 2008.

2 Gizycka, F. 1981, "John Wort and Cal Carrington." *Teton Magazine* (Vol. 14): p11.

3 Budge, B. Pers. comm. w/author, 2013.

4   Furniss, O. Pers. comm. w/author, 2004.

5   Piquet, M. Pers. comm. w/author, 2008.

6   Breckenridge, D. Pers. comm. w/author, 2004

Cal's Encinitas property holdings were verified through San Diego probate records on file at the country assessor's office. But the date of purchase, when Cal obtained the properties, could not be determined. When he actually began spending winters there isn't known for certain, probably already off and on in the late 1930s, and after Cissy's death through the 1950s. His correspondence with Goldie (*Felicia Gizycka Collection*) indicates a long association with the San Diego area. There is some indication Goldie worked in real estate. Cal had other friends there, too, which he refers to as: the Leanharts and a Mrs. Hillman.

In the winter of 1941, he wrote Goldie, "I don't think I will come to San Diego this winter." Instead he spent time in Mountain Home, Idaho. Mountain Home has a relatively mild winter climate and was also a place he may have escaped from the hard winters of Teton Valley or Jackson in his early years.

7   Piquet, M. Pers. comm. w/author, 2008.

8   September 28, 1952, letter to Goldie, *Felicia Gizycka Collection.*

9   Buxton, F. Pers. comm. w/author, 2004.

10   Berger, G. Pers. comm. w/author, 2013.

11   Thompson, G. Pers. comm. w/author, 2004, 2008, and 2013; also, Laren Piquet, 2013.

Chapter 25

1   Forbush, H. Pers. comm. w/author, 2004. Forbush believed that Cal lived without any modern conveniences. If he did, it was to save money. But Oren Furniss said Cal did have electricity and a spring for water. The fact Cal bought a radio

in 1941 indicates he did have electricity at that time. Felicia called his cabin a "hovel."

2   Breckenridge, D. Pers. comm. w/author, 2004.

3   Gizycka, F. 1965, "Jackson Hole, 1916-65..."op. cit. p 206.

4   Craighead, C. 2006. *Meet Me at the Wort: History, Legends, and Lore of the Wort Hotel*, Jackson Hole, Wyoming, 145p.

5   Ibid.

6   Gizycka, F. 1977, "Cissy Patterson, The Countess..." op.cit., p 45; and, "John Wort and Cal Carrington," 1956, op.cit.

7   Ibid.

8   Ibid, p 46. In spite of Remington's threat, Cal continued to go back and use the cabin as evidenced by correspondence to Goldie and Felicia in the *Felicia Gizycka Collection*. Cal was keyed up and angry at the confrontation with Remington.

9   Martin, R.G. *Cissy...*, op.cit.

10   Taylor, C. Pers. comm. w/author, 2013.

11   *Felicia Gizycka Collection.*

12   Albright, J. Pers. comm. w/author, 2004.

13   Gizycka, F., 1977, op.cit. p 46.

14   Ibid.

Chapter 26

1   Buxton, F. Pers. comm w/author, 2004.

2   Ibid.

3   Piquit, L. Pers. comm../with author, 2013.

4   Piquit, M. Pers. comm.. w/author, 2008.

5   Kreps, B. 2006, *Windows to the Past*, Jackson Hole Historical Society and Museum, Jackson, WY. p 68.

6   Martin, R.G. 1979, *Cissy...*op.cit.

7   August 5, 1952, letter to Josephine Albright from Carrington.

8   Gizycka, F. 1981 "John Wort and Cal Carrington," op.cit., pp 10-11, 56.

9   Gillette, "The Memorable Character..." op.cit. and 1958 interview, op.cit.

10 Craighead, C. 2006, *Meet Me at the Wort*, op.cit.

11 Shultz, M. Pers. comm. w/author, 2007.

12 Gizyka, F. 1965, "Jackson Hole, 1916-65..." op.cit.

13 Kent, D. Pers. comm. w/author 2013.

14 Gizyka, F. 1965, op.cit. p 210, The "...my grass is green and tall" statement meant Cal felt he had done well financially (and in life) and he distrusted the reason his siblings were showing up then, believing that it was to win him over in his last years to share his financial wealth. There is evidence Zeneiph Julin tried to make contact with Cal as early as 1946 (see February 19, 1960 Earle and Sadie Harris letter in the *Felicia Gizycka Collection*).

15 *Felicia Gizycka Collection.*

16 Various sources–Gillette, L. Piquet, and others.

17 Gizycka, F. 1965, op.cit.

18 Ibid.

19 Ibid.

20 E.C. Carrington 17 Dec 1959. *Last Will and Testament.* State of Wyoming, Cheyenne, Archives.

21 Bressley, G. Pers. Comm. w/author, 2007.

22 Gizycka, F. 1981, op.cit. p56 and 1965, op.cit. Also notes on file at JHHS&M. The primary source is a 12/10/1959 letter to Felicia, Earl Harris describes in detail Cal's battle to reclaim his health, including going to St. Anthony for electrical shock treatments and sweat baths, and his giving up his prescribed medications and special diet. Earl Harris said Cal "looked like hell" when he returned from those treatments. He checked into the Driggs hospital again some days afterwards. Harris wrote, "Cal is still anxious to be independent, so makes it a little difficult." Also important are Cal's November 12, 1959

letter to Goldie and Earl Harris December 10, 1959 letter to Felicia. Those letters are primary source materials for Cal's childhood (*Felicia Gizycka Collection*).

23 Sadie Harris at www.ancestry.com. Felicia also writes about the Harris's, too.

24 Gizycka, F., 1965, op.cit., p209.

25 Ibid. Also pers. comm. w/L. Piquet and others,

26 Felicia's handwritten notes on the back of an envelope in the *Felicia Gizycka Collection*. Cal had been closed mouth about his childhood and birth place even with Felicia up until near the very end. It had always been a taboo subject for him with anyone. He finally opened up to Earl Harris, who documented what Cal told him in letters to Felicia and also in conversation to her (*Felicia Gizycka Collection*). See also: University of Wyoming 1957 interview transcription where Cal says, "That subject is out..." The impression Cal was hiding something was right. It wasn't an outlaw past, it was his birth family. He refused to talk about them or make any recognition of them until the very end of his life. Cal's childhood, as described in Chapter One, exposes some of what today might be considered a dark side of a religious movement.

27 Carrington obituaries in local newspapers.

28 Gizycka, F. "Jackson Hole, 1916-65..." op.cit., p 209.

29 Gizycka, F. 1965 and 1981, op. cit.

Chapter 27

1 Gizycka, F.1965, "Jackson Hole, 1916-65: A Reminiscence." *Vogue*. p 210. Felicia may have removed more from the cabin than just $50 from Cal's boot that she mentions in this article, as evidenced by some of Cal's personal letters showing up fifty years later in the *Felicia Gizycka Collection*. Robert Rudd informed the author that Gillette told him about visiting the cabin and the trunk being in the attic right after Cal passed

away. A few days later it was gone. The *Gizycka Collection* is currently in the possession of Felicia's granddaughter, Felicia Cameron, in San Diego. Gene Downer was named executor of Felicia's published works with the intention that someday they would be transferred to the American Heritage Museum at Laramie. The author did not have opportunity to view the entire collection.

2. *Felicia Gizycka Collection.*

3. Rudd, R. Pers. Comm.w/author 2004. Gillette 1979, op.cit. Gillette may have left copies of his photographs with the JHHSM, but no one has been able to locate them. They had not been accessioned or made available as of this writing. They are printed in his publication.

4. Thompson, G. Pers. Comm. w/author 2008 and 2013.

5. Furniss, O. Pers. Comm. w/author 2004 and 2008. Oren remarked to the author, "Lots of people had thought they might find money hidden there."

6. Probate records, Teton County, Idaho, courthouse; San Diego courthouse probate records; Carrington's Last Will and Testament; Pers. Comm. w/H. Forbush, 2004; and Gizycka, F. 1965, op.cit.

7. Ibid.

8. Mary Ake obituary and Gizycka, F. "Jackson Hole, 1916-65" op.cit. The author contacted Montgomery families in the Seattle area in an attempt to locate any of Mary Ake's relatives. They would be under her sister's married name Montgomery, but had no success in finding any living relatives of Mary's brother-in-law Paul Montgomery.

9. *Felicia Gizycka Collection.* Letter was written on Hotel Mellen stationary (January 1941 letter to Goldie),where we might assume he was staying.

10. Cal Carrington 1959 *Last Will and Testament.*

Chapter 28

1   Martin, R.G. *Cissy...*, op.cit. This was most likely a reference to Mary Ake, I'm assuming Martin, in researching Patterson family papers, saw a letter written by Cissy that derided Cal for having had a baby with Mary Ake.

2   Smith, A. pers. comm. 2008, regarding a letter by Cissy in the J.M. *Patterson Papers* at Lake Forest, IL.

3   Penciled notes by Wendell Gillette and Felicia Magruder (Gizycka), Wort Hotel, 23 Oct 1987 in the *JHHSM Carrington file.*

4   Gizycka, F. 1965, "Jackson Hole, 1916-65, op. cit.

5   Downer, G. Pers. comm. w/author, 2004.

6   Gillette, B. 1992 Homesteading with the Elk, op.cit.

7   Albright, J. Pers. comm. w/author, 2004.

Chapter 29

1   Gizycka, F. 1965, "Jackson Hole, 1916-65..."op.cit. p 210.

2   Eleanor Patterson's June 3, 1944, letter to Joseph Patterson, *Patterson Papers*, Lake Forest College, IL.

Bibliography

Books

Adare, S. *Jackson Hole Uncovered*. Seaside Press (1997), pp108-09.

Alexander, T.G. *The Rise of Multiple-Use Management in the Intermountain West: A History of Region 4 of the Forest Service*. USDA Forest Service, FS 399, (1987), pp 15-53.

Anderson, A.A. *Experiences and Impressions–The Autobiography of Colonel A.A. Anderson*. MacMillan Company, NY, (1933), pp 89-116.

Back, J. Horses, *Hitches and Rocky Trails*. The Swallow Press, Chicago (1959), 117p.

Beal, M.D. *Intermountain Railroads: Standard and Narrow Guage*. Caxton Printers, Caldwell, ID (1962).

Betts, R.B. *Along the Ramparts of the Tetons*. Colorado Assoc. Univ. Press, Boulder, CO (1978).

Bonney, O.H. and L.G. Bonney. *Bonney's Guide: Grand Teton National Park and Jackson's Hole*. Houston, TX (Trip 12, 1972), pp122-23.

Brown, D. *Wondrous Times on the Frontier*. August House Publishing, Little Rock, AR (1991), pp 86-105.

Burt, N. *Jackson Hole Journal*. Univ. of Oklahoma Press (1983).

Burt, S. *The Diary of a Dude Wrangler*. Charles Scribner's Sons (1924).

Calkins, F. *Jackson Hole*. Alfred A. Knopf., NY (1973).

Craighead, C. *Meet Me at The Wort: History, Legends, and Lore of the Wort Hotel.* Paragon Press, Salt Lake City (2006), 145p.

Daugherty, J. *A Place Called Jackson Hole.* National Park Service, Moose (1999), 403p.

Driggs, B.W. *History of Teton Valley, Idaho.* Arnold Agency, Rexburg (1970 edition).

Dyke, J.C. *The West of the Texas Kid, 1881-1910: Recollections of Thomas E. Crawford.* Norman, University of Oklahoma Press (1962).

Forbush, H. *Tales of the Big Hole Mountains.* Idaho Falls, ID (2000), pp 115-16.

Gillette, B. *Homesteading With the Elk.* Jackson Printing, Jackson, WY (1992).

Gizycka, E. *Glass Houses.* Milton, Balch and Company, NY (1926).

Healy, P.F. *Cissy: A Biography of Elenor M. "Cissy" Patterson.* Doubleday, NY (1966).

Hoge, A.A. *Cissy: A Biography of Eleanor Medill Patterson Publisher and Editor of the Washington Times-Herald.* Random House (1966).

Holmes, B.M. *Victor, Idaho, 1889-1989.* Bound mimeo, Teton Valley Library (1989).

Huyler, J. *And That's the Way it Was in Jackson Hole.* Jackson Hole Historical Society and Museum, Jackson, WY (2003).

Kreps, B. *Windows to the Past: Early Settlers in Jackson Hole.* Jackson Hole Historical Society and Museum, Jackson, WY (2007), pp 61-80.

Layser, E.F. *I Always Did Like Horses and Women: Enoch Cal Carrington's Life Story.* Self-Published printed by BookSurge (2008).

Layser, E.F. *The Jackson Hole Settlement Chronicles.* Dancing Pine, Alta, WY (2012).

Lawson, J. *Men to Match our Mountains.* Pronghorn Press,

Greybull, WY (2007), pp 98-100.

Marsh, S. *"Abandoned Trails" in Stories of the Wild.* (Ed. by Susan Marsh), White Willow Publ., Jackson, WY, (2001): 237-243.

Martin, R.G. *Cissy: The Extraordinary Life of Eleanor Medill Patterson.* Simon and Shuster, NY (1979), 512p.

Moulton, C.V. *Legacy of the Tetons: Homesteading in Jackson Hole.* Tamarack Books, Boise (1994).

Mumey, N. *The Teton Mountains: Their History and Tradition.* Artcraft Press, Denver (1947).

Nelson, F. *This Was Jackson's Hole.* High Plains Press, Glendo, WY (1994), 380p.

Platts, D. *John Cherry: His Lies, Life and Legend.* Bearpaw Press, Jackson, WY (1991).

_____. *The Cunningham Ranch Incident.* Wilson, WY (1992).

_____. *Robert Miller: An Enigma.* Wilson, WY (2003).

_____. *Teton Jackson: Chief of Horse Thieves.* Pine Hill Press, SD (2007).

Smith, A. *Newspaper Titan: The Infamous Life and Monumental Times of Cissy Patterson.* Alfred A. Knopf, N Y (2011). 656p.

Smith, B, E. Cole, and D. Dobkin. *Imperfect Pasture.* USF&WS and Grand Teton Natural History Association, Jackson, WY (2004), 155p.

Thompson, E.M. S. and W. L. Thompson. *Beaver Dick: The Honor and the Heartbreak.* Jelm Mt. Press, Laramie (1982).

Wilson, C. A. *The Return of the White Indian Boy.* University of Utah Press, Salt Lake City (bound with *The White Indian Boy* by Elijah N. Wilson), (1985), pp 151-375.

Wister, O. *The Virginian.* MacMillian Company (1902).

Woods, F.E. *The Arrival of Nineteenth Century Mormon Emigrants in Salt Lake City.* Religious Study Center, Provo (2011).

Periodicals, Journals, Memoirs

Anderson, M. "Last of Jackson's Hole Horse Thieves." *The Westerner* (August 24, 1929). (The author Mark Anderson was Stanley Baker's cousin. Draft version given to the Bonneys by Rex Ross).

Bailey, E.H. "The Dairy of a Dudine." Unpublished MS (undated), Jackson Hole Historical Society, 28p + photographs.

Buchan, D. "Ties to the Past." *Teton Valley Magazine*, Driggs, ID, (Winter 2007-08): 74-83.

Burt, S. "The Most Unforgettable Character I've Met." *Reader's Digest* (Oct 1948): 83-86.

Cheny, L. "The Countess of Flat Creek." *Annals of Wyoming History* (Fall 1983): 28-32.

Draper, R. "21st-Century Cowboys: Why the Spirit Endures." *National Geographic.* December 2007, 114-135.

Forbush, H. Interview with E.G. Adams, *Voices from the Past* #163, Bringham Young University, Rexburg, Idaho (1956).

Gillette, W. "The Memorable Character–Cal Carrington." A Quarterly of Idaho History. *Snake River Echoes*, Teton County, Idaho, Edition, Vol. 8:3 (1979): 54-62.

Gizycka, Countess Eleanor. "Diary on the Salmon River." *Teton Magazine*, Vol 23, pp 11-12, 34-40; and Vol. 24. Jackson, WY, 1991. (submitted by Felicia).

Gizycka, E. "Diary on the Salmon River." *Field and Stream* (May and June, 1923).

_____. (undated copy) "Two Bear." *Field and Stream*, pp 596-598.

_____. "Sheep Hunting in Alberta." *Field and Stream* (July 1925): pp 14-15.

Gizycka, F. "Forgiveness at Flat Creek." *Teton Magazine*, Vol. 20. (1988), pp 8-9, 26-32.

_____. "John Wort and Cal Carrington." *Teton Magazine*, Vol. 14, (1981), pp10-11 & 56.

_____. "Cissy Paterson: The Countess of Flat Creek." *Teton Magazine*, vol. 10. (1977),pp 37-48.

_____. "Jackson Hole, 1916-65: A Reminiscence." *Vogue* (April 1965), pp 200, 203, 205, 208-10.

Hoyle, R.C. "To the Tetons by Train." CRM, No. 10 (1999), pp24-29.

Hoffman, L.A. "The Last Bustin' at the Bow-Gun." *Scribners*, Vol. 42(8), (1907), pp75-87.

Layser, P. "The Flat Creek Ranch: Old West, New West, But Always the Real West." *Wyoming Homes and Living Magazine.* (Summer 2005),pp 20-29.

_____. "Tracking the Wilderness Wapiti." *Bugle Magazine*, Mar/Apr 2009, 44-51.

Martin, R.G. "Letters to Rose." *Teton Magazine*, Vol. 12. (1979), pp 8-11, 27-28, 44-62.

McDaniel, La Rae Tyler, "Dorus Harvey and Lenora ... Tyler: Their Ancestry and Their Posterity". Bound Mimeo (2001), 468p.

Moss, W. "Those Were The Days My Friend." *Teton Valley Top to Bottom*, Driggs, ID. (Winter 2005), pp 56-61.

_____. "Tracks to the Tetons." *Teton Home and Living*, Driggs, ID. (Fall/Winter 2006), pp 64-69.

_____. "The Avenues of Driggs Tell a Story." *Teton Valley Top to Bottom*, Driggs, ID. (Summer 2006), pp 50-55.

_____ . "Friend or Faux." *Teton Valley Top to Bottom*, Driggs, ID. (Summer 2003), pp 62-67.

Odel, R. "Cal and the Countess." *Teton Magazine.* (Summer/Fall 2002), pp 62-68.

Rees, A. "A Classless Society: Dude Ranching in the Tetons, 1908-1955." *Annals of Wyoming*, Vol. 77 (2005), pp 2-21.

Romanelli, J. "Winchester Lever Action Legacy." *Pennsylvania Game News*, September 2012, pp 60-63.

Walker, S. "Cissy is a Newspaper Lady." *The Saturday Evening Post*, May 6, 1938; pp22-23,55,62.

Newspapers

Bill Barlows Budget, 8 June, 1892.

Owen, W. "Matterhorn of America: An Attempt to Ascend the Grand Teton Mountain." Reprinted in the *JHHS Chronicle*, Vol. XXVI, No. 3, (Fall 2006).

Dannatt, A. "Obituary: Countess Felicia Gizycka." *The Independent*, London, May 18, 1999.

Lahurd, J. "Sarasota's Rich and Famous," *Sarasota Herald Tribune*, October 7, 2010.

"Obituary, Cal Carrington." *Jackson Hole Courier*. December 31, 1959.

"Obituary, Cal Carrington." *Jackson Hole Guide*. December 24, 1959, Dec 31, 1959.

"Obituary, Cal Carrington." *Teton Valley News*. December 24, 1959, Dec 31, 1959.

"Obituary-Worldly Magruder, 93, was early valley 'dude.' *Jackson Hole News*, March 10, 1999.

Owen Collection. "John Carnes Obituary: Pioneer Civil War Vet Passes at 85 Years." (Bonney and Bonney personal files,Kelly, WY.) July 16, 1931.

Sarasota Herald Tribune, "Cissy Patterson Purchases $80,000 Beach Home Here", January 8, 1946.

Sarasota Journal, "It's Called Name Dropping," May 1, 1975.

Teton Views, "A Trip Few Have Taken: Flat Creek and Dry Hollow." Vol. 2, Issue 30, Jackson, WY, October 27, 1999.

Wilkerson, T. "Gov Made Poor Pick for G&F Commission." *Jackson Hole News and Guide*. (9 March 2005): 6A.

Interviews and Personal Communication

Albright, J. Pers. Comm. (conversations w/author), Jackson, WY, 2005.

Arnold, D. Pers. Comm. (telephone conversation w/author), Laramie, WY, 2005.

Arnold, J. Pers. Comm. (conversations w/author), Laramie, WY, 2005/2006.

Bonney, L. Pers. Comm. and access to the Bonneys' Carrington notes, Kelly, WY, 2007.

Brazil, A. Pers. Comm. re. Alice Arlen grizzly bear hide, Dubois, WY, 2013.

Breckinridge, D. Pers. Comm. (conversation w/author), Tetonia, ID, 2004 and 2012.

Budge, B. Pers. Comm. (conversation w/author), Jackson, WY, 2009 and 2013.

Buxton, F. Pers. Comm. (telephone conversation w/author), Bates, ID, 2004.

Buxton, J. Pers. Comm. (telephone conversation w/author), St. George, UT, 2004.

Chambers, R. Pers. Comm. (telephone conversation w/author), Jackson, WY, 2004.

Downer, G. Pers. Comm. (telephone conversation w/author), Calif. and New Mexico. 2005.

Forbush, H. Pers. Comm. (telephone conversations w/author), Rexburg, ID, 2004.

Furniss, O. Pers. Comm. (conversations w/author), Bates, ID, 2004.

Gillette, B. Pers. Comm. (telephone conversation w/author), Victor, ID, 2004.

Gillette, W. and F. Gizycka 1987 Interview penciled notes re. Cal Carrington on file at Jackson Hole Historical Society, Jackson, WY.

Gressley, Gene M. Pers. Comm. (telephone conversation) re. 1957 Carrington University of Wyo. Interview) 2007.

Hansen, C. Recorded oral interview conducted by C. Hansen, G. Bressley, and others at the Univesity of WY, Laramie (transcribed by the Bonneys and filed with their personal notes) 1957. The original tapes are likely at the Wyoming Heritage Center, but were not located.

Hansen, C. Pers. Comm. (telephone conversations w/author), Jackson, WY, 2004, 2007 & 2008.

Haven, J. Pers. Comm. (telephone conversation w/author, Cascade, ID, 2013.

Kent, Dawn. Pers. Comm. (telephone conversation w/author), Kelly, WY, 2013.

Petersen, C. Interviews in his home by author, Jackson, WY, 2004/2005.

Petersen, C. Transcribed Oral Interviews (Last of the Old West series by Jo Ann Byrd), Jackson Hole Historical Society, Jackson, WY, 1972 & 1982.

Piquet, L. Pers. Comm. (telephone conversation w/author), Driggs, ID, 2008 and 2013.

Piquet, M. Pers. Comm. (telephone conversation w/author), Idaho Falls, ID. 2008.

Rudd, R. Pers. Comm. (conversations w/author), Wilson, WY, 2005.

Ryan, J. Pers. Comm. (telephone conversation w/author), Jackson, WY, 2005.

Taylor, C. Pers. Comm. (telephone conversation w/ author), Jackson, WY, 2013.

Shultz, M. Pers. Comm. (telephone conversation w/author), Jackson, WY, 2007.

Smith, A. Pers. Comm. (telephone conversations and correspondence w/author), Alta, WY, 2008 and 2013.

Stone, D. Recorded Interview with Cal Carrington. Tape on file at Teton Valley Historical Society, Driggs, ID, 1958. (Also transcribed in part and on file at Jackson Hole Historical Society.)

Stone, R. Pers. Comm. (telephone conversation w/author), Victor, ID, 2004.

Thompson, G. Pers. Comm. (telephone conversations w/author), Victor, ID, 2004-2011.

Whittlesey, Lee H. Pers. Comm. (telephone conversation) re. Yellowstone National Park history, 2007.

Government Publications

Brandegee, T.S. *Annual Report U.S. Geol. Survey*, 1897-98, Re. Teton Forest Reserve. GLO, Wash., DC.

U.S. Fish and Wildlife Service, National Elk Refuge (undated). "Timeline of the Miller Ranch and National Elk Refuge."

National Archives

USDI BLM General Land Office Records, Desert Entry Case File No. 3116. Wash., DC.

USDI BLM General Land Office Records, Homestead Entry Case File No. 07481. Wash., DC.

US Census Records/Ancestry.com

Online GLO Records: http://www.glorecords.blm.gov/

State and Local Archives

Jackson Hole Historical Society and Museum, Jackson, WY (Cal Carrington file folder and photographs).

Jackson Hole Historical Society and Museum Files, Maggie McBride, 1896. "My Diary."

State of Idaho. Hodges, K. Idaho Historical Society Curator and Research Specialist. 2005. (Mary Ake materials and Carrington genealogy research.)

State of Wyoming. Univ. of Wyoming, American Heritage Center. Laramie, WY (General – Northern Pacific Railroad, ranching and period photographs. The Carrington tapes were not found, but could still be there somewhere.)

San Diego County, California, Courthouse Records: County Assessor Maps BK 257 and 9764 and Superior Court Petition Settling the Estate of Cal Carrington.

Teton County, Idaho, Courthouse, Deed and Patent Records (the original records were held in St. Anthony, but were transferred to Driggs when Teton County was formed – includes: naturalization sworn declaration, probate records, decree to quiet Bates title.)

Teton County, Idaho, Courthouse Records of Decreed Water Rights (the original records were held in St. Anthony, but were later transferred to Driggs, Idaho – Mahogany Creek water right).

Teton County, Idaho, Driggs Museum files. Tales of the Big Hole Mountains: Enoch Cal Carrington (unpublished notes and interviews).

Teton County, Wyoming, Courthouse, Deed and Patent Records (deed recordings and ownership transfers for the Flat Creek Ranch).

Wyoming State Archives, Cheyenne. Last Will and Testament of E.C. Carrington. Teton County District Court Probate File 546.

World Wide Web

http://www.flatcreekranch.com/history.html

http://www.culturaltourism.org/dch.

http://www.Ancestry.com

http://www.wyomingtalesandtrails.com/tetons.html

http://www.cr.nps.gov/history/onlinebooks/grte/chaps.htm

http://ultimatewyoming.com/sectionpages/sec1/Jackson/jackson/html

http://www.idahohistory.net/Ref%20Series/0451.pdf

http://www.glorecords.blm.gov/

http://www.blm.gov/nhp/landfacts/DesertLand.html

http://www.reference.com/browse/wiki/Desert-Land

http://rondiener.com/JHIW.htm (Diener, R.E. The Jackson Hole Indian War of 1895. 2006)

http://www.media.utah.edu/UHE/c/Carrington (Summary of Albert Carrington's life and career)

http://www.genealogi.se/roots/hull.htm

http://en.wikipedia.org/wiki/Law_of_Adoption

http://historytogo.utah.gov/utah/perpetualmigratingfund

http: //findagrave.com

http://en.wikipedia.org/wiki/Roaring_Twenties

http://idahoptv.org/outdoors/shows/riverofnoreturn/scow/cfm

http://www.onlineutah.com/smithfieldhistory.shtml

And a host of other websites for fact finding and checking.

Other

Selected letters from *Felicia Gizycka Collection* courtesy of the Arnold family through Amanda Smith (at this writing the collection was located with Felicia Cameron in San Diego, California).

Selected letters from the Joseph Medill *Patterson Papers*, Lake Forest College, Lake Forest, IL, through biographer Amanda Smith.

Ralph Martin interview with Hank Crabtree notes.

Jackie Martin Collection at Syracuse University, which, besides photographs, contains a number of magazine articles on Cissy.

The Jackson Hole Flat Creek Ranch (Joe Albright) and the Arnold family in Laramie (Felicia Gizycka's grandchildren) contributed documents, photographs, and personal knowledge.

Carrington Items

Catalogued at the
Jackson Hole Historical Society and Museum as of 2013

Spanish ring bit

Lariat

Quirt

Pipe

Horsehair strap

Branding iron

Coffee grinder

Certificate of Assistant Forest Ranger appointment

Cissy Patterson's angora chaps given to her by Cal Carrington

Brass plaque that was to be attached to Carrington's grave marker

Cal Carrington's saddle

The author at the old Horn Ranch in the upper Gros Ventre River valley, c 2007.
Photo by Pattie Layser.

About the Author

Earle F. Layser is originally from a rural and mountainous region of Pennsylvania near the village of Cedar Run. After an enlistment in the military, at age twenty-one, he drove his 1957 Chevrolet to Missoula, Montana, beginning a life-long adventure with the West. He matriculated in forestry at the University of Montana and was a smokejumper. After completing a Master of Science degree at the New York College of Environmental Science at Syracuse, he worked for federal land and resource management agencies and as a private consultant throughout the western United States and Alaska. He has authored a number of scientific research papers on land-use planning, plant ecology, and wildlife, including grizzly bear and mountain caribou, and a book: Flora of Pend Oreille County, Washington. In 1976, his career took him to Jackson Hole and the Greater Yellowstone, where he discovered a connection that has lasted a lifetime. In 1990, he retired from government service and returned to the Tetons as a natural resources consultant, photographer, and writer. Since then he has authored numerous articles on Western history, natural history, travel, and two other books: *Green Fire: Stories from the Wild* (2010) and *The Jackson Hole Settlement Chronicles* (2012). Earle, and his wife, Pattie, also a writer and a source of inspiration, and their dog, Benji, at the time of this writing, happily made their home on the west slope of the Teton Mountains in Alta, Wyoming.

PRAISE FOR OTHER TITLES
BY EARLE F. LAYSER

Green Fire: Stories from the Wild (2010)

The Jackson Hole Settlement Chronicles (2012)

Praise for
Jackson Hole Settlement Chronicles

A fascinating account of the first inhabitants of Jackson Hole: illegal squatters, rustlers, game poachers, and other outlaws rubbing up against legitimate homesteaders and ranchers. True tales of shootouts, Indian fights, and vigilante confrontations share the pages with respectable men who quietly built cabins, guided sport hunters, dug irrigation ditches, gardened, and peacefully made the Tetons their home. Oh, and once you've read the author's book, you'll no doubt want to wear a red bandana while in Jackson Hole.

> – Jim Hardee, editor, *Rocky Mountain Fur Trade Journal*,
> and author of *Pierre's Hole: The Fur Trade History of
> Teton Valley, Idaho*, Tetonia, Idaho.

A new and different perspective on Jackson Hole's earliest settlers: living in total isolation and braving brutal winters, they relied on wild game and predator bounties for subsistence and livelihood. Based on extensive research and richly illustrated with historic photographs, the author details the lives of the first settlers and Jackson Hole's infamous frontier rabble. A must read for anyone who loves Wyoming and Jackson Hole.

> – Robert C. Rudd, artist and local historian, author of
> *They Settled Here: Homesteads and Cabins of
> Jackson Hole*, Victor, Idaho.

I've read many accounts of early Jackson Hole, but this one presents the history from mostly a new and different point of view. The author leads us through the man versus nature hardships in the settlement of this remote country, but conversely, he also shows us how the early settlers depended on and benefited from nature, and how that evolved into some local citizens recognizing a need for game laws and conservation. *The author gives us a taste of whom the early rugged, non-conforming pioneers were, how they lived, where they lived, and perhaps why they came to Jackson Hole, from those that stayed in the valley only a few years to those whose descendents still leave their footprints on the ongoing history. It's a story about the valley put in a context we haven't previously seen, with episodes that I had not heard of before.*

– Harold Turner, outfitter, guide, Triangle X Guest
Ranch partner, life-long resident Jackson Hole.

The author melds human and natural history into a dramatic tale of how wildlife abundance has attracted people to Jackson Hole and sustained them from the earliest human inhabitants up through contemporary time; and how the conservation of its iconic species continues to set Jackson Hole apart from much of the modern world. While the glorious mountains made Jackson Hole a Mecca for travelers, its wildlife actually gave the valley its uncommon power of place. This is a book that speaks to the values of Nature; it will leave you inspired.

– Todd Wilkinson, editor, the on-line *Wildlife Art Journal*,
national environmental journalist and columnist,
biographer of media mogul and bison baron Ted Turner,
Bozeman, Montana.

Praise for
Green Fire: Stories from the Wild

This is a book for people who love wild animals. It is a collection of thirteen original animal stories about wildlife and wildlands. Centering on the Rocky Mountains, from the Greater Yellowstone Region to the Arctic National Wildlife Refuge, these very readable narratives incorporate current issues, history, science, natural history, and folklore. What forester Aldo Leopold first named green fire is a flame that burns within all wild creatures, a glow that reflects the indomitable and resilient spirit of untamed Nature.

The author has managed to blend science, myth, animal behavior and his own professional experience into a great contemporary natural history read. I learned things I didn't know about the creatures in my own backyard in Grand Teton National Park. I like this book a lot.
> – Charles S. Craighead, filmmaker, *Arctic Dance:
> The Mardy Murie Story* and author of *Who Ate the
> Backyard* and *Meet Me at the Wort.*

A champion of wildlife and nature, the author presents animals as the heroes in his stories as they overcome challenges rooted in both nature and the encroachment of people into their habitat. Green Fire brings greater understanding and a desire for the protection and conservation of wildlife and the Earth's landscapes.
> – Thomas D. Mangelsen, internationally acclaimed
> wildlife photographer and author of *Images of Nature
> and The Natural World.*

Green Fire is a highly readable collection of wild animal stories ranging from the whimsical to the informed scientific. I would have to consult a dictionary to come up with enough good words to say about it. This book can serve as an ecological primer for the subject Rocky Mountain animals, their history and conservation, and their possible future prospects. I heartily recommend this book as a good read.

    – Bert Raynes, naturalist and ornithologist, and
Jackson Hole News and Guide nature columnist, Director
of the *Meg and Bert Raynes Wildlife Fund,* and author
of *Valley So Sweet, Winter Wings, Birds of Grand Teton
Park and Birds of Sage and Scree.*

70499022R00215

Made in the USA
Columbia, SC
08 May 2017